THE
CHINA
GUIDEBOOK

DEDICATED

to the promise of enhanced

understanding among nations

on the occasion of the establishment

of full diplomatic relations

between the People's Republic of China

and the United States of America,

January 1, 1979

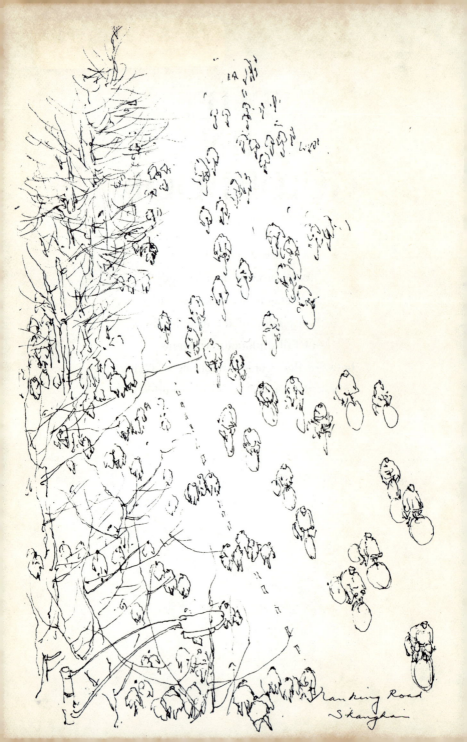

Nanking Road
Shanghai

1979/80 Edition

THE CHINA GUIDEBOOK

A traveler's guide to the People's Republic of China

ARNE J. deKEIJZER
FREDRIC M. KAPLAN

with an Introduction by
ESTHER GOLLOBIN

Eurasia Press
FAIR LAWN, NEW JERSEY

J. B. Lippincott Company
PHILADELPHIA AND NEW YORK

Distributed in the United States of America and
Canada by J.P. Lippincott Company
□
Distributed in Hong Kong by Cosmos Books Ltd.,
30 Johnston Road, Wanchai, Hong Kong.

FIRST EDITION

Typography by U.S. Lithograph Inc.
Cover and book design by Kathie Brown
Cover photograph by Audrey Topping
Frontispiece and drawings, pages 45, 107, 139,
167, and 273, by Chen Chi

Color maps prepared by Hammond, Inc.,
Maplewood, New Jersey

LIBRARY OF CONGRESS CATALOGING
IN PUBLICATION DATA

deKeijzer, Arne J.
  The China Guidebook.
    Bibliography: p. 280.
    Includes index.
      1. China—Description and travel—1976-   —Guidebooks.
  I. Kaplan, Fredric M., joint author. II. Title.

DS712.D4   1979   915.1'04'5   79-37
ISBN 0-397-01358-2   ISBN 0-397-01359-0 (pbk.)

CONTENTS

INTRODUCTION
Some Advice to the China-bound Traveler
by Esther Gollobin 13

I   TRAVELING TO CHINA

II   TRAVELING IN CHINA

III THE CHINA TOUR: CITIES AND SITES

CITIES ALPHABETIZED BY PINYIN SPELLING

MAPS

TABLES AND CHARTS

NOTES AND ACKNOWLEDGMENTS

As this edition was going to press, President Jimmy Carter and PRC Chairman Hua Kuo-feng simultaneously announced the stunning news that China and the United States, after a lapse of 30 years, would soon establish full diplomatic relations. For at least two years prior to that announcement, China travel had been undergoing a revolution. As recently as the mid-1970s, there were few places on earth less accessible to the Western tourist than China. In 1977, however, China travel officials began to reexamine the policies that had for nearly three decades kept the country off limits to all but a select group of specialists, traders, and sympathetic observers. By early 1978, China began to welcome the first of what promised to be an expanding procession of general tour groups from the Americas and Western Europe. A new age for China travel had begun.

This is not to say that travelers may now blithely pack a bag and board a plane for Peking, much as they might for Rome, Bombay, or Tokyo. Although China appears to be less concerned about who comes to visit, how and when they come are matters that remain subject to a variety of conditions.

The overriding condition—and the one that sets a China visit apart from travel to many other places —is that most visitors come to China as part of an organized tour. In 1978, for the first time on any large scale, the specific authority to form such tours was granted to a number of airlines, travel agents, and private organizations. While in China, these tours are conducted according to fixed itineraries arranged by the official China International Travel Service.

Despite the requirements for advanced booking and the rigors of exacting, prearranged scheduling, the initial response to these tour offerings has been overwhelming, and the reaction of the first returned travelers has been almost universally enthusiastic. Whatever the group experience loses in the way of spontaneity, it gains in efficiency. One's time in China is precious. When one begins to consider all that has happened in China and all that is going on there now, barely a moment is to be wasted.

The purpose of this guide is to help visitors make the fullest use of their time in China. Although getting there is no longer as arduous a procedure as it was just a few years ago, a number of special steps are still required, especially for special-interest groups or individuals seeking to initiate visits for purposes other than general travel. The first section of the guide includes information on venues and agencies (inside and outside China) for categories of visitors other than general tourists (e.g., professional organizations and business persons). In addition, the guide discusses the special procedures and protocol required by the circumstance of group travel in China.

The section on China itineraries focuses on all major cities and sites included in general tours through the late 1970s. Each city is discussed in a dual context—its importance in traditional China and its significance in the contemporary life of the People's Republic. For the Chinese, the past is used as a means to better serve the present. The preeminent stress for visitors is on how China lives today. For that reason, each discussion attempts to account for each city's importance in contemporary China, its role in the revolution, its economy and culture, and its measured achievements in improving life for its citizens. Similarly, under the Highlights section for each city, modern structures, factories, and social institutions are discussed along with monuments from traditional China.

Time for free activity is short. For larger cities, the guide suggests some brief walking tours (usually requiring no more than an hour) to enable maximum use of the free time available. In addition, step-by-step tours of major shopping areas are provided to facilitate "freelance" excursions.

The last section of the guide contains some useful Chinese phrases (including both pronunciation and Chinese characters) and suggestions for background reading.

With a few minor exceptions, the transliteration of Chinese place-names and references follows the Wade-Giles system, the method still most commonly used in the West. For cities, alternate spellings in *Hanyu pinyin* (the PRC's official system) are indicated at the start of each section and in the glossary on pp. 291-2.

Every effort has been made to present information that is accurate and up-to-date. The authors welcome the comments and criticisms of readers, as well as suggestions for additions to future editions.

The staffs of Eurasia Press and A.J. deKeijzer & Associates played an indispensable role in assembling, editing, and producing this edition. They include Arlene Posner, Martha Cameron, Lorna Harbus, and Mary Elizabeth McCarry. Many good friends of China lent good sense and experience to the project, notably Esther Gollobin, Norval Welch, Meyer Harbus, Hugh Deane, Richard Pastor, Helen Scarcella, Ruth Misheloff, Gary Schoener, and Helen Ewer. For their spirit, friendship and criticism, special thanks are owed to members of the 1978 USCPFA East Coast Leadership Tour: Anna Singletary, Sylvia Wineland, Kathleen Chamberlain, Dell Bisdorf, Barbara Jones (Omolade), Mark Powers, Jeffrey Berger, Marion Ford, Stephen Niemiec, Jane Pelletier, Anthony Lentini, Douglas Price, Roger Pattes, Tak Matsusaka, Arthur Weinberg, Joel Mlecko, Margaret Ricketson, Russel Ricketson, Suzanne Dollard, Irene Hensel, Amanda Powers, Judith Jenkins, and Kenneth Grimes. Kathie Brown of U.S. Lithograph Inc. is owed a special note of thanks for lending her care and special skills to the book. Numerous colleagues in publishing and allied fields generously shared their experience and expertise; these included Moshe Y. Sachs, Seymour Barofsky, Aristides Kambanis, Stella Heiden, Gladys Topkis, Fred Grayson, Shaie Selzer, Helmut Kapsczinski, Gary Goff, Henry Noyes, Paul Feffer, and Stephen David Price.

A heartfelt acknowledgment is due the many friends in China— among them representatives of the Chinese People's Association for Friendship with Foreign Countries (YOUXIE) and the Chinese International Travel Service (LUXINGSHE)—whose gracious hospitality and patient explanations made possible what we hope will be a small contribution to mutual understanding. Many US colleagues shared their insights as well. The National Committee on US-China Relations, the National Council for US-China Trade, and the US-China Peoples Friendship Association were the true pioneers in areas of US-China travel. Much of the information represented here derives from the experience gained through contact with these organizations.

The American Region Staff of Japan Air Lines played an important role in the publication of this book's predecessor, the *JAL Guide to the People's Republic of China*. Appreciation in this regard is owed especially to Yasutake Matsumoto, Mike Nagai, Ken Shiba, Norman Bacon, and Jackie Cole.

On a more personal level, one can never adequately acknowledge the support of long-standing friends. Arne deKeijzer singles out M. for carrying it all from the beginning and for all that was; B. for fine choruses of "Tangerine"; L. for giving more than a bookhouse full of wisdom; M. for making Irish pluck contagious; H. for sharing what can be; and his parents for gifts beyond measure. Fredric Kaplan thanks Bernard Bess and Mildred Kaplan Bess.

A.J. deK. and **F.M.K.**
New York, New York
January 1, 1979

PREFACE

A trip to China is unique among travel experiences. The dominant characteristics of the People's Republic of China—its size, cultural heritage, and political environment—suffice to give an impression of a universe unto itself. Moreover, in the course of the past three decades, China has been experiencing a transformation which, in its scope, intensity, and pervasiveness, has few if any parallels in the contemporary world. Whether or not one agrees with its ideological premises, it is evident that the Chinese Revolution and its effects have taken root everywhere—in China's streets, farms, factories, schools, homes—and even in the hotels, restaurants, and conveyances used by tourists. For the Chinese, the economic and social accomplishments of this new era are matters of consuming interest and the source of unconcealed pride and enthusiasm.

Virtually all aspects of work, culture, and even recreation are perceived in terms of their contribution to moving China forward. More than likely, the tourist will find his own visit being addressed in the same light. As a function of state policy, tourism helps to expand the economy and, not incidentally, win more friends for China. Thus, even tourists with the most modest outlook and expectations are apt to find themselves cast in the role of international emissaries, there to build bridges of understanding between their own country and the new society being forged in China. And since foreign visitors are a relatively new phenomenon in the People's Republic—tourism from the West was virtually unheard of in the 1950s and 1960s—they are visible symbols of a new policy that seeks to bridge the vast gulf which has separated the PRC from the West.

For most visitors, China's past and present have a common remoteness, and while this cultural distance may stimulate a desire to see China, it may also inhibit full appreciation of the experience. There are real cultural distances, and many who put off learning anything about China until their arrival in Peking are likely to leave having absorbed very little.

Aside from the special qualities of the country itself, the uniqueness of a trip to China is underscored by how the Chinese organize it. The Chinese assume that travelers who have taken the effort to come there have a serious intent to learn about the country, and most activities planned for visitors proceed from that assumption. Since a visit to China is seen primarily as a learning experience, the Chinese seek to exert as much control as possible over the content and quality of

11

that experience. Thus, although the treatment of visitors is invariably thoughtful and courteous, the Chinese are not content with a role as affable, fawning hosts. In the short time available (usually less than three weeks), they attempt to convey as coherent and as comprehensive a picture as possible of the salient aspects of their country's social, economic, and cultural development.

It is from this rationale that the highly organized nature of most trips proceeds. Almost all Western visitors (apart from specially invited individuals and those on business ventures) travel as part of an escorted group. Participants sightsee and take most meals together and stay at the same hotels. They are invariably accompanied on their daily excursions by an official interpreter. Tour itineraries are for the most part settled in advance and finalized within a day after arrival in China. Likewise, daily schedules of activities and visits are prearranged around tight (and frequently rigorous) schedules. The time allotted for independent activities is limited, whereas much time is devoted to organized group discussions of what's being seen. Throughout, the visitor's willingness to abide with the special circumstances of China travel is key to maximum use and enjoyment of the experience.

Fredric M. Kaplan

SOME ADVICE TO THE CHINA-BOUND TRAVELER

Are you a seasoned traveler with mementos from several continents in your living room? Or are you planning your first trip abroad? In either case, the China experience is bound to be unforgettable, for you'll be seeing another world—exotic, challenging, with ever-present evidence of an ancient civilization trying to cope with profound 20th-century transformations.

One of the best ways to prepare for a China trip is to read about China's history and about the changes that have taken place there since 1949, when Mao Tse-tung announced to the world that "the Chinese people have stood up." Also, talk to returned travelers and seek out films and slide shows that can impart a "feel" for China's people, streets, and landscape.

The most important preparation, perhaps, is to try to rid your "mental luggage" of Western notions about China's values. Try to understand the Chinese people in terms of their pre-1949 "bitter past," their stated goals, and their efforts to build a society of their own making—after about 150 years of foreign interference.

Here's how a Texas couple described their 1978 trip:

> Over the years it has been our good fortune to have visited over two dozen countries, but we have never felt more welcome than we did in China. Every effort was made to show us as much as possible and to tailor-make our tour to suit the desires of the group. Our three guides were most pleasant. And everywhere we went we were received with enthusiasm and a warm welcome. Several of our group who chose to do things on their own were allowed complete freedom to do so.
>
> Yes, the people are very curious about us round-eyed people who speak in strange tongues, and they followed us or gathered around wherever we went. Most often there were large groups applauding our arrival at various places, waving and clapping as they bid us a fond farewell.

After you reciprocate the welcoming applause at a school, hospital, courtyard, museum, or rural commune, the introductory remarks by your hosts may refer to freedom and democracy, leadership, women's equality, idealist thinking, and dictatorship. Such terms generally mean one thing to the Chinese and something quite different to Westerners. Why? Because different interpretations stem from varying historical and political experiences and value systems. Let's talk briefly about some of these.

Legacies from China's Past

When Marco Polo first found his way to Cathay some 700 years ago, his attention was drawn not only to the inventiveness—technological and artistic—of the people, but also to the fact that there were "altogether 1,200 cities, besides a great quantity of castles and towns, all fair and rich." In these walled cities, even in remote areas, Marco Polo found a well-demarcated line of administration that was able to survive dynasty after dynasty, with town guilds, occupational groups, and family societies participating in public affairs.

Specialists in Chinese history have noted the traditional reliance on the counsel of elders, the use of persuasion and arbitration rather than adjudication, and the mutual help of the extended family and adjoining courtyard.

Many aspects of these age-old norms are alive and well in the People's Republic, with socialist content added. Gone, however, are forced marriages and the triple female subservience to father, to husband (and, by extension, to mother-in-law), and to elder son. Gone are the oppressive taxes and capricious abuses by the emperor, the local warlord, or the landlord.

And no longer are intellectual pursuits the exclusive domain of the few who are deemed fit to rule, and manual labor the fate of the many who are ruled. Almost everyone in China participates in the "two-join" movement: workers join in some decision-making in the management process, and technicians and supervisors spend some time at manual labor. Everyone is encouraged to be both a doer and a thinker—to combine theory with practice. The more one understands the workings of society and of nature, the better one will be able to "serve the people."

Freedom in China

The wolf and the lamb, Abraham Lincoln once commented, do not agree on the definition of freedom. The lamb sees it as the right to live undisturbed, while the wolf defines freedom as the right to prey on that very lamb!

For the Chinese today, freedom means "the five guarantees" for everyone: a job, a place to live, an education, health care, and a decent burial—once the privileges of only 10% of the people. Freedom is defined, further, in the provisions of the March 1978 PRC Constitution: the right to own a home, to provide and claim an inheritance, to strike, to practice religion or atheism, and to register a complaint against an elected or appointed official without fear of reprisal. Freedom is also measured in the oral history transmitted to younger generations by the veteran worker or respected retiree: "My son doesn't have to make the agonizing decision of his ancestors to drown an infant because it's an extra mouth to feed, to indenture or sell a seven-year-old as a servant to the landlord, or to rely on remittances from a teenage daughter forced into prostitution."

On my third visit to China in October 1976, I was co-leader of a delegation representing national US religious, sports, social welfare, and cultural organizations. In Nanking, eight of us spent a memorable evening with K.H. Ting, a former Anglican bishop who now heads the Theological Seminary there. In the course of a conversation that ranged from the status of Christianity to current events (the "gang of four" had just been arrested), Dr. Ting, who had lived in Canada and Switzerland, cited the price of milk as a means of contrasting daily life in China and in the West:

> In a capitalist country you raise the price of milk if there is scarcity, keeping the product available for those who can pay. Here there is not yet enough milk for everyone; we get it two out of every three days. But the price remains the same and it is distributed to babies, older people and patients. For parents to have their children better fed makes them feel freer.

Late-1978 travelers report animated debates—both in conversations and in the unique "large-character posters" seen in big cities—about the changing nature of freedom and democracy in socialist society. To witness these changes, and to sense the growing openness to foreigners, will add another "plus" to your China trip.

Chinese Ideas of Privacy

What Westerners may perceive as an invasion of privacy is to the Chinese a commonsense good-neighbor policy. For example, if a teenager suddenly appears with a bicycle and his parents haven't mentioned to their neighbors any plan for such a major purchase, the local residents committee will make an inquiry. When two families frequently quarrel about shared kitchen facilities or noisy radios, the committee will be involved in "resolving contradictions among the people" through persuasion and consensus.

Individual and group evaluations—at work, in high-rise apartment buildings, or in commune courtyards—are an ongoing feature of the peer group to which almost all Chinese belong. The group provides a framework for ongoing political education, for mutual cooperation in personal and community goals, and for a sense of identification with nationwide campaigns that aim to enhance the quality of life for everyone.

Speaking of privacy, you'll find the Chinese *very* discreet about matters sexual. Public display of affection is rare, pornography and suggestive ads or clothing are nonexistent, and inquiries about pre-marital sex and out-of-wedlock births are generally met with a polite, even terse, "It does not happen here."

15

On the other hand, some visitors have broached the subjects of courtship, marriage customs, and changing family patterns in the course of a one-to-one conversation and acquired unique insights. So it's suggested that you first consider how you'd feel if a stranger from another country started asking about the intimate details of your life!

Political Life

One hundred fifty years ago a Frenchman visited the United States to report back to curious Europeans on a new form of government. Alexis de Tocqueville's admiring account, *Democracy in America*, singles out the pioneering civic role of the average US citizen:

> How does it happen that everyone takes as zealous an interest in the affairs of his township, his county, and the whole state as if they were his own? It is because everyone, in his sphere, takes an active part in the government of society.

The United States depicted by de Tocqueville in the 1830s had but recently shed the monarchy, adopted a Constitution and Bill of Rights, and blazed new trails with a budding universal public education system. Its population of 13 million could readily expand westward, diversify the economy, and attempt to keep in touch with the citizenry through a network of town meetings.

Imagine, then, China's effort—without precedent in human history—to govern almost 900 million citizens, to feed a nation once known as "the sick man of Asia," and to move from a war-weary feudal economy to that of a modern state. Large-scale campaigns and grass-roots mobilizations to instill cooperative values are credited with impressive changes in less than 30 years.

Here is the text of some bulletin boards and widely circulated pamphlets seen by visitors in recent years:

> "*The people, and the people alone, are the makers of history.*"

> "*Times have changed. Women can do everything that men can. Women hold up half the sky.*"

> "*Philosophy is no mystery.*"

> "*Serve the people!*"

A highly developed network of street offices (similar to the neighborhood city halls of some American cities) for every 10,000-20,000 persons, is China's mechanism for handling local problems. These offices serve as a coordinating center for overall community planning and maintenance, for security, education and culture, and for such public services as clinics, nurseries, local factories, cooperative laundries, and repair shops.

Learning from the West

"We have learned many things from capitalist and other socialist countries," visitors are told. "The West has a superior transportation system, but we do not plan to make automobiles for individual ownership. Your factories produce more goods faster than we can, but they empty waste into the rivers. Chinese law prohibits this, but we're still unable to control pollution due to industrial smoke.

"And when rural people migrate to urban centers for jobs—both in capitalist and socialist countries—the results are overcrowding, social alienation and family dislocation. Therefore, we hope to reverse that trend: we want to decentralize industry so that provinces have a diversified economy and the load on our transport system is reduced. We are seeking to improve amenities in the countryside to deter the lure of the city. And, as you know, we engage in extensive family planning campaigns to limit the birth rate."

People-to-People Contact

China's people—young and old—are bound to make the most vivid impression on you. They work hard, but they also relax at outings and family get-togethers. They stop at snack-shops for a bun or candy, and they take pictures of grandma cuddling the new baby. They're avid sports fans—of basketball in particular—and the afternoon spectator at the stadium is most likely an early morning jogger or a table-tennis or badminton player. Favorite pastimes include films and variety shows that feature "a cross-talk"—a two-person dialogue that oftentimes satirizes bureaucrats and male chauvinists.

The most effective diplomats of good will are the children—lovable, loved, and taught to greet their visiting "aunties and uncles" by reciting in unison, "We have friends all over the world!" Expect to acquire an entourage of 75 to 100 smiling consultants if you're shopping or taking a stroll. Many a gracious "How do you do!" will greet you in the most unexpected of places because English is the most popular second language today. It is taught from the fourth grade up in many schools, and over 300,000 people of all ages are now studying English in Shanghai alone.

Finally, don't be surprised if, at one point, your hosts say: "We see that you want to stay longer, but we must move on to the next appointment. On this visit, it is as if you are observing flowers from a galloping horse. When you come again, there will be more time!"

Have a great trip!

Esther Gollobin
New York, New York
January, 1979

I
TRAVELING TO CHINA

The Monkey King,
a traditional Chinese
literary character,
made a great journey
westward.

The People's Republic of China— At a Glance

China's People

The People's Republic of China (PRC) is far and away the most populous nation on earth. In 1979, the Chinese population totaled over 900 million, making China the home of one out of every five persons in the world. China is also distinguished by one of the oldest continuous civilizations on earth, with roots traced as far back as 2200 BC. The Chinese written language—using a unique, nonalphabetic script —is a thread that links modern-day China with its ancient past. The written script remains constant throughout the land. In its spoken form, however, Chinese has numerous dialects, although about two-thirds of the people can now understand *putunghua*—the national dialect.

China's Political System

A revolutionary movement that began in the 1920s culminated in the founding, on October 1, 1949, of the People's Republic of China. Rejecting both the traditions of China's imperial past and the weak, inept systems that dominated Chinese government in the first half of the 20th century, the new revolutionary government, under Mao Tsetung, set out to restructure the country along socialist lines.

The highest organ of legislative power in China is the National People's Congress, which elected 3,444 deputies to its fifth session in February 1978. The leading political force in the country, as stipulated by the Constitution, is the Chinese Communist Party. Overall policy decisions in China—political, economic, and social—are made by the Party and its leadership. Mao Tse-tung, Chairman of the Party from 1935 until his death in 1976, was by virtue of that position the preeminent leader of the People's Republic. Mao was succeeded as Party chairman in October 1976 by Hua Kuo-feng.

Mao's death in mid-1976 was followed by considerable political turmoil in China. A group of ultraradicals, branded as the "gang of four" and including Chiang Ch'ing, Mao's widow, attempted to usurp state power. By late 1977, however, stability was restored under the leadership of Hua and Teng Hsiao-p'ing, a former target of the "four." The post-Mao period has since been marked by new outpourings in the areas of cultural and political expression, as well as by a renewed emphasis on productivity and modernization, and new Chinese initiatives toward economic, technological, and cultural exchanges with the West.

New construction in Peking

China's Economic System

China has always been, and remains today, a predominantly agricultural country. For almost three decades prior to 1949, the incessant ravages of civil disorder, foreign interference and aggression, and gross economic neglect had reduced China to a state of helpless dependence. The first task of the new government, therefore, was to restore the economy to levels of self-sufficiency. By the early 1950s, mass starvation had been virtually eliminated and, by the end of the decade, China had begun to mobilize its vast natural and human resources to lay the base for major industrialization. Despite severe setbacks, especially in the early and late 1960s, China has continued its remarkable expansion, aided by the discovery of tremendous oil reserves and the effective mobilization of the nation's mammoth workforce. Still, China in the late-1970s remained, by its own admission, an underdeveloped country with large gaps in infrastructure and technology as yet awaiting remedy.

In spring 1978, China's leadership placed the "four modernizations" at the core of an economic development strategy that would provide the country with a "powerful socialist economy" by the year 2000. This modernization thrust, which was to focus on the areas of agriculture, industry, national defense, and science and technology, articulated a broad scope of interim goals—including some 120 specific areas of expansion—to be achieved by 1985.

China's economy is centrally planned and centrally controlled, although a considerable degree of local initiative is encouraged in most sectors. Beginning in the mid-1970s, foreign trade policies took a dramatic turn as the country sought to broaden its technological and industrial base through major purchases from the West. In an interview in late 1977, a leading Chinese trade official reiterated China's willingness to "develop and expand foreign trade relations with any country on the basis of mutual demand and mutual benefit."

This low-keyed statement was to presage a veritable explosion in China's trade policies, beginning in February 1978 with the signing of an eight-year (1978-85) agreement with Japan covering about US$10 billion in exchanges (largely Chinese oil and coal to Japan; industrial plants and technology to China). In the wake of the announcement of normalized US-China relations in December, major US-China trade agreements were concluded, including the construction of large tourist hotels in China by PanAm's Intercontinental Hotels, the sale of commercial aircraft by Boeing, the sale of Chinese petroleum to US refiners, and an arrangement by which Coca-Cola would be marketed in China. Major purchases from Canada, France, the UK, the Federal Republic of Germany, and other West European countries were also concluded during 1978.

TRAVEL TO CHINA IN THE LATE 1970s

For more than two decades after its founding, the PRC remained virtually off limits to most travelers from the West. Since 1971, however, restrictions on travel to China by Westerners have been progressively eased, with an unprecedented surge in tourism beginning in 1978. In 1978, more than 100,000 foreign tourists and 30,000 invited guests visited China—more than twice the figures for 1977 and equal to the total number of visitors during 1964-77 inclusive. Added to the 1978 total were some 400,000 overseas Chinese from Hong Kong, Singapore, Macao and other points of origin around the world. By 1980, the total volume of visitors to China was expected to exceed 1 million.

Until 1978, private travel to China had been limited mainly to those who had received a direct invitation from the Chinese government or to groups formed by PRC-oriented organizations officially designated to sponsor such trips. Beginning in 1978, however, China had clearly begun to view foreign travel in a new light. Foreign airlines (including PanAm, Japan Air Lines, Swissair, Canadian Pacific, and Iranair) and selected commercial travel agents were granted the right to form their own tours to China.

Although organized group travel remains the norm, the criteria for selection of travelers in the general tour category have been left largely to the discretion of commercial tour operators. For these groups, virtually all prior requirements for screening of applicants have been set aside, with the result that selections are now made purely on a "first come, first served" basis. The only real limitations on such trips remained the availability of accommodations in China. But here, too, new policies in effect since 1978 have aimed at rapid expansion and upgrading of hotel and transportation amenities. Indeed, the era of China's isolation from the myriad travelers who have waited decades for a chance to visit is drawing rapidly to a close.

Categories of China Travel

Official Visitors Apart from diplomatic exchanges, the PRC government has tendered official invitations to a variety of individuals and groups to visit China. For the most part, such invitations are issued on the PRC's initiative and usually have some bearing on PRC foreign policy, trade, or national political objectives. Such visits are characterized by sanction from the visitor's government, special status as guests of the host country, and high-level coordination with counterpart organizations in China (e.g., Chinese Academy of Sciences, All-China Sports Federation, China Council for the Promotion of International Trade). The frequency of such exchanges, especially with Western Europe and the United States, has been increasing dramatically since mid-1978.

Professional Groups The Chinese regard these as "people-to-people" exchanges. Groups are composed of 12-25 persons working in a common profession or belonging to a specific professional, civic, or other association. Thus, they are also characterized as "affinity groups." The range of people invited has been broad, from academics (university trustees, high school students) to civic organizations (League of Women Voters, Women for International Understanding); from economists (American Economic Association) to scientists (American Federation of Scientists); from museum curators and textbook publishers to dairy farmers.

A common denominator is the professional bond within a group and the joint submission of a tour proposal to Chinese authorities (such proposals are discussed in the section on "The Application Process").

China-Friendship Delegations A substantial number of visitors from the West fall in the category of what the Chinese call "friendship" delegations, the majority of which are formed by private, non-governmental (independent) "China-friendship" organizations. Such organizations exist throughout the Western Hemisphere (including more than 110 local chapters in the US and 8 in Canada) as well as in virtually all countries in Western Europe (see listing, pp. 24-25). Their stated purpose is to promote "people-to-

William Hinton shares his farming methods with Chinese officials

people" friendship between China and their own countries. In addition to sponsoring tours, most engage in volunteer educational and cultural activities that promote general-level interest in China. These are not "political" organizations *per se*, and most eschew involvement in issues not directly tied to China. With respect to China's revolutionary practices and goals, many see themselves as interpreters (rather than advocates) of Chinese policy. All maintain liaison with the Chinese People's Association for Friendship with Foreign Countries ("Youxie") in Peking.

Friendship tour participants are drawn from a variety of occupations and interest groups, including students, professionals, farmers, and factory workers, as well as representatives of minority groups, community agencies, trade unions, and political organizations. For such tours an informal national quota system has apparently been in force, with Japan and the US allotted large contingents into the late 1970s. Many tours are set aside for members of China-friendship organizations (such membership is open to all who seek to join). Groups pay their own way (scholarships may be available for low-income members) and are usually allotted 12-21 day itineraries. Their visits are arranged through the China International Travel Service ("Luxingshe"). These tours have traditionally sought to focus on specific aspects of China's economic, social, and political development, although cultural sites have increasingly become part of their itineraries, especially since 1978.

23

China Friendship Associations in Australia, Canada, Japan, Latin America, and Western Europe

AUSTRALIA

Australia-China Society, 228 Gertrude Street, Fitzroy 3065, Victoria

CANADA

Canada-China Friendship Association, Box 3304, Halifax, Nova Scotia

Canada-China Friendship Association, CP 872, Station A, Montreal, Quebec

Canada-China Friendship Association, 3630 Argyle St., *or* Box 3531, Regina, Saskatchewan

Canada-China Friendship Association, Box 373, Station Q, Toronto, Ontario

Canada-China Friendship Association, 33 East Hastings, Vancouver, British Columbia

Canada-China Friendship Association, Box 5074, Station B, Victoria, British Columbia

Canada-China Friendship Association, 2862 Henderson Hwy., Winnipeg, Manitoba

Canada-China Friendship Association, Box 305, Wolfville, Nova Scotia

COLOMBIA

Asociación de la Amistad Colombo-China, A.A. 17028, Bogata

DENMARK

Venskabsforbundet Danmark-Kina, Studiesstraede 18, DK 1455 Copenhagen

Venskabsforbundet Danmark-Kina, Ravnsborg Tvaergade, 2200 Copenhagen N

FEDERAL REPUBLIC OF GERMANY

Gesellschaft für Deutsch-Chinesische Freundschaft, Dreysestrasse 17, 1000 Berlin 21

Gesellschaft für Deutsch-Chinesische Freundschaft, Postfach 16328, 6000 Frankfurt am Main

THE US-CHINA PEOPLES FRIENDSHIP ASSOCIATION

Friendship Through Understanding

B Y WAY OF INTRODUCTION: The US-China Peoples Friendship Association (USCPFA) is a non-profit, tax-exempt, volunteer organization whose goal is to develop and strengthen understanding and friendship between the peoples of the United States and the People's Republic of China. We are Americans of differing viewpoints, from all walks of life, working in local associations throughout the nation. In existence since 1974, when several independent local groups united, the national USCPFA now includes more than 100 affiliated chapters and organizing committees, organized into four regions (East, Midwest, South, and West—including Hawaii).

The Association is financed by individual donations, membership dues, tours to China and local fundraising activities. It receives no financial contributions from China or the US government.

Activities of local chapters include film showings, slide-lectures, exhibits, dramatic performances, festivals, Chinese banquets, and study groups for their members, other organizations, and the general public. National and regional centers coordinate activities of and provide resources for local Associations, including films for rental and speakers on tour.

US-China Peoples Friendship Association

NATIONAL AND REGIONAL OFFICES

USCPFA National Office
635 S. Westlake,
Suite 202
Los Angeles,
CA 90057
(213) 483-5810

USCPFA Eastern Region
PO Box 63
720 Massachusetts Avenue
Cambridge, MA 02139
(617) 491-0594

USCPFA Midwest Region
407 S. Dearborn,
Suite 1200
Chicago, IL 60605
(312) 922-3414

USCPFA Southern Region
4384 Varsity Lane
Houston, TX 77004
(713) 747-1502

USCPFA Western Region
50 Oak Street,
Suite 502
San Francisco,
CA 94102
(415) 863-0537

Statement of Principles

As of the September 1978 USCPFA National Convention

GOAL: To build active and lasting friendship based on mutual understanding between the people of the United States and the people of China.

Toward that end we urge the establishment of full diplomatic, trade, and cultural relations between the two governments according to the principles agreed upon in the joint US-China communiqué of February 28, 1972, and that US foreign policy with respect to China be guided by these same principles: respect for sovereignty and territorial integrity; non-aggression; non-interference in the internal affairs of other states; equality and mutual benefit; and peaceful coexistence.

We call for the removal of all barriers to the growing friendship and exchange between our two peoples. We recognize that a major barrier is the US diplomatic recognition of and military presence in Taiwan. In the Joint Communiqué signed by the governments of the United States and the People's Republic of China, both parties acknowledge that Taiwan is an inseparable part of China and that the Taiwan question is an internal affair of China. We recognize that the People's Republic of China is the sole legal government of China.

Our educational activities include production and distribution of literature, films and photo exhibits; sponsoring speakers and study classes; speaking out against distortions and misconceptions about the People's Republic of China; publishing newsletters and pamphlets; promoting the exchange of visitors as well as technical, cultural, and social experiences.

It is our intention in each activity to pay special attention to those subjects of particular interest to the people of the United States.

Everyone is invited to participate in our activities and anyone who agrees with our Statement of Principles is welcome to join.

TOURS

Since a major way to understand anything is to see for yourself, USCPFA sponsors tours to China. This is an especially exciting time to visit. The Chinese have begun a campaign to modernize agriculture, industry, defense, and science and technology by the year 2000. Every commune, factory, neighborhood, and school is alive with new and creative approaches to this task. Arts and crafts, operas and films are flourishing. Areas and cities in China not previously visited by foreigners are now being added to itineraries.

Response to the tours has been very enthusiastic, and many participants, not already members, are joining the USCPFA on their return from China.

The USCPFA sponsors various types of tours:

FRIENDSHIP STUDY TOURS
These are three-week tours (17 days in China) offered to members who agree to work with the Association to promote friendship on their return from China, and who understand and accept the purposes and goals of the USCPFA. Candidates apply through a local chapter of the USCPFA and are approved by their Regional Tours Committee.

CHINA STUDY TOURS
These tours are 19 days (13 days in China) and are open to all. These tours enable Americans to gain a better understanding of China through first-hand observation, which they can then share with others in their communities. Those wishing to participate should apply to the CST office in their region.

CHINA STUDY TOURS—Special Tours for Educators

A special program for teachers who wish to visit China and then share their experiences in their classrooms. These tours are open to educators at all levels. They provide opportunities to become familiar with many aspects of Chinese society, including educational facilities and policies in China. University credit can be arranged through the Center for Teaching about China. Applicants should contact the China Study Tours office in their region.

NATIONAL SPECIAL INTEREST TOURS

Each year the USCPFA sponsors several national tours with a specific focus. These tours spend 21 days in China. Their purpose is to send to China individuals who are prominent in their fields and nationally recognized. Delegations for 1979 will include groups of (1) prominent women, (2) trade union leaders, (3) leading scientists (especially in mathematics and physics research), and (4) leaders of organizations. Interested persons should send biographical statements to the National Tours Office or to their local or regional travel committee.

USCPFA China Study Tour Offices

National Office
635 S. Westlake, Suite 205
Los Angeles, CA 90057
(213) 483-5810

Eastern Region
80 Eighth Avenue
Suite 303
New York, N.Y. 10011
(212) 255-8377

Hawaii
PO Box 1613
Honolulu, HI 96806
(808) 941-6727

Midwest Region
PO Box 793
Detroit, MI 48232
(313) 868-0082

Western Region
635 S. Westlake, Suite 204
Los Angeles, CA 90057
(213) 483-6060

Southern Region
PO Box 5939
Austin, TX 78763
(512) 454-6607

The Center for US-China Relations

The Center for US-China Relations was established by the USCPFA in March 1978 to aid and focus a widespread campaign among the American people for immediate establishment of full diplomatic relations between the US and China, a guiding principle of the USCPFA since its inception. Much of the work of the Center and the USCPFA as a whole came to fruition with the establishment of full relations and the visit to the US of leading PRC officials in January 1979. The USCPFA had the unique opportunity to co-host a private dinner for Vice Premier Deng Xiaoping (Teng Hsiao-ping) and his associates during the Vice Premier's visit as a non-governmental expression of friendship between the peoples of the US and China.

The Center monitors developments in US-China relations on Capitol Hill and shares USCPFA opinions with US government leaders and other national organizations. The Center urges continuing cooperation between the two countries in the fields of technological, student, and people-to-people exchanges as well as the further development of mutually beneficial trade. It also plays a major role in interpreting to the American public at large the significance of diplomatic relations, the deepening of cooperation and understanding between the two countries, and attempts to respond to the ongoing questions related to the province of Taiwan. The Center works with government leaders, church and civic organizations and through the national media to promote the principles of the USCPFA. In addition, the Center publishes a regular newsletter, *US-China Update*, and is a major resource on US-China relations and Congressional deliberations. The Center also coordinates arrangements for visiting delegations from China under the auspices of the USCPFA.

The Center urges all Americans to communicate with their Congressional representatives in offering their support for normalization and the ongoing process of closer ties between our two countries.

Frank Pestana of USCPFA, former US Senate Minority Leader Hugh Scott, and PRC representative Chao Ya-chin attend opening of Center for US-China Relations in Washington.

If you are interested in receiving more information about the Center, or wish to receive our mailings, please contact:

The Center for US-China Relations
422 C Street, N.E.
Washington, D.C. 20002
(202) 547-0040

The Center for Teaching about China

The Center for Teaching about China was established by the USCPFA in 1977. Its primary purpose is to assist teachers and local friendship associations in need of materials and approaches for bringing China into the classroom. The Center offers the following services: (1) Collects published and unpublished teaching resources for all grade levels; (2) consults with those who are developing teaching units to meet the needs of teachers and local chapters of the USCPFA; (3) publishes a resources catalogue and quarterly newsletter; (4) facilitates distribution of new materials through its catalogue; (5) identifies a national network of persons who wish to share ideas and develop materials on China.

The Center draws on the talents and resources of many persons both inside the USCPFA and elsewhere who have practical experience in presenting China in schools and public programs. It works closely with school personnel and local friendship associations, providing materials and assistance on China-related studies. Some of these activities include holding seminars on life in China and planning and carrying out teacher workshops or in-service courses. The Center for Teaching about China is represented at major conventions.

In addition, the Center assists in administering a section of the USCPFA China Study Tours designated especially for educators. It arranges for university credit for tour participants and designs the pre-departure orientation program. Brochures on the tour program are available from the Center for Teaching about China, the National Tour Office (Los Angeles), or the regional China Study Tour offices.

Interest in China is growing rapidly among educators. The existence of a National Center makes it possible for USCPFA chapters involved in school work and individual teachers to share their experiences and receive assistance. The Center has some funding available for projects in curriculum development. Persons interested in any of the services offered by the Center for Teaching about China should write to:

The Center for Teaching about China
407 S. Dearborn, Suite 685
Chicago, Illinois 60605

Special Outreach Efforts

The USCPFA seeks to include all sectors of the American people in its friendship activities. Special efforts are made to involve minorities and working class people in different aspects of the association's programs. Films and literature on China are made available in languages other than English. Scholarship aid for tours can be offered on the basis of need, and the position of resources coordinator is being considered to enable minorities and working class persons to know more about China.

Publications

The USCPFA publishes *New China*, a quarterly magazine, an ongoing pamphlet series, and one-page handouts. A complete brochure and order form are available from the USCPFA National Office.

Read about China in the latest USCPFA pamphlets

CHOU EN-LAI AND THE CHINESE REVOLUTION, By Davison and Selden
CHOU EN-LAI: CONVERSATIONS WITH AMERICANS,
Interviews by William Hinton

China Series No. 3, 1977, 86 pages ($1.95)

This pamphlet presents a multifaceted view of the late Premier Chou En-lai. It examines his career in the context of the Chinese Revolution. William Hinton's interviews with Chou, reprinted from *New China* magazine, present illuminating insights into Chou's personality, politics, and world view.

"THEY ALL LOOK SO HEALTHY!"
An Introduction to Health Care in the People's Republic of China

China Series No. 6, 1978 ($.50)

A comprehensive view of China's health care system, including traditional and Western medicine, the training of paramedics (barefoot doctors), family planning, and medical advances.

AMERICANS TALK ABOUT U.S.-CHINA RELATIONS

China Reprint Series No. 5, 1978 ($.50)

A collection of articles reflecting pre-1979 developments in the area of US-China relations. Articles by Senator Edward Kennedy, Secretary of Commerce Juanita Kreps, and the International Longshoremen's and Warehousemen's Union are included.

REMEMBERING KOJI ARIYOSHI:
An American G.I. in Yenan, by Hugh Deane

China Series No. 5, 1978 ($1.00)

A vibrant story of one of USCPFA's founders: a farmer and dockworker who became a U.S. Army liaison with the Communist forces in Yenan during 1944-45; his interviews with Japanese prisoners; his meetings with Mao Tsetung, Chou En-lai, Chu Teh, Generals Hurley, Wedemeyer, and Marshall; his vision of China's future; then a second look throughout China in 1972 and his reunion with Chou En-lai. Much of the story is in Koji Ariyoshi's own words, excerpted from his articles in the *Honolulu Record* and the *Star-Bulletin*.

FRANCE

Association des Amitiés Franco-Chinoises, 32, rue Maurice-Ripoche, 75014 Paris

ITALY

Associazione Italia-Cina, Via del Seminario 87, Roma

JAPAN

Japan-China Friendship Association, 1-4 Nishiki-cho, Kanda, Chivodaka, Tokyo

MEXICO

Sociedad Amigos de China Popular, A.C, Peten 460 Col. Vertiz Navarte, Mexico 12, D.F.

NETHERLANDS

Netherlands-China Friendship Association, Bermuurde,-Weerd OZ 8, Utrecht

NEW ZEALAND

New Zealand-China Friendship Society (Inc.), 22 Swanson Street, Auckland

NORWAY

Vennskapsambandit Norge-Kina, Boks 57, Blindern, Oslo

SWEDEN

Svenski-Kinesiska Vanskapsfobundet, Maria Prastgardsgata 31, Stockholm 11652
Svenski-Kinesiska Vanskapsfobundet, Malmoavdelningen Box 4180, Malmo

UNITED KINGDOM

Society for Anglo-Chinese Understanding, 152 Camden High Street, London, NW 1, England

UNITED STATES

US-China Peoples Friendship Association, National Office: 635 South Westlake Avenue, Suite 202, Los Angeles, California 90057

We [in China] have friends all over the world.

Calligraphy by Chen Chi

General Tour Groups Until 1977, the Chinese discouraged tourism per se (except for overseas Chinese), both for political reasons and due to a lack of adequate facilities and sufficient numbers of qualified escorts and interpreters. The first tourists to break this pattern were cruise ship passengers who were allowed entry to one or two port cities on the basis of a "shore pass" of two to three days. By late 1977, most international airlines having a relationship with the Civil Aviation Administration of China (CAAC, China's national airline) were also allocated tour groups and, as of early 1979, private travel agents throughout North America, Western Europe, and Asia had been granted the right to form tours. Beginning in 1978, Linblad Travel began to offer ocean liner-based tours to China. The largest beneficiaries of the new policy have been the China-friendship organizations and airlines such as PanAm, JAL, and Swissair. In 1979, for example, PanAm was given an allocation of some 5,000 individual spaces and the US-China Peoples Friendship Association 3,800 spaces, including some 69 general "study" tours of 12-day duration.

The general tours also adhere to a new format. The size of the groups has been expanded to 50-100 and groups are broken down into smaller "clusters" once inside China. All are hosted by China International Travel Service.

China's post-1977 rush to expand tourism initially overtaxed its relatively limited capacity to handle the new wave of visitors. During the spring and summer of 1978, some guests complained of brusk treatment by harried service staff, inadequately trained interpreters, overcrowded transport facilities, and hastily arranged (if not makeshift) itineraries. For their part, however, Chinese travel authorities openly acknowledged these difficulties and sought some immediate remedies by lowering the rate of tourism expansion for 1979.

Meanwhile, expenditures and programs for rapid expansion of tourist facilities were proceeding apace through 1979. New hotels were under construction in more than 30 Chinese cities, with direct participation by foreign concerns announced for the first time in November 1978 (with Intercontinental Hotels of the US). By the end of that year, more than 100 areas had been opened to tourism. Expansion of the variety of activities available in China was also being emphasized, with a major new stress given to the opening of cultural and historical sites. A government release issued in December hinted that "hunting, camel-riding, skiing, and mountaineering" as well as sojourns in "traditional herdsmen's tents" were in the offing.

Business Travelers Of the more than 20,000 European and Western Hemisphere travelers who visited China in 1978, more than half came for business purposes. Most of these were invited to attend the semi-annual Chinese Export Commodities Fair held in Kwangchow (see special section on the Fair, pp. 91-8), although others have also visited Peking and Shanghai. Business people are invited for the purpose of carrying out trade; they rarely have an opportunity to see much of China beyond the negotiating sites. On the other hand, technicians working on plant construction in more remote parts of China get a glimpse of daily Chinese life withheld from most other visitors.

Invitations to representatives of business enterprises are arranged through one of China's nine state-owned trade corporations (listed on p. 39). The Chinese have also invited commercial groups such as chambers of commerce, the Mid-America Committee, and the National Machine Tool Builders Association.

Australia – China Travel

Measured by its population, both the volume and variety of Australia's exchanges with China are proportionally among the most extensive in the world. General tours to the PRC are conducted on a regular basis by the Australia-China Society, a China-friendship group that also sponsors cultural programs, trade symposia, and radio broadcasts. A news bulletin is published by the Society's Victoria branch (Fitzroy). An array of tour options are also provided by private travel agents. Most tours enter China from Hong Kong.

Australia-Chinese student exchanges have been ongoing since the early 1970s. Exchange agreements also exist between the Chinese and Australian Academies of Science, which, for example, sponsored a Sino-Australian Plant Tissue Symposium in Peking during August 1978.

Canada – China Travel

Canada established diplomatic relations with the PRC in 1969. Since then, successive governmental exchange agreements have been concluded annually. Canada sends only government personnel from various ministries on these missions. The government also monitors the student exchange program between the two countries. The Council for the Arts administers officially sponsored tours of Chinese cultural groups. In March 1978, in an event of major cultural significance, the Toronto Symphony Orchestra engaged in a major tour of Chinese cities. Additional exchanges are carried out through private channels, most of which are handled through the more than eight branches of the Canada-China Friendship Association. In 1978, Canadian Pacific Airlines was awarded the right to organize China tours for 1,000 visitors.

For Canadian business travelers, information on China trade is available from the China Desk, Asia Division, Federal Government Department of Industry, Trade, and Commerce, 240 Queen Street, Ottawa, Ontario K1A 0H4; tel: (613) 992-9386. Free materials on

Canada-PRC marketing practices are available on request. The Canada-China Trade Council, incorporated in 1978, was to open its headquarters in Toronto in January 1979.

Hong Kong—China Travel

Hong Kong has been called China's "window on the world" and the British Crown Colony is playing an ever-increasing role in China's exchanges with the outside world. For many years, the proximity of Hong Kong to China made it the major port of entry for travelers to China, as well as a primary outlet for Chinese export goods.

Since early 1978, the China Travel Service (CTS) in Hong Kong has been organizing trips to China. Previously limited to short excursion tours to Kwangchow (Canton) and other southern cities, in 1978 CTS began to dramatically increase both the numbers and variety of its offerings.

Travel Services The Hong Kong agent of China International Travel Service, CTS, is located in Central District, Hong Kong Island, 77 Queens Road (tel: 5-259121), with a branch office in Alpha House, 23-33 Nathan Road, Kowloon (tel: 3-667201). CTS organizes its own tours to China and moreover has enfranchised over 6 local Hong Kong travel agencies to organize group tours. Most medium-sized travel agents in Hong Kong can provide the traveler with the relevant information on these trips. A number of travel agencies in the US, Canada and Europe have links with these Hong Kong agents and market the tours to the general public.

Group Trips from Hong Kong The following trips were being offered by CTS in 1979:

1 The Kwangchow Excursion Tour, including Kwangchow and the neighboring city of Foshan. This is a four-day trip that departs Hong Kong every Tuesday, Thursday, and Saturday. 25 persons per group; HK$850 per person (all prices are as of November 1978).

2 Kwangchow-Kweilin. A six-day tour leaving Hong Kong every Monday. 24 persons per group; HK$1,610 per person.

3 Kwangchow-Nanning-Kweilin. A ten-day tour leaving Hong Kong every Monday. 24 persons per group; HK$2,200.

4 Kwangchow-Kunming-Nanning. A nine-day trip leaving Hong Kong every Wednesday. 24 persons per group; HK$2,520.

5 Kwangchow-Changsha-Kweilin. A nine-day tour leaving from Hong Kong every Wednesday. 24 persons per group; HK$2,060.

6 Kwangchow-Shanghai-Nanking-Peking. A ten-day trip departing once each month (excluding April, November, and December). 24 persons per group; HK$3,720.

7 Kwangchow-Peking-Shanghai-Hangchow. An 11-day tour with one or two trips per month (excluding December). 25 persons per group; HK$3,890.

8 Kwangchow-Hangchow-Shanghai-Peking-Tokyo. A ten-day trip, one leaving Hong Kong each month (except March). 24 persons per group; HK$4,330.

Visas Three days to a week is required for a visa to be processed for the excursion trip to Kwangchow. A week or more may be necessary for a visa for the trips to the southern cities (Kweilin, Nanning, Kunming, and Changsha). Up to a month may be required for visas for trips to the northern cities.

Points to Note The above trips are organized in the main for foreign residents in Hong Kong and travelers in transit in Hong Kong. They are organized primarily on a first-come, first-served basis. It should also be noted that the CTS has annual quotas for the number of visas it can give to travelers from any one country.

Visas for group trips from Hong Kong, like those for tours from other ports, are group visas. This means that it is next to impossible to make itinerary changes in China, or even leave China from a different port than the one specified in the group visa. All arrangements for individual travel following the end of the tour should be made well in advance.

The most common means of entry into China from Hong Kong is by train. A change of train at the Lowu-Shumchun border is still required, although a direct train link between Hong Kong and Kwangchow was being negotiated in late 1978.

The train (HK$250 round trip), including service charges, begins in Kowloon. Passengers get off the Hong Kong train at Lowu and walk across a covered bridge and then through customs procedures. Lunch is served before completing the two-hour ride to Kwangchow. In late 1978, direct morning air service was inaugurated from Hong Kong's Kai Tak Airport to Bai Yun Airport in Kwangchow (HK$500 round trip). Finally, a hovercraft service was initiated in November 1978. Boats depart the ferry terminal in Kowloon three times a day for the 2-hour, 40-minute trip up the Pearl River to Whampoa Harbor (HK$320 round trip).

Japanese travelers are directed to go through Japan-based travel agencies for tours to China, unless they are residents of Hong Kong. In certain circumstances, members of the clergy are requested to apply through the Religious Committee in Peking for the organizing of tours. To date, only one delegation of Japanese monks (Buddhist) has gone to China in this manner.

Accommodations and Shopping in Hong Kong Hotel accom-

29

modations in Hong Kong can be arranged through any of the large travel agencies in the colony. CTS also provides this service for individuals and groups. It is important to note that most of Hong Kong's hotels overbook during the tourist season (May-November), requiring arrangements for accommodations well in advance.

Shopping Hong Kong is a shopper's paradise, bargains and interesting buys being an integral part of the life of Hong Kong residents. Hong Kong is also the largest outlet for Chinese manufactured consumer goods, stocking the best range of such products in the world (often surpassing what can readily be found in China). Some travelers prefer to visit a few of these stores and ship purchases home before going to China so as to avoid overloading with goods in the course of the trip. However, many local Chinese non-processed goods (e.g., textiles, bamboo-ware, and innumerable knick-knacks) are generally not available in these stores. Some of Hong Kong's major China-products emporia are:

Ywe Hwa Chinese Products, 301 Nathan Road, Kowloon;

Chungchiao China Products Emporium, corner of Nathan Road and Shantung Street, Tsimshatsui, Kowloon;

China Products Emporium, 17-31 Yee Wo Street, Tung Luo Wan (Hong Kong Island);

Ta Hwa China Products, 92-104 Queens Road Central (Hong Kong Island);

The Chinese Arts and Crafts Building in Tsimshatsui (near the Kowloon Star Ferry Terminal) stocks an extraordinary selection of Chinese jewelry, decorative furniture, and crafts.

Japan—China Travel

Japan's broad and multichanneled relationship—accentuated in 1978 by the signing of a treaty of friendship as well as a $10-billion long-term trade agreement with China—is reflected in the wide diversity of contacts between Tokyo and Peking. The two governments regularly exchange delegations, but the Chinese also unilaterally invite opposition political parties, political leaders, and special-interest groups. Japan also has a number of friendship groups that sponsor private visits. Prominent among these is the Japan-China Friendship Association (Orthodox).

In 1979, China was to accept 50,000 Japanese tourists, a 70% increase over 1978 and far and away the largest one-year allotment by the PRC to any single country. Visa formalities were to be eased and a major volume of travel by small groups would be approved for the first time.

In December 1978, PRC officials announced an unprecedented decision (for China) to permit Japanese trading firms to open offices in Peking and to receive long-term visas for their representatives. Japan's Tokyo-based coordinating body for PRC trade is the Japan-China Association for Economy and Trade.

Sports exchanges are popular between the two countries. They are sponsored by the appropriate national organizations as well as by universities, commercial enterprises, and military groups. Cultural exchanges are administered under a government umbrella organization but are usually initiated by private interests.

New Zealand–China Travel

Contacts between New Zealand and China have increased steadily since the two countries established diplomatic relations in 1973. In the late 1970s, several tours were being sponsored annually by the New Zealand-China Friendship Society, Inc. The Society's national office is in Auckland, with 15 branches located throughout the country. Most of its tours are of about three weeks' duration. The Society issues a newsletter, "New Zealand-China News," and publishes a brochure on China travel, "Helpful Information for China Tours."

One of the most prolific writers on travel and cultural subjects among Peking's foreign residents is Rewi Alley, a New Zealander.

United Kingdom–China Travel

The United Kingdom was one of the first Western countries to recognize the PRC after its founding in 1949, and the British have had a good working relationship with the Chinese since then. A great many British groups have visited the PRC, among them labor groups, friendship delegations, sports teams, and technical delegations. The UK has an official trade promotion organization called the Sino-British Trade Council, but the Chinese also deal with a private consortium known as the "48 Group," comprised of a number of firms that were the first to publicly promote trade with China. Exchange agreements are reviewed annually by the two governments.

A number of private tours are arranged each year through the Society for Anglo-Chinese Understanding (SACU), the UK's China-friendship organization founded in 1965. Membership is "open to all, irrespective of party affiliations, who are interested in the life and work of the Chinese people and support the aims and activities of the Society." SACU's 1978 tours included those with general themes as well as a Young People's Study Tour and a Social Planning Study Tour. Inclusive fares ranged from £780 to £950 with an average duration of 22 days. Its publications, "China Now" and "China Broadsheet," describe a wide range of current developments in the PRC.

A number of private tourist agencies in the UK offer cultural tours to China, among them Oriental Express Travel, Bales Tours, Regent Holidays, and Thompson Holidays.

United States–China Travel

Exchanges between the US and the PRC began officially in March 1971 when the US travel ban to China was formally lifted. The Shanghai Communiqué, issued in 1972, noted that exchange visits were an essential part of the process of establishing full diplomatic relations between the two countries. From 1972 until 1978, a total of about 15,000 persons from the US had visited China, with visa applications for that same period estimated at well over 1,000,000. In turn, about 2,000 Chinese have visited the US, for the most part trade, scientific, and cultural groups. During March-April 1978, in a notable exchange, leading officials of the China International Travel Service toured the US, visiting tourist sites and meeting with various representatives of the US travel industry.

With the establishment of full relations on January 1, 1979, exchanges with the United States were expected to enter a new stratum, with projections of an annual volume of 100,000 US visitors by 1985 considered conservative by many analysts. The first direct commercial air link between the two countries (San Francisco-Peking) was expected to be announced in 1979.

Official Contacts Official US exchanges with the People's Republic of China began in 1971 when Premier Chou En-lai personally invited the US Table Tennis Team to China. Secretary of State Kissinger soon followed. President Nixon's famous visit in February 1972 resulted in the issuance of the Shanghai Communiqué. President Ford and officials of the Carter administration have since visited China, as have 75 US senators and congressmen. On January 28, 1979, following the establishment of full diplomatic relations on January 1, Teng Hsiao-p'ing paid an official visit to the US, marking the first state visit by a PRC leader since the government's founding in 1949.

Quasi-Official Contacts Three nongovernmental organizations, the National Committee on US-China Relations, the National Council for US-China Trade, and the Committee on Scholarly Communication with the People's Republic of China, have handled what might be considered quasi-official exchanges in trade, science, technology, medicine, culture, and sports. Such exchanges and visits have been agreed to in principle by the two governments and are nominally hosted by them. Logistics and administration, however, are handled by the staff of the three organizations.

Within their areas of specialty, the three groups can advise on the likely success of a travel request, provide names of appropriate contacts in China, offer reports on previous visits in specific fields, and supply general background information. Delegations specifically organized by them, however, consist largely of officials or influential public figures, and are not accessible to the general public.

The National Committee on US-China Relations, Inc. (NCUSCR). 777 United Nations Plaza, 9b, New York, New York 10017.

The NCUSCR facilitates and administers exchange visits agreed to by the US and PRC governments in the fields of education, international affairs, performing arts, and sports. It is funded largely by the US Department of State, and works under its direction. Some of its major undertakings have included visits to China by the Philadelphia Orchestra (1973), a group of university presidents (1974), a track and field team (1975), and a group of congressional committee staff members. Groups from China have included a martial arts troupe (1974), a women's basketball team (1975 and 1978), and a performing arts troupe (1978). General services of the National Committee include travel advice, briefing kits, seminars, and a newsletter describing its programs. Also available are lists of previous exchange groups who may be contacted for more specific information. In the wake of President Carter's announcement of full recognition, the NCUSCR was expected to continue to coordinate exchanges in 1979, including the visit to China of the Boston Symphony Orchestra.

Committee on Scholarly Communication with the People's Republic of China (CSCPRC). National Academy of Sciences, 2101 Constitution Avenue, N.W., Washington, D.C. 20418.

The CSCPRC is sponsored jointly by the National Academy of Sciences, the American Council of Learned Societies, and the Social Science Research Council. It is supported in part by State Department funding and administers exchanges in science, medicine, and technology. Sponsored groups are selected on the basis of prior negotiation with the PRC government.

A multi-faceted exchange program for 1979 was concluded between the CSCPRC and the Scientific and Technical Association of the People's Republic of China. The new programs included a series of lecture visits by US and Chinese scholars, research visits by scholars from both countries, and bilateral symposia. Activities were to include the US visit of a multidisciplinary delegation representing the Chinese Academy of Social Sciences. In addition, the CSCPRC agreed to assist Chinese scholars with their plans to attend international meetings held in the US.

33

Under an announced agreement on October 23, 1978 China was to send 500-700 students and scholars to the US during the academic year 1978-79, and 60 US students were to be sent to the PRC in a federally funded program by September 1979, with more to follow based on China's ability to receive them. The Americans were to eventually include undergraduates, but initial applications were to be limited to graduate students and professors.

The National Council for US-China Trade (NCUSCT). 1050 17th Street, N.W., Washington, D.C. 20036.

The NCUSCT is recognized by both governments as the focal point for development of trade between China and the US. This organization is less directly connected to the US government than either the NCUSCR or the CSCPRC, as it derives its financial support from some 425 member corporations, banks, and individuals, and because the Chinese have been willing to move outside of government channels to engage in foreign trade and commerce. The NCUSCT assists both members and nonmembers in formulating approaches to Chinese foreign trade authorities. It assists business persons in making appropriate contacts, sponsors commercial exchanges between the two countries, and offers special services to persons attending the Kwangchow Trade Fair.

It also maintains special industry-wide committees to help promote US-China trade. The NCUSCT publishes a bimonthly magazine for members entitled *China Business Review*, with special reports on different sectors of the Chinese economy, and maintains a translation service to aid in rendering business proposals into Chinese.

Private Exchanges The largest number of US citizens to visit China prior to 1978 traveled under the auspices of the US-China Peoples Friendship Association (USCPFA). Other organizationally based or ad hoc groups in the US have succeeded in arranging tours through direct application to China International Travel Service (CITS) in Peking. In 1977-79, such tours included artists, World War II veterans, religious leaders, overseas Chinese, trade union leaders, media specialists, women financial executives, and booksellers.

US-China Peoples Friendship Association (USCPFA). National Office: 635 South Westlake Avenue, Suite 202, Los Angeles, California 90057.

The USCPFA is recognized by the Chinese as the principal sponsor of "friendship" tours to the PRC for US citizens. A non-profit educational organization founded in 1974, the USCPFA's status and purpose is similar to those of friendship organizations in other countries that are actively sympathetic to China. It supported the establishment of full diplomatic relations with China and the severance of all official US ties with Taiwan; its goal to promote the development of "people-to-people" contacts between the US and China remain a focal point of its activities following the January 1979 establishment of full diplomatic relations. USCPFA tours are organized regionally (by its 110 member chapters) as well as nationally around special interests such as community organizations, trade unions, sports, minority leaders, public-health personnel, and curriculum planners. In 1979, the USCPFA sponsored 3,800 visits to the PRC (compared with 675 in 1977), with more anticipated for 1980. The first reciprocal "people-to-people" exchange from China took place in December 1977, with the visit to the US of an artist delegation sponsored by the Chinese People's Association for Friendship with Foreign Countries. USCPFA tours are available to non-members as well as members. In 1979, the all-inclusive cost of USCPFA general tours to China ranged between $2,600 and $2,800.

APPLICATION PROCEDURES

Despite the increased tourist volume planned for the late 1970s, procedures for gaining entry to China were expected to remain relatively formal and lengthy, calling for long-range planning and awareness of special guidelines. And, although in 1979 the PRC was moving closer to acceptance of general tourism, it seemed likely that a degree of selectivity would be retained, at least for those seeking to pursue specific interests while in China. For example, special restrictions may continue to apply to Western journalists (including photojournalists) and to citizens of a few countries that do not have full diplomatic ties with the PRC (e.g., as of early 1979, Haiti, Israel, South Africa) as well as to persons with political associations considered inimical to state interests (i.e., persons with ongoing political ties to the present government on Taiwan).

Inasmuch as the number of applicants is expected to continue to outpace the availability of accommodations in China, preference (apart from participants in general tours formed by airlines and travel agents) will no doubt continue to be given to applicants whose interests or occupations have a clear counterpart in China and, by extension, to those whose experience in China is likely to have a broad impact on the occupational or social circles to which they return. Although such criteria have remained vague and largely unspecified, the Chinese seem likely to continue to regard an invitation to visit their country as a privilege to be conferred on those either well-placed or well-disposed to convey the experience to their associates back home.

Special-Interest Travel

Groups seeking to initiate a visit to China in order to pursue a special interest (i.e., commercial or professional) must be in possession of an official invitation from a PRC governmental body. The key element in securing an invitation is a written proposal. Except in the case of business travelers or persons well known in China, individual applicants will usually be advised to seek entry as part of a group.

In general, a short good-will tour is the easiest to arrange. A wide variety of occupational groups has succeeded in gaining approval, with medical, educational, legal, and technical fields accounting for a significant share. In recent years, the Chinese have been known to turn down the following proposals: a hike along the length of the Great Wall, a canoe trip down the Yangtse River, a bicycle tour of southern provinces, a mobile home trip by a retired couple, a mountain-climbing team, in-depth studies at institutes or universities, schemes for "living among the people," projects of "humanitarian" interests (e.g., missionary groups).

Once a prospective group has been formed, a detailed letter requesting permission to visit China should be prepared and addressed to the China International Travel Service or to an appropriate PRC host organization. The letter should include the following elements:

Reason for the Visit Applicants should explain why, from the group's vantage point, they seek to make the trip; why the Chinese should invite this particular group; the manner in which the trip will contribute to mutual understanding, friendship, and professional knowledge.

One-Page Biographies of Participants Chinese travel authorities seek a clear sense of the composition and balance of a group and the relevance of each member to it.

Length and Time of Year for the Proposed Trip Most group visits last from two to three weeks. In terms of optimum climate conditions, the best times for visiting China are in spring and fall.

Proposed Activities While in China Although a list of activities need not be exhaustive, proposals should include the kinds of institutions deemed relevant to the group's interests (universities, museums, factories, historical sites). The more specific the list, the better, although the final itinerary will consist mainly of what's practicable from the Chinese end.

Places to Be Visited Most groups, as a matter of course, travel to Peking, Shanghai, and Kwangchow. Other cities commonly visited include Sian, Nanking, Shenyang, and Hangchow. Requests to visit specific cities or regions should be rationalized in terms of the group's special focus. Proposals may also include general suggestions for visiting a rural commune, although the specific selection is best left to the Chinese. Rural sojourns are usually kept short, so as not to overtax local facilities or unduly disrupt work schedules.

Official Travel Contacts in the PRC

Final authority for granting permission to visit China is vested in a small number of central agencies in Peking. Initial applications from all organizations, groups, and individuals must receive approval (usually transmitted in the form of an invitation to visit China) from one of these agencies. In general, initial travel requests may also be sent to the PRC's overseas diplomatic representatives. Although the embassies are not themselves empowered to extend invitations, they may expedite such requests and handle visas and other formalities.

China International Travel Service The China International Travel Service (CITS) carries out two functions. On the international level, it has responsibility for all general tour groups, i.e., those that come for nonprofessional reasons. On the domestic level, it makes all arrangements for travel within the People's Republic of China. Most tour groups should apply to this organization; they will probably be referred to it should they apply through a Chinese diplomatic mission abroad. The CITS address is 6 East Changan, Peking.

While not maintaining any offices overseas, CITS has an official agent in Hong Kong: the China Travel Service (CTS—see preceding section on Hong Kong-China Travel).

Although CITS has no other agents acting on its behalf in other countries, it does maintain correspondence with a number of private travel agencies in Japan, Canada, the US, Latin America, and Europe, and, through them, approves applications for general and specialized groups.

PRC Agencies for Specialized Travel

A variety of organizations in China issue invitations to foreign delegations, although most of these exchanges are arranged through government (or quasi-official) channels at the other end and rarely come about as the result of private initiatives. Although it is possible for private groups to contact these agencies directly (all are headquartered in Peking), the likelihood of a positive response—except in the case of overseas Chinese—is not great.

Overseas Chinese Travel Service This organization handles all travel requests and arrangements for overseas Chinese, whether born in China or not. Visitors of Chinese origin are generally accorded trips of longer duration. While in China, they may travel in smaller groups or singly, in order to spend time with relatives.

Chinese People's Institute of Foreign Affairs An advisory and research body, the institute usually invites prominent public figures and government officials. Opinion leaders, members of the political opposition, influential journalists, or prominent business figures are handled under the auspices of this institute.

Chinese People's Association for Friendship with Foreign Countries This association invites cultural figures, orchestras, artists, dance companies, and other groups concerned with art, literature, and other cultural interests. It maintains a consultative relationship with China-friendship associations in other countries.

All-China Sports Federation This federation invites foreign athletic teams and sponsors international competitions in China.

Chinese Scientific and Technical Association This group is almost a direct counterpart of the US Committee on Scholarly Communication with the People's Republic of China. It seeks to bring scientists and scholars to China.

China Medical Association This agency invites medical delegations.

China Council for the Promotion of International Trade This group's counterpart in the US is the National Council for US-China Trade. It arranges exchanges of business and commercial delegations.

Chinese Architecture Society To date, a group of US women architects, among others, has been invited to China by the society. CAS members paid a reciprocal visit to New York and Boston in late 1978.

Chinese Ministry of Education This agency invites educational administrators as well as delegations from foreign schools and universities.

China's State Trading Corporations

Foreign trade in the PRC is a state monopoly, controlled by the Ministry of Foreign Trade and conducted through ten foreign trade corporations. The corporations are organized according to kinds of commodities, and businesses seeking to initiate trade—either import or export—can do so by writing directly to the appropriate foreign trade corporation (see listing, p. 39).

The most important event on the China trade calendar is the semiannual Chinese Export Commodities Fair, held in Kwangchow (Canton) April 15-May 15 and October 15-November 15. Invitations to the Fair may be solicited by contacting the appropriate foreign trade corporation.

Head Offices of China's Foreign Trade Corporations

China National Arts and Crafts Import and Export Corporation
82 Tung An Men, Peking, People's Republic of China
Cable: ARTCHINA PEKING

China National Chemicals Import and Export Corporation
Erh Li Kou, Hsi Chiao, Peking, People's Republic of China
Cable: SINOCHEM PEKING

China National Native Produce and Animal By-Products Corporation
82 Tung An Men, Peking, People's Republic of China
Cable: CHINATUHSU PEKING

China National Light Industrial Products Import and Export Corporation
82 Tung An Men, Peking, People's Republic of China
Cable: INDUSTRY PEKING

China National Textiles Import and Export Corporation
82 Tung An Men, Peking, People's Republic of China
Cable: CHINATEX PEKING

China National Cereals, Oils and Foodstuffs Import and Export Corporation
82 Tung An Men, Peking, People's Republic of China
Cable: CEROILFOOD PEKING

China National Machinery and Equipment Export Corporation
Erh Li Kou, Hsi Chiao, Peking, People's Republic of China
Cable: EQUIPEX PEKING

China National Machinery Import and Export Corporation
Erh Li Kou, Hsi Chiao, Peking, People's Republic of China
Cable: MACHIMPEX PEKING

China National Metals and Minerals Import and Export Corporation
Erh Li Kou, Hsi Chiao, Peking, People's Republic of China
Cable: MINMETALS PEKING

China National Technical Import Corporation
Erh Li Kou, Hsi Chiao, Peking, People's Republic of China
Cable: TECHIMPORT PEKING

Hong Kong's China Resources Company, an official agency of the PRC, is authorized to deal directly with foreign business persons. This company handles commercial matters for the Chinese corporations dealing with machinery, chemicals, and metals and minerals. It also acts as an intermediary for the China National Technical Import Corporation.

PRC Diplomatic Missions Abroad

In general, PRC diplomatic missions deal with governmental exchanges rather than with private travel requests, although special sections may be available to assist commercial travelers and overseas Chinese. Since permission to visit China can be secured only from an appropriate host organization in Peking (and not from a PRC embassy), inquiries regarding general travel—especially in the case of first trips—are likely to be redirected to CITS.

Diplomatic representatives may occasionally grant appointments to professional groups wishing to visit China. They may be helpful in framing a proposal, indicating the appropriate agency to write to in Peking and informally evaluating the merits of the application. Commercial sections of embassies are more active in arranging travel. In addition to contacting the appropriate foreign trade corporation in Peking, traders are advised to seek assistance from these sections.

 ### Selected Overseas Diplomatic Missions of the PRC

Argentina: Conesa 1964, Buenos Aires

Australia: 247 Federal Highway, Watson, Canberra, A.C.T. 2602 Australia

Belgium: Boulevard General Jacques, #19, 1050 Brussels

Brazil: Embaixad Republica Popular da China, MPWS cj 43 It 4, Brazilia, DF

Canada: 411-415 St. Andrews St., Ottawa, Ontario K1N 5H3

Colombia: Carrera 15 80-25, Bogota

Denmark: Oregaardsalle #25, DK 2900 Hellerup, Copenhagen

France: 11 Avenue George V, 75008, Paris

FRG: 5307 Wachtbergniederbachen, Konrad-Adenauer Str. 104

Italy: Via Giovanne, Paiseillo 39, Roma 00198

Japan: 5-30 Minami-Azabu, 4-Chome, Minato-ku, Tokyo

Mexico: Avenue San Jeronimo 217, Mexico City 20, DF

Netherlands: Adriaan Goehooplaan 7, Den Haag 070-55.15.15

Norway: 11 Inkognitojaten, Oslo 12

Peru: Jr. Jose Granda 150, San Isidoro, Lima

Sweden: Bragevagen #4, Stockholm

Switzerland: Kalcheggweg 10, Berne

United Kingdom: 31 Portland Place, London W1N 3AG

United States: 2300 Connecticut Avenue, N.W., Washington, D.C. 20008

Venezuela: Quinta Mama, Calle Mohedne, Country Club, Caracas

The Embassy of the PRC in the US The Embassy of the People's Republic of China to the United States, which functioned as a "Liaison Office" until March 1, 1979, plays an important role in evaluating travel and trade proposals. Once an invitation has been received from the host organization in China, the Washington office will also process visas. A copy of trade or travel proposals sent to China should be forwarded to the Embassy, with a covering request to discuss the proposal further. The Commercial Section of the Embassy can provide assistance in making introductions in China, in ascertaining whether there is interest in the kind of business proposed, and in solving problems once a commercial relationship has been established.

What to Pack

For visits to the People's Republic of China, just as to other parts of the world, a simple rule applies: bring twice as much money as may be needed and half as many clothes.

The Chinese are an informal people, therefore obviating the need to pack formal clothing, several changes in wardrobe, or any "special" items for a special occasion. Women will find pantsuits, everyday dresses, and other casual clothing appropriate, and should minimize flamboyance in makeup and jewelry. Such adornments will seem out of place in China. Shorts, halters, or other revealing clothes are frowned upon. Men should choose a wardrobe of conservative color. For most visitors there is no need to take anything more formal than a sports jacket and, perhaps, one tie. Shorts are acceptable for men in the summer, as are jeans for both men and women.

Only a few changes of clothing are necessary. Laundry and dry cleaning services are excellent in China, and are performed overnight in most hotels. Comfortable walking shoes are a must, perhaps with a dressier pair reserved for dinners or special occasions (women should avoid high heels).

The seasons must be taken into account, of course, and in cool weather it is better to wear several layers than to rely on bulky outer garments. In the winter, warm socks, thermal underwear, and head-gear are recommended for both men and women. A sweater is appropriate for almost any time of year, as is a light raincoat. Cottons are most comfortable for hot weather. Open-neck, short-sleeved shirts will blend in with the attire of Chinese guides.

Other practical items to include are:

Toiletries Facial tissues, toothpaste, shampoo. (As most brands can be replenished in Hong Kong, quantities should be kept to a minimum.)

Pharmaceuticals Prescription medicines, vitamins, aspirin, and other health aids as required on a regular basis. As a precaution, cold and digestive remedies might be included. Mosquito repellent can also be useful.

Books As of late 1978, there were no Western publications available at newsstands in China, so magazines, books and maps may be brought along.

Liquor and tobacco Apart from a new concession at the Peking Hotel, Western liquor is unobtainable in China and the ubiquitous Chinese cigarettes may seem strong and raw to Western tastes.

Camera and film The rule about film is that one can never take enough. Western film brands are generally unavailable in China (and time considerations usually do not permit developing). An ample supply of batteries, flashbulbs, and, for the fastidious, replacement parts should also be brought along.

Instant coffee Many find the Chinese variety quite palatable, but those who are particular should bring their own.

What Not to Pack

"Street" drugs, pornography, firearms, inflammatory political or evangelical literature, contraband.

INTERNATIONAL AIRLINE CONNECTIONS

While China may still seem "on the other side of the world" —psychologically and culturally—getting there is no longer an exotic or complicated procedure.

Air Links The most common points of entry into China by air are Peking and Shanghai. In October 1978, China's CAAC inaugurated regular charter air service connections between Hong Kong and Kwangchow (although rail service was expected to remain the most common means of travel between those two points. For details on Hong Kong-Kwangchow rail and hovercraft connections, see section on Hong Kong-China Travel). In every case, entry and exit points are specified by China International Travel Service. All travel connections within China are prearranged.

CAAC Boeing 707 at Peking Airport

Twelve international carriers now fly directly to Peking or Shanghai, among them CAAC, China's official airline. For those living in the Western Hemisphere, the Pacific is the shortest route, with direct flights via Tokyo available on Japan Air Lines, Canadian Pacific, PanAm and other carriers. Connections via the Atlantic and Europe are also possible. For those living on the Atlantic seaboard this route may mean a modest financial saving. Atlantic routings entail a longer flight time, however, since there are at least three stops en route to China, often including a change of planes and, usually, an overnight layover in France, Switzerland, Romania, or Pakistan.

Arriving by air in Peking or Shanghai, passengers first proceed to customs for a passport check. A representative from the group's host organization will then assist the delegation in moving through customs (waived for official groups who are guests of the state). From Shanghai Airport, most hotels can be reached in about 15 minutes by bus or taxi; in Peking, the trip takes about 40 minutes.

PRC Customs

China's customs formalities have tended to be rather exacting. In late 1978, however, PRC officials announced that measures were under way to simplify procedures. The most important document the visitor must fill out before arrival is the customs declaration form. It requires an itemization of cameras, watches, jewelry, and money being taken in. Foreigners who are not residents of the PRC are allowed to bring in four bottles of liquor, three cartons of cigarettes, an unlimited amount of medicine for personal use, any personal effects, and a virtually unlimited quantity of currency (the amount to be declared).

There is no restriction on film, but professional film equipment (i.e., 16 mm. or 35 mm. cameras) is not allowed in without special permission. There is no restriction on tape recorders and recording tape.

Overseas Chinese or foreign citizens of Chinese origin who come to visit relatives are placed in a special category under Chinese customs laws; these travelers should consult their PRC embassy for further information.

There are four cardinal rules to observe with respect to customs procedures:

1. Declare everything that is asked for.

2. Do not attempt to bring in any contraband or other illegal items (e.g., weapons, drugs).

3. All personal possessions taken into China must be taken out (cameras, watches, jewelry). In no case should such items be given away. Losses should be reported as soon as they are discovered.

4. Scrupulously record the full amount of money (including travelers checks) taken in. Save all currency-exchange vouchers and all receipts for major purchases. Upon departure, the amount of money taken out must be noted on the original currency declaration form, and should correlate with the amount spent in China. Chinese currency may not be taken out of China (except Bank of China travelers checks).

II
TRAVELING IN CHINA

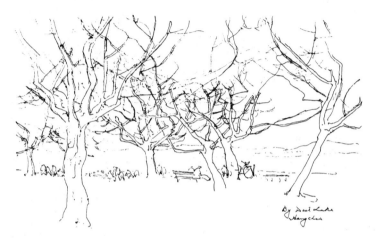

Itinerary

While every effort is usually made to fix an itinerary within China before arrival, tour groups traveling under arrangements made by China International Travel Service may find themselves subject to sudden changes. Due to an extreme shortage of hotel space in Peking, for example, groups have arrived in the morning only to find themselves on a train to Nanking that night. Cities on a preliminary itinerary may also be changed depending on availability of hotels and transportation.

Climate

Visitors to the PRC should be prepared to experience a wide range of climatic conditions, particularly if visits are made during the spring and autumn when temperature changes can be frequent and abrupt. The enormous north-south extent of Chinese territory—roughly from the latitude of Winnipeg to that of Jamaica—in part explains the great contrasts.

Before discussing specific regions, several general characterizations about China's climate can be made:

—Seasonal temperatures differ greatly in nearly all parts of the country.

45

China's climate ranges from cold, snowy northern winters . . .

to humid summers, as here in Kiangsu Province

TEMPERATURES AND PRECIPITATION IN CHINA

MEAN READINGS°	JANUARY (°F)	(°C)	APRIL (°F)	(°C)	JULY (°F)	(°C)	OCTOBER (°F)	(°C)
PEKING								
Max.	35	1.7	69	20.5	89	31.7	69	20.5
Min.	14	10	43	6.2	71	21.7	44	6.7
Precip.	.2		.7		9.6		.6	
SHANGHAI								
Max.	47	8.3	67	19.5	91	32.8	75	23.9
Min.	32	0.0	49	9.5	75	23.9	56	13.3
Precip.	1.9		3.6		5.8		2.9	
KWANGCHOW								
Max.	65	18.3	77	25.0	91	32.8	85	29.5
Min.	49	9.5	65	18.3	77	25.0	67	19.5
Precip.	.9		6.8		8.1		3.4	
KWEILIN								
Max.	55	13.1	74	23.4	93	33.9	81	27.2
Min.	41	5.0	59	15.0	76	24.5	62	16.7
Precip.	1.6		9.4		8.0		2.6	
CHANGSHA								
Max.	45	7.2	70	21.1	94	34.5	75	23.9
Min.	35	1.7	56	13.3	78	25.6	59	15.0
Precip.	1.9		5.7		4.4		3.0	
WUHAN								
Max.	46	7.8	69	20.5	93	33.9	74	23.4
Min.	34	1.1	55	12.8	78	25.6	60	15.6
Precip.	1.8		5.8		7.0		3.1	
CHENGCHOW								
Max.	40	4.4	70	21.1	90	32.2	70	21.1
Min.	20	−6.6	50	10.0	70	21.1	50	10.0
Precip.	.4		.9		7.0		.7	
NANKING								
Max.	58	14.5	70	21.1	93	33.4	80	26.7
Min.	24	4.4	45	7.2	75	23.9	60	15.6
Precip.	2.1		4.2		5.0		2.8	
SHENYANG								
Max.	20	−6.6	55	12.8	78	25.6	58	14.6
Min.	2	−16.7	40	45	7.2	38	3.3	−12
Precip.	.2		.8		9.2		1.0	

°Daily readings for temperatures; monthly readings (in inches) for precipitation.

—Although rain and high humidity are common in summer throughout the PRC, the length of the rainy season is longer and the amount of rainfall considerably greater south of the Yangtse River.

—Winters are dry, with little precipitation, particularly in the north and northeast where spring may also bring little rain.

Northeast This area includes Shenyang and Harbin, and comprises the huge northeast plain that extends some 600 miles north-south. Summers are hot and dry, and winters bitterly cold; the climate over-all is similar to that of Minnesota and southern Alberta.

North-central This region includes the middle and lower valley of the Yellow River, the intensively cultivated North China Plain, and the hills and mountains to the west. Cities in this area include Peking, Chengchow, and Sian. Temperatures are roughly similar to that of Kansas or Nebraska although there is year-round precipitation. Haze and duststorms can occur during late winter and early spring.

Southeast The lower Yangtse valley and its many tributaries are characterized by warm temperatures and substantial rainfall. Rice is grown in virtually all lowlands and the long growing season permits at least two crops a year in most regions. Climatic conditions are semi-tropical, comparable to the Gulf Coast (except that winter storms are rare). Summers are long, hot, and sticky, often subject to incessant rain. The fall is more pleasant, and winters are brief with cooler temperatures. Shanghai and Hangchow are often overcast, damp, and drizzly during the winter.

Language

Visitors to the People's Republic of China can expect that tour escorts and representatives from their host organization will speak the group's language, be it English, French, Spanish, or Urdu. These personnel have been trained at universities or special language institutes and are often quite skilled at discoursing with foreigners on many subjects—from politics to culture. Some younger escorts still in training may not be quite so proficient. The flow of conversation will be aided if visitors take care to speak slowly and distinctly, avoid jargon, and adopt a patient demeanor.

English and other foreign languages are now widely taught over radio and television, and one may be greeted on the street with a friendly "Hello!" However, it is not common for most Chinese to speak a foreign language. In all parts of China, the dominant dialect is *putunghua* (the "common language"), a derivative of Peking dialect (sometimes referred to as "Mandarin"). The individual native dialect of each region (e.g., Shanghai, Kwangtung, Hunan) is also used, making most Chinese effectively "bilingual." Of course, any attempt to master some rudimentary Chinese phrases (no matter how horrendous the resulting pronunciation) will be appreciated (see Chinese Phrases for Travel, p. 284).

Currency

China's Currency The official name for the currency of the People's Republic of China is the *renminbi* (RMB—the "people's money"). It is denominated into the *yuan*. Within China, it is also informally counted out as *k'uai* (unit). Notes in common use are printed in denominations of 1, 2, 5, and 10 *yuan*. The *yuan* is in turn divided into *fen* (cents). Paper notes are issued for the 50-*fen* unit (called 5 *jiao*), the 20-*fen* unit (called 2 *jiao*), and the 10-*fen* unit (called 1 *jiao*). Coins are in denominations of 1, 2, and 5 *fen*.

The RMB is not traded on international markets and can be purchased or exchanged only within China or in Hong Kong (in exchange for travelers checks only). The amount of foreign currency allowed into the country is unlimited, but the full amount must be declared and accounted for upon leaving. It is forbidden to remove Chinese currency from the country, and remaining RMB must be reconverted before leaving China.

CHINESE CURRENCY (RMB) EXCHANGE RATES

COUNTRY		BUY	SELL
Australia	$100	183.3	180.3
Belgium	F100	5.9	5.8
Canada	$100	134.9	132.7
France	F100	38.0	37.4
Germany (FRG)	DM100	87.1	85.7
Hong Kong	$100	33.8	33.2
Italy	L100,000	194.9	191.7
Japan	Y100,000	812.2	798.9
New Zealand	$100	170.2	167.4
Sweden	K100	37.0	36.4
Switzerland	F100	96.0	94.5
United Kingdom	£100	321.2	315.9
United States	$100	160.6	158.0

Sources: Bank of Tokyo, January 25, 1979; *Wall Street Journal*, January 25, 1979.

Travelers Checks Travelers checks usually bring a slightly higher exchange rate than currency. They are accepted from most of the world's leading banks and issuing agencies (as of January 1979, 41 types of checks were accepted). A Bank of China check was introduced in 1978 (they are sold at the Bank's branches in Hong Kong at a HK$3.00 service charge). Others negotiable in China include Bank of America, Barclays, Thomas Cook, Lloyds, Midland, National Westminster, Bank of Tokyo, Fuji, Mitsui, Sumitomo, Algemene Bank of Nederland, Australia and New Zealand Banking Group, Bank für Gemeinwirtschaft, Banque de Bruxelles, Banque Nationale de Paris, National Bank of Australia, Credit Lyonnais, Deutsche Bank, Hong Kong and Shanghai Banking Corporation, Standard Chartered Bank, and Swiss Bankers. In addition, China accepts money orders drawn on Manufacturers Hanover Trust and the Royal Bank of Canada.

There is no black market in China. Checks and foreign currency should be converted only at branches of the Bank of China.

It is possible to arrange for a letter of credit payable to the visitor through the Bank of China. This can be done through most large international banks for a service fee. The procedure is cumbersome, however, and is not recommended except in cases where it might be necessary to transfer some emergency funds to someone already in China. As of January 1979, the only bank in the US that had a direct "correspondent" relationship with the Bank of China was the First National Bank of Chicago.

It is usually recommended that the traveler exchange money as needed; this prevents having to contend with a large stack of Chinese notes (the largest denomination, a Y10 note, was worth $6.16 as of December 1978, and will avoid minor losses from reconversion at the end of the trip.

Postal Service and Telecommunications

China maintains good mail and telecommunications links with the outside world. Telex and phototelegraphic facilities are available for business transactions. Most communications services are available at hotels.

Mail Postal rates for international mail were sharply increased in 1977. The following is a brief summary of rates (in Chinese *yuan*):

Postcard	(airmail)	.60
Letter	(airmail)	.70 for first 10 g.
	(surface)	.40 for up to 20 g.
Aerogram		.60
Small packets	(surface)	.60 up to 100 g.
	(airmail)	.60 + .15 for every 10 g. or fraction thereof

Telephone Long-distance calls to North America are charged at the rate of Y9.60 (US$5.85) per minute, with a minimum charge of three minutes. A service charge of Y4 (US$2.44) is made on all calls, whether or not completed. Charges may be reversed to most countries. Long-distance calls may be booked at hotel service desks and usually take 5-15 minutes to be completed.

Cable Telegram rates to overseas destinations vary considerably from country to country, but generally fall within Y1.20-1.50 per word. The per-word charge to the US is Y1.30 ($0.79). The rate is doubled for "express" (four-hour) delivery and is halved for "regular cable" (night letter). Because of the high cable rates, it may be worth considering a phone call in some instances.

Telex Telex facilities are available at main and branch post offices in large cities. Only three hotels have telex: the Chin Chiang Hotel in Shanghai and the Tung Fang and Bai Yun in Kwangchow. Patrons must punch their own tapes. Rates to all overseas destinations, excluding Hong Kong, are Y8.40 ($5.12) per minute, with a minimum three-minute charge.

Incoming Correspondence Delivery of mail from North America or Europe generally takes a week to ten days. For most tours, it is thus impractical to request mail from home. Since exact daily itineraries and hotels are rarely known prior to arrival in China, mail should not be addressed to hotels or cities. To facilitate such contacts the proper address to use is:

Name of Individual, Name of Group, c/o Host Organization (e.g., China International Travel Service), Peking, People's Republic of China.

Cables can reach the visitor in the same manner (the cable address of China International Travel Service is its acronym, LUXINGSHE). Every effort is made to deliver cables promptly. For business travelers spending some time in one place, it is advantageous to register a cable address (for a small fee).

Incoming telephone calls are connected by an overseas operator. Callers should instruct the operator to contact the host organization in Peking in order to locate the delegation and the individual being sought. This procedure can be remarkably efficient—one party received a phone call from the US in less than three hours on a Sunday night, even though they were on an "unscheduled" side trip to a small resort hotel in central China.

Health

A valid smallpox shot is required for entry to the People's Republic of China. Although a physician or local public health authority should always be consulted, other shots that may be recommended include cholera, tetanus, typhus, and gammaglobulin.

Many visitors have commented on the extraordinary concern shown by the Chinese for their guests' health and have praised the excellent care provided by Chinese hospitals and medical personnel. Medical services are available to visitors at hospitals and local clinics in all major cities and in the countryside. There is clearly great interest in doing everything possible in terms of both preventive measures and treatment.

The most common maladies afflicting travelers in China are respiratory problems such as head colds, bronchial conditions, and sore throats. Diarrhea or constipation may also be problems, and appropriate remedies should be taken along on the prior advice of a physician. Visitors should be sure to pack ample supplies of prescribed medications, since many prescriptions may be difficult to obtain in China.

Sanitary conditions are generally excellent. Tap water is not potable in China, even in large cities. Hotel rooms are supplied with boiled water in thermos bottles or carafes. Ice is made from purified water and local beverages are safe. Restaurants take the sensitivity of their foreign guests' stomachs into account, and even meals prepared on rural communes will have been carefully supervised.

Tour guides are extremely solicitous about health problems, and at first sign of illness will recommend seeing a doctor.

Hospitals Should an illness require hospitalization, both Western and Chinese medicines are available. Visitors will be given their choice of treatment (it is in no case advisable, however, to go to China with the expectation of getting long-standing rheumatism or gall bladder disorders cured by herbs or acupuncture). The Chinese do not have RH-negative blood, and their blood banks do not store it. Persons with this blood-type should consult their physician before departing for China.

In case of serious illness, it is possible to have relatives summoned, and the Chinese will facilitate special invitations, visa clearance, and other necessary arrangements. At the same time, one should notify one's embassy in Peking.

Some visitors may be put off by what may appear to be primitive medical facilities. There are no luxury hospitals in China, no carpeted waiting rooms, and few examples of the complex diagnostic equipment found in the West. Considering the barrier of language (although an interpreter will always come along to help) and the strange surroundings, it is natural to feel uncomfortable. Such qualms

53

are unfounded, however, since Chinese physicians are well trained and their diagnostic techniques sophisticated, time-honored, and judicious.

 ## Selected Foreign Diplomatic Missions in Peking

Australia: 41 San Li Tun (tel: 522331).

Austria: Chien Kuo Men Wai, Hsiu, Shui Nan Chieh, 5 (tel: 522061 or 522063).

Belgium: 34 San Li Tun (tel: 521736-38).

Canada: 16 San Li Tun (tel: 521475).

Chile: 22 San Li Tun (tel: 521287).

Denmark: San Li Tun (tel: 522431).

Federal Republic of Germany: Diplomatic Office Building, 39 San Li Tun (tel: 521161-65).

Finland: 3 Kwang Hua Road (tel: 521817).

France: 10 San Li Tun (tel: 521331-35).

Greece: 19 Kwang Hua Road (tel: 522250).

Italy: Diplomatic Office Building, Apt. No. 1-71/72, Entrance No. 1, San Li Tun (tel: 522131).

Japan: 48 San Li Tun (tel: 522055).

Mexico: Diplomatic Office Building 2, 72; 29 San Li Tun (tel: 522055, 521396, 522070).

Netherlands: 2 San Li Tun (tel: 521731).

New Zealand: No. 1 Building, No. 2 Street, East Temple of the Sun (tel: 522731).

Norway: 11 San Li Tun (tel: 552262).

Peru: 2-82 San Li Tun (tel: 522178, 522005, 521480).

Spain: Building 45, San Li Tun (tel: 521436-39).

Sweden: 22 San Li Tun (tel: 521770, 521252).

Switzerland: 25 Tung An Men Nan Chieh (tel: 551914, 551259).

United Kingdom: 5 Kwang Hua Road, Chien Kuo Men Wai (tel: 521961-64).

United States: 17 Kwang Hua Road (tel: 522033).

Hotel Accommodations

For most travelers, hotel accommodations are prearranged by CITS or other host organizations. Hotels in China generally meet first-class international standards, with good service. Rates and facilities vary somewhat from city to city, but most hotels that serve foreigners are equipped with similar amenities.

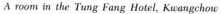

A room in the Tung Fang Hotel, Kwangchow

Room Amenities Hotel rooms in China are simple and functional, but comfortable. They generally contain twin beds, a desk, easy chair, bureau, and bathroom. A carafe of preboiled drinking water is provided, as is a thermos of hot water for tea. Lighting is sometimes inadequate, especially for reading or writing at night, and travelers who expect to do a lot of reading may wish to pack high-wattage bulbs for the trip.

Services Most hotels have postal, banking, and telegraph and cable facilities on the premises. Hotel shops sell snacks, general travel items, and handicrafts. Room service is available. In addition, each residence floor has a service counter which will handle laundry and dry cleaning (laundry normally takes one day, dry cleaning two) and book long-distance telephone calls. Service counters also sell mineral water, beer, and Chinese liquor. Most hotels are now equipped to supply ice.

Food

Of the world's two great cuisines, the Chinese is as varied as, and, in fact, much older in tradition than the French. Chinese chefs are masters at creating culinary triumphs from the barest necessities. Indeed, some of the most prized delicacies are said to have been concocted during times of famine—many from substances never before

55

considered edible. The manner of serving even the simplest dishes appeals at once to the eye, the sense of smell, and the palate.

Hotel Dining Generally speaking, most tour groups and visiting delegations take all of their meals at the hotels (except for welcoming banquets). Meals are served at predesignated times (usually 8, 12, and 6), at preassigned tables, and from a menu preselected by the hotel cooks. Unless special requests are made, breakfast will be Western style (eggs, toast, jam, coffee, a cake or pastry); lunch and dinner are Chinese. It is usually possible to order a Chinese-style breakfast a day in advance, and if enough people to fill a table (eight or ten) require it. The hotel dining rooms will also be glad to serve Western food for lunch and dinner, again if the request is made well ahead of time and if enough persons in a group ask for it. It is often difficult to order individually prepared dishes (which in any case cost extra), although the Chinese will prepare special meals for visitors with special dietary requirements. Most beverages, including beer, are considered part of the meal, the cost of which is included in the tour package. Yoghurt is sometimes available, at a small charge.

Hotels will waive charges for meals that are cancelled, given ample notice.

Restaurants Although it will entail an additional expense, eating at a local restaurant is highly recommended, both for its atmosphere as well as for noticeable improvements in the quality and variety of food. Excursions can be arranged by forming a group and making reservations through a tour escort, the main service desk at the hotel, or at the

restaurant itself (this usually requires a Chinese-speaking person). The custom is to establish a price range (Y10-15 per person is standard) and make advance requests for special dishes.

Banquets It has been customary for the host organization in China to give a welcoming dinner in honor of visiting groups or delegations. Depending on the protocol required, the dinner can be an elaborate banquet—complete with formal invitations and a detailed seating plan—or a simpler affair. In both cases, many of the same procedures apply.

All meals in China—including banquets—start at the announced time. Tardiness is considered rude. Formal dinners are timed to last about an hour and a half. Arriving guests are usually ushered into an anteroom and offered tea, hot towels, and about 10 to 15 minutes of light conversation with the hosts. The principal host will then signal that dinner is ready, and guests will be seated according to protocol. The host will preside, sitting at a head table (Chinese tradition dictates that the seat of honor faces the door), with the highest ranking guests (i.e., the delegation's leaders) arranged to his left and right. It is customary for hosts to serve guests with special chopsticks and implements.

A typical setting will include a small plate, a pair of chopsticks resting on a holder (forks and knives are always available), and three glasses: for beer or soft drinks, wine, and the customary *mao t'ai* (a fiery 140-proof liquor). Dishes are served in sequence, starting with cold appetizers and continuing to ten courses and beyond. A well-

A restaurant menu

balanced meal will contain, at a minimum, the five basic tastes of Chinese cuisine (acidic, hot, bitter, sweet, and salty). Dishes alternate between crisp and tender, dry and heavily sauced. Soup usually concludes the main courses; in the south, fried rice or noodles come last. Dessert is usually fresh fruit with pastries.

It is polite to eat (or at least appear to eat) a bit of each dish served, pacing oneself through the course of the meal. In formal settings, it is impolite to drink alcohol alone, and thus toasts are usually offered either among neighbors or to the table as a whole. At banquets, it is appropriate for the tour leader to offer toasts to the entire assemblage. The host usually begins the toasts after the first course. Excessive toasting should be avoided, however. Inebriation is frowned upon. Individual restaurant recommendations and local dishes are discussed in the sections on individual cities.

Entertainment

Two themes dominate cultural life in the PRC: the pervasive use of arts forms as a means of political education, and the encouragement of broad participation in cultural activities by all segments of the population—from school children to factory workers to farmers. In the course of most China tours, visitors will have a chance to attend a variety of cultural performances, many of which will have some sort of political message at their core (acrobatic and circus performances are an exception). In this respect, culture is no different from all other forms of collective activity in today's China. Art may serve to promote enjoyment, excitement, and good feelings among its practitioners and observers as well as make a concrete contribution to the goals of nation-building.

Approached in this context, an evening's entertainment in China can provide a rewarding cross-cultural experience for foreign visitors. As is their intent, these performances offer a means for better comprehending central values in PRC society. Not incidentally, many of these bright, exuberant displays also succeed delightfully as entertainment.

Performing Arts A wide range of performing-art genres are practiced in today's China. In addition to their general stress on political themes (these have been present with less regularity since late 1977), most presentations—be they in the form of opera, dance, film, or theater—are marked by a high degree of stylization (e.g., lots of posturing and broad gestures) and by an outward freshness and enthusiasm conveyed by the performers. In addition, visitors must be cautioned that most cultural presentations in China are not known for their brevity.

Peking Opera, probably the best-known of China's traditional art forms, was undergoing a revival in the late 1970s. Operas with both classical and modern themes were being performed in great profusion and variety throughout the country. Many regions in China have developed their own operatic styles. For most, however, plots can be obscure and intricate; if possible, story-lines should be consulted and sorted out before the performance. Ballets such as *The White-Haired Girl* and *Red Detachment of Women* are among the modern classics of this genre, which combines dance, choral singing, and visual effects in a manner designed to engulf the senses. Similarly, Chinese theater makes extravagant use of action, color, and forthright emotion. Acrobatic performances are now common to most tourist itineraries. Here, subtle skill and visual impact are stressed over displays that court bodily danger. Chinese puppet theater, which retains a level of humor, skill, and verve matched in few other countries, seems to strike Western audiences with delightful immediacy. By early 1979 Western classical music was frequently performed and neighborhood moviehouses were showing Japanese and English films.

Shopping

The Chinese are continually nonplussed by the Westerner's penchant for shopping, but are certain to arrange at least one group visit to the local Friendship Store or department store so that visitors may exercise their curious compulsions. China is not a consumer society and there is no equivalent of Fifth Avenue in New York, the Ginza in Tokyo, or the Champs Elysees in Paris. The emphasis in Chinese products is on the everyday and the practical, with the notable exception of some splendid handicrafts. The tourist will find that basic items are inexpensive, but that there are few bargains, even among such common "Chinese" items as jade, jewelry, and antiques. In fact, some "luxury" goods may be cheaper and available in wider varieties in Hong Kong. Other shopping hints will be found in individual shopping sections in the city itineraries.

Friendship Stores Friendship Stores have been established in the major cities specifically to sell export items to foreign visitors. Thus,

59

New Friendship Store, Kwangchow, opened in 1978

they offer many products that do not circulate in the local economy (i.e., exclusive silks, jewelry, or intricate lacquerware). Guides will encourage visitors to do most of their shopping in these stores.

Other advantages include sales personnel who speak foreign languages, a wide selection of merchandise, and the best quality range available for most items. Friendship Stores have uncrowded counters, facilities for packing and shipping large items home (in Peking), and the helpful presence of tour guides. In nearly all cases, the prices of items will be the same as in regular stores.

However, the very attributes of Friendship Stores can also be disadvantages: visitors are deprived of the experience of mingling with Chinese shoppers. Also, mundane items that may be unusual outside of China are not carried in the Friendship Stores (for example, books, posters, and crockery).

If possible, both types of shopping should be tried. Friendship Stores are located in Peking (the largest and best-supplied), Shanghai, and Kwangchow, and are being added in scaled-down versions in many other cities.

Local Stores There are usually several major shopping areas in most cities visited, many close to the hotel. The best approach is to go out and explore them on your own. Prices are almost always marked. If communication becomes difficult, Chinese shopkeepers will usually write out the price (in Arabic numerals) on a slip of paper. Veteran travelers will note the absence of inflation in China. Prices are set by the state and will not vary from store to store. (A can of "Ma Ling" peanuts has been Y1.43 for the past five years, no matter where in China it was seen.) There is absolutely no bargaining.

The Chinese are scrupulously honest. If visitors can't figure out the exact payment from the assortment of bills and coins, the sales staff will offer to fish out the correct amount. Receipts are usually provided and, especially in the case of large purchases, should be retained.

Except in Friendship Stores, a number of items are rationed: cigarettes, cottons, and "luxury" fabrics such as silk. Local department stores or clothing shops abide strictly by these rules. If one is "waved off" from an item, offense should not be taken; it simply means ration coupons are required (in some cases, purchase of such items can be arranged with the help of the Chinese tour escort, but may cause some difficulty).

There is another aspect of shopping to keep in mind, especially in areas where foreign visits are less frequent. Expect to be stared at (in a friendly way) and even followed. This should not be interpreted as hostility or a discourtesy but merely as an expression of curiosity and interest. Under such circumstances, it's best to smile and continue on.

Antiques Persons who come to China expecting to find an antique-buyers paradise are likely to be disappointed. First, antiques are sold only in licensed shops in Peking, Shanghai, Kwangchow, Wuhsi, Kweilin, and some other middle-sized cities. Second, authorities have generally restricted sale of items older than 100 years. They regulate what is purchased by marking it with a special red wax seal and requiring a special customs declaration form, issued at the time of purchase. Third, the Chinese are well aware of the international market prices of antiques and charge accordingly; there simply are no bargains left. Finally, the stores—especially in Kwangchow and Peking—have been thoroughly "picked over" during the past several years as visitors to China have increased in number. This is not to say that the pursuit itself will not be rewarding. The availability of many unusual "non-antiques"—jewelry, ceramics, and even paintings—may make the venture worthwhile.

Items Recommended for Purchase Individual taste will always dictate what is a good buy and what isn't, though the following indicates some of the most popular items bought in China over the past years and the best places to get them:

Rugs (Peking, Shanghai, Tientsin)

Ceramics (Kwangchow, Changsha)

Ivory (Kwangchow, Peking) (note: as products from endangered species, illegal for US import)

Clay figurines (Peking, Wuhsi, Kwangchow)

Cloisonné, lacquerware (Peking, Shanghai)

Jewelry, including jade (Peking, Shanghai, Kwangchow)

Silk (Hangchow, Soochow, Wuhsi, Shanghai)

Embroidery (Changsha, Soochow)

Furs and suedes (Peking, Shenyang)

Scroll paintings (Peking, Shanghai)

Woodblock prints and stone rubbings (Peking only)

Papercuts (everywhere)

Mao t'ai and other liquors (everywhere—beware, *mao t'ai* will leak through the bottle seal)

Other Items to Look for: chops (signature seals); postage stamp sets; miniature carvings in stone, cork, or wood; sandalwood fans; brushes and art supplies; knives; books; posters; acupuncture dolls; and clothing (don't despair—somewhere among China's vast population there are likely to be people who take the same size as you). Always look for the unusual: in Shanghai and Kwangchow, cold cream comes packaged in a charming double sea shell and is sold for about 30 *fen* ($0.20).

Restrictions and Duties on PRC Purchases

Import regulations vary widely from country to country and prospective travelers should consult their country's regulations before departing. In the United States, special conditions apply to the import of certain products from the People's Republic. Since, as of January 1979, China had yet to be granted "most-favored-nation" status, duties on a variety of items remained high, if not prohibitive.

Common Rules-of-Thumb There is a general US ban on importing objects made of ivory (aimed at protecting Asian elephants), so Asian ivory may be confiscated by customs. Similarly, if you plan to purchase furs, you should check which are endangered species since there is a US ban on objects made from the fur or other parts of endangered species. Agricultural items such as seeds and plants may be held for inspection or quarantine and eventually denied entry.

Medical equipment and drugs purchased in China may be confiscated for inspection. They are required to have full details as to their contents, manufacture, and instructions for their use. Sometimes this extends to acupuncture needles and dolls, which have at times been sent to the FDA for examination.

Problem Areas Challenges to the originality of artwork: This distinction is relevant since original artwork is duty-free, whereas massproduced artwork carries a 25% duty. To be "original" the work should be the only one of its kind and should be signed. You can argue past the absence of a signature. If it's indeed original, hold your ground and make your case.

Challenges to the authenticity of antiques: True antiques are duty-free, but non-antique porcelain, bronzes, and jewelry can range from 25% to 110% duty, depending on the item. The formal requirement of US customs is a signed receipt from the dealer certifying that the item is more than 100 years old.

In the PRC any item more than 100 years old has a red seal on it. These receipts, however, are in Chinese so that the name of the item and even the name of the store are not verifiable by the average customs agent. Record the name of the store from one of your guides and print it along with the description of the item on the receipt. If possible, have the shopkeeper print the age of the item on the receipt—otherwise, determine the age and print it yourself. Thus armed, you may argue forcefully at customs, pointing out the red seal.

A SAMPLING OF US DUTIES ON
ITEMS IMPORTED FROM THE PRC

ANTIQUES

More than 100 years old	Free (with proof of age)

CERAMICS

Coarse, earthenware	15%
Fine grain, pottery	25%

CLOTH

Silk, cotton, synthetics	See scale for clothing below

CLOTHING

Leather	35%
Silk	60%
Ordinary apparel—cotton, wool	45%
Fancy lace or knit—cotton, wool	90% (note that the duty doubles on "fancy" goods)

JEWELRY

Ivory	It will probably be confiscated
Cheap (without precious metals or stones)	110%
Fine (with silver, gold, or gemstones)	80%

PAINTINGS

Original artwork	Free (with proof)
Mass-produced	25%

RADIOS, TVS, TAPE-RECORDERS 35%

RUGS Tends to follow scale for clothing; thus, fine rugs can be as high as 90%

TRANSPORTATION IN CHINA

Most travel between the major cities of China is by air. Shorter inter-city excursions are by train. With the exception of commercial travelers, foreign visitors will not have to buy their own tickets for air or train travel; the host organization handles all reservations, ticket purchases, and appropriate clearances with the public security bureau (a "foreigners check post" is set up at all major airports and train stations).

Domestic Air Travel The Chinese airline, the Civil Aviation Administration of China (CAAC), has expanded its services greatly over the past several years. Its eleven international routes total 40,000 km. (24,840 mi.), covering all continents (except the Western Hemisphere). Domestically, CAAC has 100 routes totaling 147,543 km. (91,264 mi.) and linking 80 different cities with the capital, Peking. CAAC uses an array of jet aircraft—Boeing 707s, British Tridents, and Soviet Ilyushins—between the three major cities of Peking, Shanghai, and Kwangchow as well as between other points. Propeller planes such as the Soviet Antonov are used between small- and intermediate-sized cities.

Air travel in China has become increasingly more comfortable (the Soviet planes are exceptions, with their notorious lack of leg room) and schedules more convenient. Flights are often crowded, mainly with officials, People's Liberation Army personnel, and foreigners. All passengers are limited to 30 kilos (66 pounds) baggage allowance in first class, 20 kilos (44 pounds) in economy class. Excess baggage charges amount to 1% of the applicable one-way fare, making the charge for an additional kilo (2.2 lbs) on the Peking to Kwangchow sector Y2.44 ($1.49).

Airports, whether new or old, are spartan, with vacant, unadorned waiting rooms. Each airport usually has a small retail shop (selling regional specialties) and a restaurant. The largest air terminal facility in China is expected to be opened in Peking in 1979 (other new airports have been built at Tientsin, Harbin, and Urumchi). Shanghai has the second largest. Some airports also serve as military bases, especially in the interior of China. Photography is not allowed aboard an airplane, either in the air or while taxiing.

CAAC serves meals on its longer flights, although these do not enjoy a favorable reputation. On shorter flights, fruits or pastries, accompanied by tea, are often served. Liquor is not served, but cigarettes, lapel pins, candy, gum, and address books are handed out as souvenirs of the flight.

Train Travel Train travel is by far the most enjoyable way to see China, since it is not only comfortable, but affords an excellent view of

DISTANCE BETWEEN MAIN TOURIST CITIES

Shortest Railway Distance

1,000 = kilometers
621 = miles

	Peking	Shanghai	Tientsin	Kwangchow	Changsha	Nanking	Hangchow	Tsingtao	Sian	Chengchow
Shanghai	1,462 / 908									
Tientsin	137 / 85	1,325 / 824								
Kwangchow	2,324 / 1,445	1,822 / 1,132	2,461 / 1,530							
Changsha	1,587 / 986	1,187 / 738	1,724 / 1,071	737 / 458						
Nanking	1,157 / 719	305 / 190	1,020 / 634	2,127 / 1,322	1,492 / 927					
Hangchow	1,651 / 1,026	189 / 118	1,514 / 941	1,633 / 1,015	998 / 620	494 / 307				
Tsingtao	887 / 551	1,361 / 846	750 / 466	2,688 / 1,671	1,951 / 1,213	1,056 / 656	1,550 / 963			
Sian	1,165 / 724	1,511 / 939	1,302 / 809	2,140 / 1,330	1,403 / 872	1,206 / 750	1,700 / 1,006	1,570 / 976		
Chengchow	695 / 432	1,000 / 622	832 / 517	1,629 / 1,012	892 / 554	695 / 432	1,189 / 739	1,059 / 658	511 / 318	
Shenyang	841 / 523	2,029 / 1,261	704 / 438	3,165 / 1,967	2,428 / 1,509	1,724 / 1,071	2,218 / 1,379	1,454 / 904	2,006 / 1,247	1,536 / 955

the Chinese countryside. Fares are also considerably lower than air travel.

The Chinese divide their trains into "hard seat" and "soft seat" compartments, with the latter reserved for foreigners and high-ranking Chinese such as army personnel and government officials. On long-distance trains there are sleeping coaches reminiscent of European trains, accommodating 32 passengers—four each in eight separate compartments, each with its own bunks, wood-paneled walls, fan, curtains, and a small potted plant. Such trains also have dining cars (as does the Kwangchow-to-Hong Kong train).

Chinese trains invariably run on time. A long, ringing bell is the signal for departure. As the train pulls out of the station, it is accompanied by martial music carried over loudspeakers in each compartment or coach. The music continues sporadically during the trip—dining, conversation, even slumber are frequently interrupted by loudspeaker announcements of stops, time, news reports, and interludes of music. If the traveler prefers, it is possible to turn off the speaker system, either in the individual compartments where the switch is located under the table, or near the door at the end of each car. Carriages are meticulously serviced by attendants, who regularly mop the floors, clean woodwork, serve tea and other beverages (unlike airplanes, trains serve beer and, occasionally, wine), and turn the loudspeakers back on. Since 1977, 87 newly-built passenger trains have been put into service. New railway stations have been opened at Changsha and Kweilin.

Urban Transport Within cities, visitors are conveyed by bus, private car, or taxi. High-ranking visitors are often chauffeured in "Shanghai" sedans, while heads of state or guests of ministries may be provided with the larger and more elegant "Hung Ch'i" (Red Flag) limousine.

Tour groups usually travel on 25-passenger Chinese buses or 16-seat Japanese minibuses. (Kwangchow now uses Romanian "Icarus" tour buses for large groups.) Although newer models are perfectly comfortable, none are air-conditioned.

Taxi fleets (usually Toyotas) serve the major hotels in the cities of Peking, Shanghai, and Kwangchow. Fares are computed on a formula incorporating both time and distance. For a fixed hourly rate, the driver will wait while the visitor goes about business or sightseeing; an afternoon's excursion can cost US$10-15. Some travelers regard Chinese taxis as not only convenient but also as something of an adventure, especially at night when vehicles in China dart through the streets without lights (used only as warning signals). Taxi dispatchers are situated in the lobbies of hotels. Store or restaurant staff will help summon one on request.

66

Travel on China's efficient and inexpensive urban bus and trolley systems is possible but somewhat complicated. Ticket prices are based on distances traveled, making it vital to know one's final destination. This requires some knowledge of Chinese or the services of an interpreter. For those able to read Chinese there are convenient route maps at most major stops. Buses are usually crowded, but people are extremely courteous to foreigners and it is not unusual for a young Westerner to be offered a seat by an elderly Chinese.

As of 1978, coastal ships carried passengers between Dalien, Tientsin, Tsingtao, and Shanghai. Ferries cross major rivers, such as the Whangpoo in Shanghai or the Pearl in Kwangchow. Such rides are recommended in leisure time, since they may allow exploration of areas not often visited. Fares are usually less than 10 *fen* (US$0.06).

GROUP TRAVEL IN CHINA

All visits to China are directly coordinated by the host organization that provided initial authorization for the trip. Upon arrival, the host organization assumes all responsibility for domestic travel and accommodations.

General tour groups, including friendship groups and study tours, will be accompanied by representatives from the China International Travel Service (CITS). Professional groups will be hosted by representatives of their counterpart organization in China. Official, government-hosted delegations will be accompanied by a ranking member of the host organization. This person fulfills both protocol and escort functions, and works closely with the visiting group's leader. Business representatives, by contrast, are left much more to their own devices, mainly since they do not usually travel from city to city. Business persons are expected to arrange appointments by themselves, although the Chinese may provide escorts for first-time visitors to Peking or Shanghai. If a business representative's schedule allows for sightseeing or for travel between cities, an escort and/or interpreter from the appropriate Chinese trade corporation can be provided on request.

Arrival Representatives of the host organization will be on hand to welcome visitors upon their arrival in China. They are likely to accompany the group throughout its stay in the PRC. These personnel serve as escorts, guides, and interpreters, and will have themselves made all prior arrangements for the tour. Upon arrival at the preassigned hotel, people may go directly to their rooms (also preassigned). Usually, a meeting with the host is arranged shortly thereafter to discuss the proposed itinerary and work out details of the stay. Initial meetings with host representatives are important. They serve to mutually acquaint escorts and guests, work out the itinerary, and generally set the tone for the visit. After guests are formally welcomed to China, a schedule is proposed. The Chinese usually prearrange trips in accordance with the interests of the group as expressed in their initial tour application. The schedule should be gone over in detail since it will be nearly impossible to make changes afterwards, especially those that involve alterations of travel dates between cities or of appointments at particular institutions. Likewise, suggestions for splitting up into subgroups are rarely accommodated.

Adjustments in the tone and organization of tours are made for political groups, friendship tours, general study trips, professionals, and commercial visitors. Each type is handled according to a different set of expectations. Thus, a business representative who continually quotes Chairman Mao may be looked upon with curiosity. The Chinese zeal for categorization of tour groups is well intentioned, the point being to make the sojourn in China as relevant as possible to the group's major interests. Inevitably, however, groups of more diverse makeup may find themselves being unduly stereotyped.

Group Leaders The Chinese are sensitive to leadership responsibilities and will expect their guests to appoint a group leader. Leaders of foreign groups are treated with some deference. For their part, leaders are expected to assume responsibility for introductions at the places visited and to act as intermediaries for complaints and suggestions. Most delegations also select a "secretary" who can serve as the first point of contact with Chinese personnel in making room assignments or working out schedule details.

Escort Procedures A pattern of organization becomes apparent during the first few days of a stay in China. Escorts and interpreters will meet with the group at the outset of any planned activity, make the introductions at the institutions or sites visited, and help with any problems—from protocol to travel, from shopping to laundry—that may arise.

A group may not always be in the company of the same guide, since each factory, school, museum, park, or other site maintains personnel who specialize in meeting "foreign friends." There will, however, be at least one interpreter assigned to the group at all times. Most delegations have found translators to be quite competent (although the recent growth in tourist volume has occasionally resulted in students temporarily pressed into service before their training has been completed). All interpreters have a particularly grueling task, since they bear the major burden of making Chinese society comprehensible to the foreigner. They are called upon to translate briefings, speeches, signs, and conversations for many hours each day,

often having to sift through a muddle of accents, jargon and temperaments.

Free time between scheduled appointments can be used for shopping, walking around, or other leisure activities. Such excursions do not require an official escort.

On-Site Briefings When visiting a factory, school, commune, or other institution, the tour group or delegation is normally escorted to a room to have tea and receive a briefing from a "leading member" of the institution. Remarks usually take note of changes since the revolution, the effect of the current policy line, and general statistics. Guests are usually invited to ask questions as they tour the site. If time allows, the group may return to the briefing room for further follow-up.

Questioning is always encouraged, but visitors should be sensitive about the style of questions and the areas probed. Unanswered questions should not be pursued beyond the bounds of courtesy. Reticence on the part of a spokesman should not be taken as a sign of evasion or deception. From the Chinese standpoint, briefings serve to fill a narrow, specific context. Most Chinese in this situation are not given to extemporizing and, lacking either information or the authority to give a complete answer, they will prefer to give none. Hosts at sites generally prefer to take all questions at once, answering them in as much detail as time and discretion allow. While this method works fairly well with larger tour groups, smaller delegations may seek to ask their questions one at a time so that appropriate follow-up inquiries can be made.

Norms of Behavior and Decorum

Under the special conditions imposed by escorted group travel, visitors should seek to exercise courtesy and patience. It is always best to try to relax and "flow" with the visit. A willingness to experience China on its own terms will result in a more satisfying visit, whether its purpose be business or general travel. The accumulated experience of recent visitors has produced some guidelines that will facilitate relationships.

General Conduct The Chinese expect their guests to behave as representatives of their own society and are respectful of cultural and national differences. Visitors should act themselves, and feel free to speak openly about differing political, economic, religious, or social beliefs. Spirited disagreements, however, should not be allowed to degenerate into remarks that are indiscreet or disrespectful towards aspects of Chinese society or particularly towards its leaders.

While Western manners need not be abandoned in China, some restraint is advisable. The Chinese do not appreciate a "hail fellow, well met" style and are sparing in their use of direct physical contact. A courteous handshake is acceptable. As one gets to know the Chinese, greater familiarity becomes possible. Public displays of affection among members of visiting groups are also regarded as unseemly. Likewise, visitors should attempt to keep a pleasant demeanor and not show hostility or anger in public either towards the Chinese or fellow group members.

Norms of etiquette in the PRC do not differentiate between men and women, and members of both sexes are treated equally.

Terminology Terms for China in Western usage such as "Red China," "Mainland China," or "Communist China" may cause offense, as may references to Taiwan as the "Republic of China" or "Free China." The preferred name for China is the People's Republic of China or, simply, China.

Punctuality and Protocol Punctuality is expected for all business and social appointments. Except in extenuating circumstances, all planned activities and meetings should be attended. This is as important for general visitors as for business representatives. Even the most mundane arrangements may have required considerable preparation on the part of the Chinese. At many institutions, especially schools, guests are usually greeted upon arrival by applause. It is polite to return the gesture.

Smaller tour groups and delegations visiting an institution (or arriving at a negotiating session) should be cognizant of protocol requirements. The leader or senior member of the party should enter first since the Chinese will have lined up their hosts in protocol order. It is also appropriate to introduce group members individually after the Chinese have made their own introductions, noting those who may have special expertise in the subject at hand.

Voicing Complaints Individuals should not be criticized or chastised openly. If complaints about arrangements must be raised, they should be broached first in private with an escort or interpreter. For example, if a group visits a commune and is advised that it is "inconvenient" to tour the local hospital, members should not insist on being taken there, even if they have just walked by it. When there is an opportunity, it may be mentioned in friendly terms that the group has a special interest in hospitals and it hopes there may be another opportunity to visit one. If, indeed, another opportunity is possible, efforts will be made to grant it.

Expressing Gratitude Tipping, whether in cash or gifts, is strictly forbidden in the PRC. The only appropriate gesture, in the case of official or specially invited delegations, is to arrange a return banquet for the host organization (at the end of the trip) and to present the host organization with a collective gift, such as plaques, technical or scientific books, and the like. Tour groups and delegations sometimes take lapel pins, postcards, small flags, or other tokens from home. These can be presented to a school, commune, factory, or other collective entity. Instant pictures are popular. It is thought unseemly for business people to present gifts in China. They are likely to be instantly returned, to great mutual embarrassment.

The Chinese have a justified reputation for honesty. They will endeavor to return any items that have been misplaced, including some that have been intentionally discarded or left behind. If one wishes to dispose of belongings such as worn clothing or books, they may be given directly to workers at the service desk, with an explanation that the items are no longer needed and may be disposed of. Such efforts are well taken, since stories abound of discarded sandals or mystery novels following their original owners across the breadth of China.

VISITING CHINA'S SCHOOLS

"A Miscellany of Edifying Advice for the Intrepid Schoolmarm About to Embark Upon a Teachers' Tour of the People's Republic of China"

John Israel

Those who embark on a China trip expecting to unearth some heretofore unsuspected aspect of official policy are bound to be disappointed. Talmudic China analysts in government and academia devote their lives to ferreting out every nuance concealed between the lines of the *People's Daily*. A brief tour is not likely to reveal very much about high-level policy and official attitudes that cannot be gleaned from their writings.

The most important thing that can be brought back—something that the desk-bound expert cannot match—is a feeling for the realities of China. Visitors will see China's schools not as abstract models but as living institutions where human teachers interact with flesh-and-blood students. After meeting these people, each with his or her own personality and perceptions, one will never again find oneself thinking of the Chinese as undifferentiated "blue ants." The sense of China as a living reality may be an intangible benefit, but it is an invaluable one. If you come back with nothing more than this, the trip may be deemed a success.

But you should come back with a great deal more. One way to learn as much as possible is to take the broadest possible view of education, which is in fact the Chinese view—that education is not confined to the schools but permeates the whole social order. In addition to institutions that are "educational" in the narrow sense, your group may visit communes, factories, clinics, homes, theaters, bookstores, restaurants, museums, and tourist attractions. You will observe people at work and at leisure, in groups and individually, reading, strolling, and playing poker. You will see political posters and billboards, as common as commercial advertising is in the United States. Once it is realized that education is all-pervasive, you will be sensitive to one of the fundamental realities of contemporary China and will be better able to evaluate what you see in the schools you visit.

On a typical China education tour there will be few days on which you fail to visit at least one school and many days on which you visit two. At each school, you will be greeted at the gate by your hosts, including, usually, the principal or chancellor and their assistants and possibly some teachers. Then you will be ushered into a conference room, seated around a table, furnished with tea and cigarettes, and treated to that standard fare of China visitors, the "brief introduction." The "B.I." is a 10-to-20-minute discourse on the history of the school, its academic structure, and its vital statistics. Almost invariably there will be some mention of national political, social, and educational goals, which recently have emphasized support for the post-1976 leadership, recovery from the depredations of the "gang of four," and construction of a strong modern socialist state by the year 2000. You will hear, either in general or specific terms, that the institution you are visiting is overcoming obstacles and doing its part in reaching these goals.

What you learn beyond the brief introduction depends upon how thoroughly you have prepared for the trip, the acuteness of your observations, your aggressiveness in seeking out information, and a bit of luck. There are two kinds of information that you should have when you start out. One is the kind of general background on the educational scene that you can acquire from preparatory readings (see list at end of this section). Even more important, however, if you want to probe deeply, are up-to-date reports on educational conditions in various parts of China available for the period immediately preceding your visit.

Fortunately, such material is available in translated press accounts and radio broadcasts regularly published by American governmental agencies. For example, the *Foreign Broadcast Information Service* provides daily verbatim news reports from radio stations all over China. These are available in major university libraries or your group leader can request a file of translations on Chinese education from the National Committee on US-China Relations. A careful reading of these will make it possible to go beyond the formulaic generalities of the brief introduction. You may learn, for example, that policies presented by your hosts as centrally approved and nationally enforced are so controversial that "bitter and prolonged struggles" are taking place in schools all over China. Such information from Chinese sources will enable you to ask incisive questions with some assurance.

Sometimes even a simple query may lead to a startling reply. For example, a member of our group once asked an innocuous question about the number of books in the school library and drew the answer

A primary class in a commune school

that there were not so many since Red Guards had burned the library to the ground during the Cultural Revolution.

Some of your questions may have to wait, for immediately after the brief introduction you probably will be taken on a tour of the school. In the classroom, you are on familiar turf and can draw freely from your own teaching experience. What is the teacher-student ratio? In a given classroom, it is likely to be on the order of 1:40 or 1:50. What teaching methods does the teacher use under such conditions? From your own experience and reading on Chinese educational traditions, you will not be surprised to learn that the teacher resorts to that time-tested rote education that Chairman Mao derisively called "stuffed duck" learning. You might also take note of the conventional physical layout, the teacher's desk facing a neatly-aligned arrangement of old-fashioned wooden desks. Both the tone in which the teacher speaks and the attitudes of the students will tell you much about the learning experience even if you do not understand a word of Chinese. You may also look over students' shoulders or borrow one of their books, which will be especially interesting if you are observing an English-language lesson. Your school hosts will probably try to include such a class on your tour.

You should take careful note of the decorations and displays on classroom walls and elsewhere on the school grounds. You will understand the significance of the omnipresent portraits of Chairman Hua and the late Chairman Mao, though you may react with surprise when you recognize Benjamin Franklin staring at you from a bulletin board in a school yard. (Franklin is admired as a paragon of science and patriotism and not, for example, as an exemplar of 18th-century America's bourgeois virtues and 18th-century France's aristocratic vices.) If you have time, ask for translations of some of the attractive multicolored displays adorning school courtyards. If there is no time to obtain a translation, take a close-up photo and get help from a Chinese-reading friend when you return home. And don't forget to seek out English-language displays; the words will be familiar, and the contents will tell you much about official values in China's school system.

Who Decides What You Will See in China?

Your itinerary will probably be a compromise between what your group asks to see and what the Chinese want—or find it logistically possible—to show you. Well in advance of departure for China, your group leader should compile a "shopping list" of members' interests, general and specific. This will be sent to your Chinese hosts; then you sit and wait. Do not expect to learn details of your itinerary until you arrive in China. In some cases, even the cities that you will visit will remain a mystery until you have crossed the border.

Most Americans want to see what is "typical" or "average" or at least a spectrum from best to worst. Your hosts, understandably, want you to see their proudest achievements. "Key schools" favored with government subsidies, hand-picked teachers, and selected students may represent a small proportion of all the schools in China, but will account for a disproportionate number of the schools you visit. It is easy to find out whether or not a specific institution is a key school; just ask.

Arriving in China, you will be met by your chief guide and interpreters from the host organization, and these will be joined in each city en route by local guides and interpreters. You will soon discover that despite the highly centralized Chinese political structure, many decisions are made on the local level. Your centrally appointed guides can be invaluable in handling problems, requests, and complaints, but they, like you, are guests in strange cities and must defer to their local hosts.

To illustrate: On its final day in Chengtu, my group visited a local "Temple of 500 Buddhas." This was a 500 Buddhas temple to beat all 500 Buddhas temples, and we spent three hours there, first picnicking among the ancient artifacts, then seeing and gawking at the exquisitely carved and painted Buddhist saints, each of them uniquely different from the other 499. That evening we overheard our chief guide on the phone, long distance, to our next city, Wuhan:

"But you can't take them to a 500 Buddhas temple. They've just been to one!"

Next afternoon we checked into our Wuhan hotel and were taken to—you guessed it—Wuhan's Temple of 500 Buddhas.

Although it is difficult to add to your itinerary or to exchange one institution or attraction for another, it sometimes is possible to cancel a visit in favor of free time. In the packed agenda of a China trip, that is no small blessing. For example, having visited an industrial exhibition just before leaving Shanghai, we were about to be taken to a handicraft exhibition just after we got off the plane in Peking. Instead, we requested—and got—free time to shop, stroll, and rest. Such changes are easiest to arrange in instances when an entire commune or school is not geared up and waiting to entertain its foreign friends.

Difficult though it may be to change your itinerary, you may find it easy to adapt scheduled visits to your special interests. You should try to inform your group leader and guides in advance of your particular needs, e.g., a desire to visit an art class or to meet with a professional counterpart. But even if things cannot be arranged in advance, opportunities may well arise upon arrival at the school. Most groups are too large for everybody to visit the same classroom at once, so you will have to split up anyway. After the brief introduction, it is perfectly all right for the group leader to approach one of the hosts and ask if members may visit a particular kind of class. If such a class is in session, they will probably be happy to accommodate you.

While walking through the school, you will generally be free to stop, ask, and look, provided that you do not hold up the group. For example, one of our group's most fruitful encounters occurred during an impromptu visit to a teachers' lounge, where we were able to talk informally to the teachers and even to ask questions about their teaching schedules (which were posted on the blackboard). My wife's curriculum developers group gained permission on several occasions to break up into three or four units to talk informally with counterparts—master teachers, administrators, curriculum specialists, etc. Pursuing your own interest will be beneficial to your group as well as to you when you return to your hotel and compare notes with colleagues who had different kinds of encounters.

Use of Cameras and Tape Recorders

Your hosts would not take you to an institution or tourist site if they were not prepared to have you record your experience. Cameras and tape recorders may generally be used without special permission. In

fact, frequently visited schools are so accustomed to camera-happy foreign friends that you often can take photos at point-blank range without distracting your subject. Flash photos are permitted at dramatic performances, both school and professional. The only places where I was forbidden to take photos was from airplanes (though I received permission to photograph a strategic airfield from the terminal!) and in certain museums where signs forbid photos until the exhibits were completed in their final, approved form.

Educational Souvenirs

In a country where politics rather than the marketplace determines the price, the more educational the commodity, the cheaper the cost. For a few dozen *yuan* you can fill your suitcase with souvenirs that will dazzle your friends, fascinate your students, and make you the most popular show-and-teller in your school.

You can buy all sorts of picture books readily comprehensible to non-Chinese readers, as well as English-language translations sold in friendship stores and hotels. Equally educational and even cheaper are the colorful political posters that sell for 11 to 40 *fen* (ca. US $.08-.30) in bookstores and special poster shops. (When we returned, we held a Chinese poster exhibit that was warmly received.) Postage stamps, available in all major hotels, reveal much about political values and aesthetic standards. Games can be useful as well. Among the not-easily-found but highly-prized items in 1978 was an anti-"gang-of-four" dartboard. Models, charts, and English-language publications on acupuncture can be purchased on the ground floor of the Shanghai friendship store, among other places.

There is no limit to souvenirs save your own ingenuity. Beer labels have become such a tourist favorite that some hotels will furnish, on demand, new ones that never have touched a bottle. Even toilet paper wrappers, if properly read, have a story to tell.

After Your Return

Some method for sorting out and building upon your group experience is highly desirable. You may exchange slides, notes, or taped transcriptions by mail or you might want to get together for a day or two reunion or "debriefing." It is best to wait a few months for such a meeting. By then, your photos will have been processed, your notes typed, and you will be able to exchange ideas on how you have been conveying your knowledge and enthusiasm to the unfortunate majority of your fellow citizens who have not yet been to China.

What to Read Before the Trip

It is not difficult to find useful books and articles on education in the People's Republic of China. What is difficult is to find good up-to-date material. Descriptions of conditions during the decade from the beginning of the Cultural Revolution to the death of Chairman Mao

(1966-76) became outdated following the ouster of the "gang of four" in October 1976 and the launching of a program of rapid modernization. Nonetheless, even studies of the pre-1976 educational scene can be enlightening. One such book is Ruth Gamberg's *Red and Expert* (Schocken, 1977), based upon the author's trips in 1973 and 1975. Briefer but more recent is Theodore H.E. Chen's, "Changes in Chinese Education," *Current History*, September 1978, pp. 73-82. Donald J. Munro's *The Concept of Man in Contemporary China* (Michigan, 1977) brilliantly elucidates the ideas, values, and attitudes that underlie educational policy and practice.

Among the most useful materials are reports by earlier groups of visiting educators, for example, "China's Schools in Flux," *Wingspread Brief*, April 1978 (available from The Johnson Foundation, Racine, Wisconsin 53401). Thoughtful reflections on the whirlwind education-oriented tour are to be found in Ward Morehouse's "Academic Tourism Reconsidered: The Case of China" (October 1973), available from the Foreign Area Materials Center, 60 East 42nd Street, New York, New York 10017. The National Committee on US-China Relations, 777 United Nations Plaza, 9b, New York, New York 10017, is an excellent source for all kinds of information, including up-to-date lists of other educational tour groups and their reports, topically defined packets of newspaper clippings and press and radio translations, and a five-page "Bibliography on Education in China." The National Committee will also prepare comprehensive China briefing kits.

VISITING CHINA'S HEALTH
CARE FACILITIES

Ruth Sidel, Ph.D., and Victor W. Sidel, M.D.

O ver the past 30 years, the People's Republic of China has fundamentally reorganized China's health services. In a country once ravaged by starvation and communicable disease, and possessing extremely limited personnel and facilities for modern medicine (and those few concentrated in urban areas), a radical and rapid change has been achieved.

Following the establishment of the PRC in 1949, a National Health Congress in Peking established four basic principles for health work: serving the workers, peasants, and soldiers; putting prevention first; coordinating the practices of traditional Chinese and Western medicine; and integrating public health work with mass movements. From 1949 to 1965, large numbers of doctors and middle-level health workers (assistant doctors, nurses, and midwives) were trained. During the same period, large numbers of new hospital beds were built; in 1965, a Ministry of Health official reported that each of China's 2,000 counties had at least one hospital. A number of medical schools and other "centers of excellence" were established.

At the same time, the government was also fostering mass participation in health care and preventive medicine. Through the "patriotic health campaigns," sanitation was improved and pests such as flies and mosquitos were largely wiped out. Opium addiction was brought to an end and venereal diseases were essentially eliminated by campaigns conducted by locally recruited and briefly trained workers with community support. Vast numbers of people participated in campaigns against schistosomiasis and other parasitic infestations. Mobile health teams brought initial measures of preventive medicine to isolated areas.

In June 1965, foreshadowing the Cultural Revolution, Chairman Mao Tse-tung criticized the Ministry of Health for its sparse provision of services in rural areas; for its emphasis on theoretical knowledge and the duration of its training of physicians; and for its lack of attention to the prevention and treatment of common disease in research. In response to this criticism, and as a result of policies generated during the Great Proletarian Cultural Revolution (1966-69), highly professionalized methods standard in industrialized countries were at least temporarily abandoned and were replaced by much more vigorous attempts at the popularization of medical services. One million "barefoot doctors" (part-time paramedical workers trained in simple techniques of diagnosis and treatment) and 3 million rural health aides were trained, and local cooperative medical care systems were developed and expanded in the rural areas.

Health Care in Rural Areas

Health care is now available at each level of rural organization. The smallest subdivision of a Chinese rural commune is the production team, with a membership of 100-200 people. Members of a production team live close to one another, usually in one or more small villages, and form the basic social unit in the countryside. A group of teams, usually 10-20, combine to form a production brigade; a typical commune is composed of 10-30 production brigades. The commune is the lowest level of formal state power in the rural areas, analogous to the "neighborhoods" in the cities; it is responsible for overall planning, education, health, and social services, and for the operation of small factories that produce goods for members as well as for outside distribution. Health care for the production teams is provided by barefoot doctors and, in some areas, by part-time volunteer health aides who deal with problems of sanitation under the supervision of the barefoot doctors. The barefoot doctors provide health care and medical care, including health education, preventive medicine, and the treatment of minor illness by means of their sparsely equipped health stations. They also provide care in the fields, taking their medical bags with them while taking part in agricultural work. The production teams choose health aides, whose primary role is to teach people about sanitation, to collect night soil, and to ensure that it is adequately stored (usually for ten days, in cement vats) before being used as fertilizer. The health aides work during their lunch hour or after their regular work and are not paid for this duty.

Health facilities at the brigade level vary widely in different parts of China. Care at this intermediate level is also provided by barefoot doctors, although in some areas at somewhat more elaborate health stations. The stations are generally furnished with an examination table, a desk, a few chairs, a medicine cabinet stocked with traditional and Western medicines, and an acupuncture chart. Midwives also work out of the brigade health stations; they perform normal deliveries in the mother's home and deal with birth control.   81

A doctor visits Khalkhas nationality peasants in their fields, Sinkiang Province

Many large communes have their own hospital facilities to which patients are referred from the production brigade health stations; each county in China is now said to have at least one general hospital, which serves the people of the immediate area as well as patients referred from the commune hospitals.

Health Care in the Cities

Health care in China's cities, as in the countryside, is provided at each organizational level. The smallest unit in the urban area is usually the "lane" (or "residents' committee"). The lane health station, which may serve from 1,000 to 5,000 people, is near the residents' homes; its major functions are preventive work—including health education and immunization, birth control, and the treatment of minor illnesses. Health workers at the lane level are local housewives, called "street doctors" and in some places "Red Medical Workers." Health care is also provided in factories, either by "worker doctors" or by fully trained physicians. Most factories have a central clinic as well as health stations staffed by worker doctors in individual workshops; some large factories have in-patient hospitals for short-term stays.

The back-up institution for lane and factory health stations is the neighborhood "hospital" (which often has no beds and thus might be more appropriately termed a clinic). Neighborhood hospitals, which may serve as many as 50,000 people, are generally staffed by physicians fully trained in both traditional and Western medicine, and by "middle" medical workers (nurses, technicians, and assistant doctors). Neighborhood hospitals are the referral centers for the local health stations and in turn refer patients to district and specialty hospitals. Facilities for simple laboratory tests and x-rays are available. In addition, the hospital acts as a center for public health work in the neighborhood. Although the equipment in the neighborhood hospital is usually sparse and relatively primitive, it seems adequate for most of the health work performed there.

Hospitals in China's cities range from these small neighborhood institutions to technologically sophisticated research and teaching hospitals. In Peking, for example, there are four research-oriented specialized hospitals functioning under the aegis of the Chinese Academy of Medical Sciences. There are also 23 municipal hospitals (10 of which have over 500 beds), under the jurisdiction of the Peking Bureau of Public Health; and there are 20 district hospitals.

The Current Scene

Since the death of Chairman Mao in 1976, the new leadership has shifted much of the emphasis in medical care—as in other aspects of China's work—toward "modernization" and technological change. Under the banner of "smashing the gang of four," medical education has been lengthened, specialty care is being expanded, and some prior efforts to "de-professionalize" medical care—e.g., the use of part-time medical workers such as the barefoot doctors and the street doctors— are being given less attention.

Nonetheless, "mobilization of the masses" still plays a crucial role in China's health care. The participation of the community in dealing with health problems remains a central issue in China. Great attention is paid to educating the population on the importance of immunizations, the handling of infectious diseases, and the need for planned births. In health, as in other fields according to the Chinese brand of socialism, there are no passive bystanders. Each person is expected to participate wholeheartedly in community public health measures, the organization of medical care, and the conduct of all aspects of his or her personal life, including health.

VIEWING ART
AND ARCHEOLOGICAL SITES
IN CHINA

Annette Juliano

For the visitor with a particular interest in art and archeology, China offers an array of unforgettable experiences. In every part of China, museums, architectural monuments, and archeological sites evidence the richness of over 7,000 years of continuous creativity—from Neolithic times to the present. Into the 1980s, more sites and monuments are expected to be opened to the public as the Chinese government continues extensive programs of restoration and preservation to make these treasures available both to the Chinese people and foreign visitors.

The science of archeology was first introduced to China from Japan and the West in the first half of the 20th entury. Some of the earliest digs in north China during the 1920s uncovered Neolithic villages and the now world-famous Bronze Age capital of Anyang, along with a nearby cemetery containing five royal tombs. By 1949, this new science, supported by the government and the universities, took firm hold. Government support—coupled with major national construction projects to build canals, reservoirs, and housing—produced a veritable flood of new finds from under the earth. The last 30 years have been enormously productive. Old sites were reworked and many new ones discovered. Vast amounts of hitherto unknown and often unprecedented material have been uncovered. As a result, the history of China's ancient cultures is being rewritten.

With few exceptions, most cities on the visitor's planned itinerary will have important art-related sites: local or provincial museums, often filled with recent archeological finds; perhaps a tomb opened to the public with a small attached exhibit hall; palaces or temples; nearby kilns; and contemporary arts and crafts centers. Be prepared: sometimes unexpected treasures are found in the most unlikely places. The following discussion summarizes briefly the various kinds of experiences a visitor interested in art and archeology can expect in China.

Archeological Sites

Generally, visitors are not taken to excavations in progress. More likely are sites which have been completely excavated and turned into museums. An example is the site of Pan-p'o, a Neolithic village outside of Sian. Among the most worthwhile excursions are visits to Loyang with its two small tombs from the Western and Eastern Han Dynasty (206 B.C.-220 AD) and to the T'ang tomb of the Princess Yung-t'ai (about 42 miles west of Sian), who died in 706 AD. As one walks down the entrance ramp, the air temperature cools rapidly, providing the visitors with some tangible insights to these underground burial chambers and ancient burial practices in China. In all three tombs, some of the *ming-ch'i* (usually clay and sometimes wood objects made specifically for burial with the deceased) are left in their original positions. The Han tombs are less lavish in scale and decoration than that of the Princess. Two exhibit halls stand near the T'ang tomb. The first contains objects removed from the tomb, including some gold ornaments, jade plaques, and ceramic wars; the second has some of the contents from nearby tombs not yet open to the public.

Yung-t'ai's tomb is one of 17 satellite tombs that surround a large tumulus marking the burial of the T'ang emperor Kao-tsung (who died in 683) and his wife, Empress Wu (who died 21 years later). The satellite graves marked by smaller mounds contain relatives and mistresses of the imperial family. The approach to the imperial tumulus consists of a "spirit" road lined with stone ostriches, flying horses, courtiers, and two armies of barbarians (with their heads knocked off). Spirit roads like this and those that have been preserved near the Ming and Ch'ing tombs are a characteristic feature of imperial burial sites.

85

Lungchuan celadon, Sung Dynasty

Primitive clan cemetery is excavated in Tsinghai Province

East of Sian is the large tumulus of the remarkable Ch'in Dynasty emperor, Shih Huang Ti. Although the imperial tomb itself has not been opened, archeologists have discovered extensive pits containing an army of life-size clay warriors and horses, estimated to total over 6,000. At present, the Chinese are building an enclosure over those sections of the pits that have been excavated. Upon completion, excavated warriors and horses will be placed back in the pits so visitors can see the original arrangement. This structure is scheduled to open to the public by early 1980. In the meantime, archeologists are working at the site reconstructing and repairing clay figures and horses. Visitors are welcome.

When visiting an archeological site or museum, groups of visitors will be met and briefed on-site. These briefings usually provide a general introduction with pertinent statistics. Occasionally, such briefings will be given by an archeologist or someone knowledgeable about the site, offering an opportunity for more technical questions or discussions.

Museums

Most art and archeological treasures are housed in an impressive network of thousands of museums all over China. Each province has a central museum which brings together artifacts drawn from all parts of the province. Many of these provincial-level museums are quite large and have become well-known for the exceptional quality of their collections; an example is the Shensi Provincial Museum in Sian and the Honan Provincial Museum in Chengchou. A veritable treasure trove resides in the Shansi Provincial Museum in Taiyuan, a city recently opened to foreigners. Aside from the sumptuous array of cloisonné, porcelains, and paintings, there is an extensive collection of Buddhist stone carvings from the 5th to the 10th centuries. Colossal stone Buddhas and animals litter the main entrance courtyard along with Buddhist stelae stacked against the enclosure walls.

In addition to these provincial repositories, many smaller towns and cities maintain local or municipal museums to preserve artifacts uncovered in the immediate vicinity. A good example is the Loyang Municipal Museum. Because of their more modest scale, local museums are often more manageable for the visitor with limited time. One of the most delightful museums of this type is the Chengchou City Museum located in the Chengchou Workers Park. Collections include superb examples of Neolithic pottery from nearby Taho village and early Shang bronze vessels. Around the back of the main buildings is an astonishing sight—several headless stone statues of

Bodhisattvas stand lashed to wooden stakes. Rows of bodiless heads rest on a stack of hollow clay tiles excavated from a Han Dynasty tomb. Many of the objects in the courtyard were discovered locally (some during the Cultural Revolution) and brought to the museum, which lacks sufficient display space at the moment.

Buddhist temple compounds are places where collections of objects are likely to be tucked away. The Lung Hsing Temple near Shihchiachuang has at least three buildings filled with local discoveries and art treasures ranging from ancient bronzes to Sung, Yuan, and Ming porcelains. Several examples had been unearthed quite recently (e.g., in 1974 and 1977). The Hsiang Kuo Monastery near Kaifeng in Honan and the Hua Yen Monastery in the city of Tatung in Shansi also have fine collections. Similar situations probably exist in other Buddhist temples.

Museums do present challenges to the visitor. Most only provide labels and explanatory materials in Chinese. Tour guides and museum staff are quite willing to provide assistance here. However, they cannot be expected to translate every label in the museum. Since museums are generally dimly lit, flashlights are useful for closer scrutiny.

Architectural Monuments

Untold numbers of architectural monuments dot the Chinese landscape. Visitors will be taken to selected monuments accessible to the cities on the planned itinerary. The Chinese will not usually allow visitors to see monuments which have not been completely or partially refurbished. Many requests are turned down for this reason.

The visitor's experience can run the gamut from magnificent palaces and temples to pagodas and bridges. All can be interesting and informative. For example, the road to the Great Wall is straddled by a magnificent stone gateway built in the Mongol period (1345), certainly worth a short stop. The surfaces of the vaulted arch are covered with excellent low-relief carvings of the four heavenly kings, Buddhas, and mandalas. Southeast of the city of Shihchiachuang in Chao Hsien stands the handsome An Chi bridge built in the Sui

Dynasty (ca. 605 AD), famous for its daring conception, structure, and elegance. This single arch bridge is 50m. long and constructed with 700 tons of stone. Original relief carvings of dragons piercing clouds and monster masks are preserved in a nearby museum. Besides the stone pagodas in Sian, Kaifeng boasts the "Iron Pagoda," built in 1049. The 13-story pagoda is constructed of masonry and faced with tiles glazed in deep browns and greens, which appear from a distance to be rusted iron. The tiles have stamped designs of apsarases, Buddhas, dragons, and musicians.

It is possible to see two types of Buddhist temples: compounds composed of several wooden buildings and rock-cut temples. Two interesting wooden compounds are the Lung Hsing Monastery in the town of Chengting near Shihchiachuang and the Hua Yen Monastery in Tatung. The Lung Hsing Monastery covers an area of 2 sq.mi. and most of the fine buildings date from the Sung and Ch'in dynasties. In the chief temple is a 71-ft. bronze image of Kuan Yin (the Bodhisattva of Mercy). At Tatung, the Hua Yen actually consists of two monasteries, the upper and lower. The lower monastery contains an exquisite wooden building constructed under the Liao in 1038. The decoration, frescoes, and particularly the sculpture are superb. Some of the greatest Buddhist sculpture in China can be found in the rock cut temples of Lungmen near Loyang and Yunkang near Tatung.

*Lungmen
rock cut temples*

Yunkang, one of the earliest such sites, has 21 caves carved from a sandstone cliff and ranging in date from the mid-5th through the 6th century AD. Colossal, powerfully conceived images, 20 to 40 ft. high, fill the five earliest caves, Nos. 16-20. The carved limestone cliffs of Lungmen rise up on either side of the Yi River about nine miles from Loyang. The majority of caves are on the western cliffs. If time allows, a small group of later T'ang caves can be visited on the opposite side.

Another important group of Buddhist temples which may soon be open to the public is located on Wutai mountain in Shansi. At the present time, no Confucian temples have been opened to visitors.

Miscellaneous

The city of Kaifeng, which remains a cultural center where handicrafts flourish, provides a contrast to other Chinese cities. Intensive urbanization is just beginning. It offers an undisturbed atmosphere of old houses, cobblestone streets, and thatched roofs. In Kaifeng's embroidery factory, the workers produced an exquisite silk embroidery reproduction of a famous Sung painting in the Palace Museum in Peking, "The Ch'ing Ming Festival on the River." Twenty workers took five years to complete the task.

Various kilns have also been opened to visitors. The most famous, which has been producing porcelains for centuries, is Ching Te Chen in Kiangsu.

Many excursions hold surprises. For instance, Taiyuan in Shansi has a small late Buddhist temple, still used by a few practicing Buddhists. The main hall contains a *sutra* library with about 5,000 texts, some illustrated with Ming paintings of exceptional quality.

For some additional information, travelers should consult the comprehensive survey of Chinese art by Michael Sullivan, *The Arts of China* (University of California Press, 1977 ed.); and two booklets published in the People's Republic of China, *New Archeological Finds in China* (Foreign Languages Press, Peking, 1972) and *New Archeological Finds in China (II)* (FLP, Peking, 1978).

VISITING THE CHINESE EXPORT COMMODITIES FAIR
(THE CANTON TRADE FAIR)

In 1979—the Year of the Sheep—China was embarked on a major new course of economic expansion that was virtually without parallel in the 30-year history of the People's Republic. China's vigorous pursuit of the newly enunciated "four modernizations"—in industry, agriculture, national defense, and science and technology—has brought with it a major new stress on foreign trade, with a key emphasis laid on the massive importation of technology from Japan and the West.

The 44th session of the Canton Trade Fair held during October-November 1978 attracted more than 25,000 businessmen from over 110 countries. The Fall 1978 Fair witnessed a record US$1.6 billion of business, with Japan's volume alone accounting for US$530 million in total turnover—an all-time record—and the US selling some $83 million in commodities (mostly industrial chemicals) and buying $62 million worth of metals, textiles, foodstuffs, and arts and crafts. US-China contracts amounted to twice the previous record set at the Autumn 1977 Fair.

Development of the Fair

The Kwangchow (Canton) Trade Fair, held twice yearly in the spring and fall, is the most important event in the Chinese business calendar. Officially known as the Chinese Export Commodities Fair, it accounts for nearly half of China's yearly export sales and about a third of the country's total trade turnover (China's total trade was estimated at US$19 billion in 1977).

The first Kwangchow Fair was held in October 1957, when 1,200 visitors from 20 countries and regions came to the Kwangtung Provincial Exhibition Hall on Pearl River Square to view some 12,000 products. The Fair has been held twice a year ever since, in the spring from April 15 to May 15, and in the fall from October 15 to November 15. The 1979 Fairs will be the 45th and 46th, respectively.

The Fair has gradually grown in size and importance, although business declined somewhat during the height of the Cultural Revolution period (1966-69) when, to use the Chinese phrase, politics took command. Since then, the pace of business has again picked up. A new Fair complex, more than twice the size of the original, opened in

April 1974. It covers 60,000 sq. meters of exhibition space, divided among 12 exhibition halls. Some 40,000 items were on display in the mid-1970s.

Attendance by US businessmen at the Kwangchow Fairs began in spring 1972 when a dozen were invited. The Fall 1978 Fair was attended by some 700 North Americans, representing 300 companies— the second largest regional contingent, after Japan.

Officials at the Fair represent ten of China's Foreign Trade Corporations, dealing in the general areas of cereals, oils and foodstuffs; native products and animal by-products; textiles; light industrial goods; chemicals; metals and minerals; machinery; and handicrafts (for which an independent trade corporation was established in January 1978).

Unlike other international trade fairs, the Canton Fair is designed to be a showcase of current Chinese export potential and industrial development as well as a venue for direct business negotiations. Thus, it is a "permanent" exhibition and, as the official title suggests, it is a place mainly used for negotiating Chinese export business. Foreign companies may not acquire display space.

As China's goods have found increased acceptance in world markets, prices have kept pace, and there are few "bargains" to be had. The most dramatic events of 1978 included a rapid increase in the price for down (as world demand for this product soared), and a new flexibility in producing export items in areas ranging from textiles to handicrafts. Ventures in compensation trade were also on China's shopping list for the first time. These agreements call for the construction of factories in China specifically to produce items for export, with products geared to meet customers' specifications.

During 1978, the Fair also saw greater numbers of participants from Third World countries as well as more overseas Chinese. Many "old friends" among Western traders now do business between Fairs, either dealing directly with the head or branch offices of the foreign trade corporations or attending specialized "mini-fairs."

Getting to the Fair

Fair Invitations Attendance at the Kwangchow Trade Fair is by invitation only. Invitations are sent to those foreign corporations that have established trade ties with China as well as to "new friends" as a means of introducing them to the China trade. Invitations are generally issued by one of China's ten state trading corporations, headquartered in Peking, whose product lines roughly define the range of commodities that China seeks to export.

Firms seeking to initiate business with China should first write to the Peking headquarters of the appropriate PRC trade corporation.

Under some circumstances, invitations to the Fair may be solicited by writing directly to the Chinese Export Commodities Fair, Pearl River Square, Kwangchow, People's Republic of China or to the China Resources Company in Hong Kong. On first approaches, it is advisable to write both to one's local PRC commercial representative and to the trade corporation's headquarters in Peking, informing each that the other has been contacted. Foreign firms should correspond with the Commercial Attache at that country's PRC embassy.

Requests for an invitation should take the form of a letter of introduction and should include detailed information on the company's history, product lines, and sales volume. Bank references, financial reports, Dun and Bradstreet ratings, and other supporting data should be included. Requests for an invitation should precede the Fair opening by 2-3 months.

The Exhibition Hall in Kwangchow

Holders of invitations are permitted to have a maximum of three representatives accompany them to China. The party may include spouses.

Visas Once an invitation to the Fair is received, the prospective visitor must apply for PRC entrance and exit visas. Standard visas are for 35 days and are valid for Canton only. They are not renewable, although they may be extended should negotiations in China so require. Many transactions at the Fair, however, can be conducted within 5-10 days. Visa application forms can be obtained from PRC embassies. Visa forms should be submitted in duplicate, together with the applicant's passport, two passport photos, and a processing fee (e.g., $6 for US applicants). Passports are usually returned with a visa stamp in one week.

Diagram of the Trade Fair
Exhibition Hall

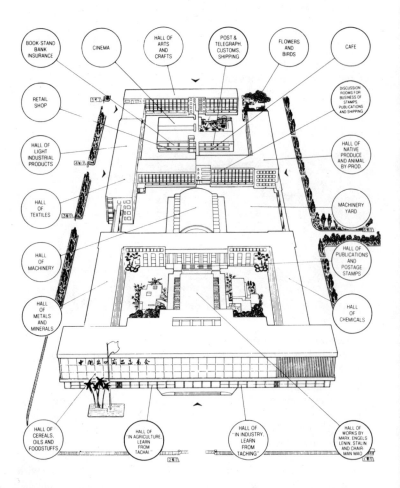

Clothing Dress protocol at the Fairs is practical and informal, with open shirts appropriate for men at both business and social occasions. Business suits are occasionally worn by visitors at ceremonial functions, although official PRC representatives usually stick to casual attire (pantssuits in the case of women). In any case, dress codes are demure and unostentatious, favoring muted colors.

Useful Items to Take Along For the businessman, an ample supply of business cards is an important asset at the Fair. Bilingual cards (in English and Chinese) can be ordered in Hong Kong or at the Fair itself.

 ## DOING BUSINESS AT THE FAIR

Advance Preparations and Contacts

Advance preparation is essential to the conduct of successful business negotiations at the Kwangchow Trade Fair. Although political and cultural differences between Chinese trade representatives and Western businessmen are not overt aspects of the negotiations process, the tone of the relationship and how it develops will often govern Chinese attitudes on who they will do business with, on how much business will be done, and on what is traded.

There is no attempt at the "hard sell" in China. On the contrary, the passive attitude of the Chinese trade representatives, who behave more as order-takers than as salesmen, has been noted by many. It is important, therefore, to form as clear an idea as possible beforehand about the nature and quantity of the purchase being sought. The wide variety of products on display will tempt window-shopping. An impulsive decision can be counter-productive, however, since it may then take two or three days simply to find the appropriate Chinese representative to discuss the product and its availability. Further, it is important to arrive prepared with the detailed specifications required, not only to save time in communicating back and forth with the home office, but also to be able to fill in specific entries in the contract. Knowledge of current pricing levels, whether they be for shoes or chemicals, is also important. Buyers will find the Chinese to be very much abreast of world market conditions.

Due consideration should be given to the choice of a company's representative to be sent to the Fair. It is vital—in the Chinese view—that representatives have the authority to sign contracts. Further, they should have a good working knowledge of the product areas to be explored. There is an advantage to having continuity of representation from Fair to Fair, since this will help promote an "old friend" relationship with Chinese negotiators. The Chinese try to discourage

95

Negotiating in the Exhibition Hall

"non-serious" buyers, meaning those who pose as businessmen in order to see something of China, those who seek to sign only token orders on behalf of a company, or those who come merely to browse.

Learning the ropes about doing business at the Fair has become easier due to the several years' experience gained by a host of China traders, including agents and trade representatives. The Chinese themselves publish guides to the Fair, and a helpful magazine called *China's Foreign Trade* is available in several language editions from PRC embassies or directly from the China Council for the Promotion of International Trade in Peking. A basic source in the US for information on the China market is the National Council for US-China Trade.

The Negotiation Process

China's negotiators at the Kwangchow Fair are representatives of the state-owned foreign trade corporations—they are not consumers, end-users, manufacturers, or suppliers. Nevertheless, these personnel are well versed in their assigned product areas.

First Contacts Business hours at the Fair are 8:30-11:30 AM and 2:30-5:30 PM daily (except Sundays). It is necessary to go directly to the section of the Exhibition Hall featuring products of interest to the foreign buyer (see Exhibition Hall Diagram), and to seek out the appropriate Chinese officials in order to set up an appointment. A business card should be presented. Because of the great number of visitors to the Fair, appointments should be secured as soon as possible. In no case, however, can they be made prior to arrival in Kwangchow. Appointment times can be set in person or through a third party such as the Fair Liaison Office at the hotel. Arriving late or missing an appointment is considered rude, and broken appointments will be difficult to reschedule.

The Style of Negotiations Business negotiations take place in individual discussion rooms or, frequently, in corridors or the exhibition halls themselves. It is not unusual to find competitors sitting at directly adjacent tables. There may be 3-4 Chinese negotiators present, some of whom may abruptly get up and leave, while others randomly wander in, perhaps interrupting the train of conversation. Such procedures are considered normal practice, and it is important to retain aplomb.

Export Negotiations The Kwangchow Fair is largely geared toward importers, but exporters are now more frequently invited and given an opportunity to hold some initial discussions. Export negotiations at the Fair are sometimes exploratory in nature. Provided there is sufficient interest, the talks will usually move on to Peking for further discussion.

Contracts

The drawing-up of a contract concludes the negotiating process. The Chinese attach great importance to the contract stage, and assume strict compliance by all parties. Contract terms and conditions vary among the foreign trade corporations and also according to the commodity being traded. It is important to specify in the contract all terms and conditions verbally agreed to during the negotiations. (Importers will also find it useful to repeat such stipulations when opening Letters of Credit.) Standard features of Chinese contracts include requirements for import and export documentation, claims settlement, arbitration, insurance, and arrangements for inspection. Buyers of Chinese products are usually required to open an irrevocable Letter of Credit—payable to the Bank of China. The BOC has established correspondent relationships with banks in many countries, including

97

the First National Bank of Chicago (the sole correspondent bank for the US) and the Canadian Imperial Bank of Commerce. Chinese trade was formerly negotiated in British sterling, but other major currencies—including the French franc, Swiss franc, Deutschemark, Belgian franc, Dutch guilder, and US dollar—have also become acceptable.

Shipping For importers, the terms of the contract usually specify C+F or CIF. The PRC operates a large merchant fleet, much of it under charter, and has shown a strong preference for making its own shipping arrangements, with Hong Kong and Tokyo the most common trans-shipment points for the US. Goods destined for Canadian ports are shipped direct from the PRC or, in some cases, via Hong Kong.

Insurance Chinese insurance coverage for CIF shipments is regulated through the Ocean Marine Cargo and Ocean Marine Cargo War Clauses of the People's Insurance Company of China. Terms accord with international practices. Many importers now prefer CIF to C+F terms, having found Chinese insurance to be a good value. China retains agents in most major international ports to handle claims.

Arbitration Arbitration clauses in standard Chinese contracts generally call for negotiations in Peking under terms set by the Chinese Foreign Trade Arbitration Committee. In actual practice, however, arbitration proceedings are found to be cumbersome and the Chinese discourage them, preferring "friendly discussion" between the parties.

III
THE CHINA TOUR:
CITIES AND SITES

Children in Peking

ANSHAN

saddle mountain

Pinyin Spelling: Anshan
("ahn-shahn")

A nshan, the steel capital of China, is located in Liaoning Province about 80 km. (50 mi.) southwest of Shenyang. The city is set amidst a densely populated agricultural-industrial area rich in deposits of iron and coal. Anshan boasts the largest iron and steel complex in China (although Wuhan is more modern and may soon supplant it). It produces about one-fourth of China's steel. The Chinese are especially proud of Anshan because of its role in providing most of the steel used in the PRC's initial industrial expansion during the 1950s.

Appropriately enough, the town is on the same latitude as a US steel center, Youngstown, Ohio. Its climate, however, is more like that of Minneapolis: hot, dry summers and bitter winters, when the temperature rarely goes above freezing.

Anshan in History

Iron and steel are also synonymous with the history of Anshan. Organized iron mining and smelting began about 100 BC. There was some expansion of activity during the 10th and 11th centuries, but during the Ch'ing Dynasty a superstitious Manchu emperor curtailed operations for fear of disturbing some ancestral graves about 10 miles away.

The modern development of Anshan began with the rediscovery of iron ore deposits by the Japanese in the early 1900s. The Japanese added the first open-hearth furnaces in 1935.

Anshan was occupied by the Soviet army in 1945, which immediately began the systematic dismantling and removal of power-generating and transforming equipment, electric motors, and all new or undamaged machine tools. Anshan's condition worsened during the civil war (1946-49), when control of the town seesawed back and forth 11 times between the Communists and the Kuomintang. The People's Liberation Army finally gained permanent control in 1948, whereupon restoration of the iron and steel plant was given the highest priority.

HIGHLIGHTS FOR TRAVELERS

Today, the iron and steel plant sprawls over an area of about 5 sq. mi., monopolizing the skyline of the northwest part of the city with its belching smoke stacks, blast furnaces, and cooling towers. Its No.7 blast furnace is the largest in the country, with an annual capacity of 1.5 million tons of steel in 1978.

In addition to iron and steel, Anshan produces agricultural machinery, construction materials, chemicals, and consumer goods. There are several parks, schools, and technical institutes (mostly related to the metallurgical industry). Chien Shan (Thousand Lotus Hill), in the outskirts of Shenyang, is one of Liaoning Province's most famous scenic spots, once a Buddhist hermitage. A hot spring lies about 6 miles southeast of the city.

Anshan possesses few sights of historical interest, although a residence of the former warlord Chang Tso-lin (d. 1928) is located here, as is the home of Henry P'u-yi, the last Ch'ing emperor who for a while served as the puppet Emperor K'ang-te of "Manchukuo" under the Japanese.

CHANGCHUN

eternal spring

Pinyin Spelling:
Changchun
("chang-choon")

Changchun, the capital of Kirin Province, is situated on the Yitung River in the central part of the Northeast Plain. A city of 1.5 million, it is primarily known as the first center of China's automotive industry.

Changchun is characterized by wide, tree-lined avenues and large administrative buildings. Much of the present city was constructed between 1933 and 1945, when, as part of the Manchurian region occupied by Japan, it was designated the capital of "Manchukuo."

In 1953, work on China's first automobile factory began in Changchun. The plant has since undergone several phases of expansion and now produces trucks and automobiles, including the famous "Red Flag" limousines. The city's industry also includes machine tools, railway cars, electric motors, textiles, and food processing.

There are two hotels in Changchun. In addition to the industrial sites, tourists are likely to have a chance to visit Kirin University and one of China's largest film studios.

Changsha, the capital of Hunan Province, is a flourishing regional center for culture and education. Situated in south-central China at the lower reaches of the Hsiang River, Changsha lies 525 km. (315 mi.) northwest of Kwangchow and 1,350 km. (810 mi.) south of Peking. It is one of three principal stops on the Peking-Kwangchow railway line (12 hours from Kwangchow, 26 from Peking). The greater municipality of Changsha has an area of 2,990 sq. km. (1,800 sq.mi.). The central city occupies about 110 sq.km. (66 sq.mi.) and supports a population of 800,000.

Physically, Changsha offers only modest historic and scenic attractions. It owes its significance to two factors: the intensively cultivated alluvial lowlands surrounding the city are among the most productive in China; and, not incidentally, the city played a major role in the lives and political careers of both Mao Tse-tung and Hua Kuo-feng.

Mao was born in neighboring Shaoshan (discussed below) and attended high school in Changsha. His observations of life in this area served as the basis of the most important of his early political works, "Report on the Peasant Movement in Hunan Province." Prior to his appointment as Mao's successor in 1976, Chairman Hua Kuo-feng held important political and administrative posts in Hunan. An agricultural specialist, Hua helped direct much of the reclamation and irrigation work undertaken in the area during the 1960s and early 1970s.

Changsha in History

The site of Changsha was inhabited as long as 3,000 years ago. Metallurgy, textile handicrafts, and lacquer work have flourished since the Spring and Autumn and Warring States periods (770-221 BC). Changsha was the site of a recently excavated tomb dating from the Western Han period (206 BC-24 AD) containing some remarkable, superbly preserved artifacts.

The city was known as an important educational center as early as the Sung Dynasty (ca. 11th century AD). A large encircling wall with nine

CHANGSHA

long sandbank

Pinyin Spelling:
Changsha
("chong-shah")

gates (portions of which are still standing) was built during the Ming period.

In 1904, an "open-door" treaty established Changsha as a foreign-trade port. Afterwards, large numbers of Europeans and Americans began to take up residence in the city. Foreign influences were soon manifested in the establishment of churches, educational institutions —including a college set up by Yale University (now serving as a medical center), and a number of small export factories.

Mao Tse-tung lived in the city as a student from 1912 to 1918. It was here that his conversion to communism began. Local guides relate that during this period Mao matured politically from a naive country lad who had never read a newspaper to a questioning student, progressive teacher, and local political organizer. One of his first jobs was editing the local *Hsiang River Review*. Many of the sites associated with those days are indispensable parts of the visitor's itinerary.

Changsha suffered acute damage during the Sino-Japanese War (1937-45), and much of it remained in ruins until after the establishment of the PRC in 1949. By 1952, reconstruction and rehabilitation were well under way and important initiatives in industrialization had begun.

Economy and Culture

Changsha served as a major trading center for more than 2,000 years. Prior to the 20th century, most commercial activity stemmed from agriculture. Hunan has traditionally been a surplus food producer, annually furnishing about 15% of China's total rice crop. At least a dozen rice mills are now in operation in Changsha and constitute the most important single economic activity in the city.

An early boost to development occurred when Changsha was linked by rail to Hankow and Peking in 1908, providing an impetus for the growth of modern light industry, particularly textiles and food processing. Today, although the city's economy is still strongly tied to its agricultural hinterland, the traditional dominance of food-processing and handling has significantly diminished. The trend toward economic diversification has featured the establishment of small and medium-sized machinery, chemical, electronics, and metal-working plants. A new railway terminus was completed in 1977.

River transportation remains another aspect of Changsha's economy. Although its cargo facilities have yet to be modernized, Changsha remains the busiest port on the Hsiang River. Food grains, construction materials, coal, and timber account for about 70% of the freight handled. Shipments arrive in long, graceful, flat-sailed cargo boats or on low-riding, utilitarian barges.

Culturally, Changsha is noted for its marionette and shadow-puppet theater. Recently, its museum has become a major attraction by virtue of the Han tomb excavation. (See below.) The city's major educational and cultural centers are located on the west bank of the river at the base of Yueh-lu Shan. These include Hunan University, Hunan Teachers College, and the Central-South Institute of Metallurgy. Changsha also boasts 13 hospitals and an Institute of Chinese Traditional Medicine.

HIGHLIGHTS FOR TRAVELERS

Changsha is a relatively new addition to the itinerary of visiting foreigners and, with the exception of the museum, there are few unique displays of Chinese antiquity, architecture, or other cultural attractions. Rather, it is the countryside and the sites associated with Chairman Mao and his early revolutionary activities that are the focal points for visitors.

Line drawing from silk funerary banner found in Changsha tomb, Han Dynasty

Hunan Provincial Museum The Provincial Museum, located in a large park in the northeast section of town (near the hotel), was formerly known mainly for its collection of documents dealing with revolutionary history. While the collection is still there, most attention now focuses on the relics unearthed from Han Tomb No. 1 at Mawangtui, a site just two miles east of the museum. The site, excavated in 1972, featured two spectacular finds: the first was the perfectly preserved corpse of a woman about 50 years old. She was apparently the wife of a royal personage and had lived around 193-141 BC. Individual organs removed from her body are on display. Details of her life have been deduced from items found in her stomach and other medical evidence. The body itself is housed in the basement of the museum and may be viewed through a plexiglass skylight.

When found, the body was wrapped in more than 20 layers of silk and linen with a silk painting draped over the inner coffin. In three layers, it depicts scenes of the underworld, of human society, and of the celestial world. Some details derive from legend, others from the society of the time. The painting retains its brilliant colors, with figures outlined by a single flowing line and colored with mineral pigments of vermilion, azurite, and malachite. Other funerary objects on display from this tomb are the three lacquered coffins, gowns of silk

105

gauze, lacquer-ware, musical instruments, and some outstanding figurines.

Lovely Evening Pavilion (Ai Wan) Situated on Yue-lu Hill on the west bank of the Hsiang River, the Ai Wan Pavilion commands a striking view of the town. It is a popular place for the people of Shaoshan to relax and picnic in their time off. The pavilion itself has a double roof with glazed green tiles.

Orange Island (Chu-tzu Chou-tou) This island is in fact the "long sandbank" from which Changsha takes its name. Lying midstream in the Hsiang River, it runs almost the length of the city. The Orange Island Pavilion, at its southern tip, affords a commanding view of river traffic. The Hsiang River Bridge, at the island's northern end, was completed in the early 1970s. Before then, ferries were the only means of transport across the river.

Museum at Hunan Normal School Mao Tse-tung attended classes here between 1913 and 1918, and later returned there to teach. Destroyed during the civil war, the school has been carefully restored to serve as a monument to Mao and the Chinese Revolution.

Former Office of the Hunan Communist Party Committee This museum includes the rooms used for early meetings, Mao's living quarters, and an exhibition of historical materials from that period.

 # HOTEL ACCOMMODATIONS

Hunan Guest House The nine-story Hunan Guest House, built in 1959, is Changsha's tallest building and offers the city's best tourist accommodations. Located at the edge of the Martyrs Park (Lieh-shih Kuang-yuan) and about a mile and a half from the main square, it has over 250 rooms and can accommodate up to 600 people. A staff of 250 presides over this rather cavernous structure which, until the recent upsurge in tourism, had remained relatively empty. Services include three modern dining rooms, a souvenir shop, a crafts emporium, and other amenities such as barber and beauty shops, telephones, post office, bank, and laundry. The lobby has a map showing bus routes to other parts of the city. Rates are Y14-18 for a twin-bedded room; a suite is Y60.

HUNAN CUISINE

Although Hunan is a province noted for its spicy, flavorful food, this feature may elude tourists whose meals are confined to the

hotel's dining room. Apparently, the hotel is under instructions to refrain from challenging its guests' palates and, as a result, blander versions of Hunan fare are the rule. The alert tour group will try to make a special request of the kitchen or try to negotiate an evening at a local restaurant with the tour guides (Shaoshan has no restaurants catering to foreigners, although the open hospitality of the local people may afford a chance to try the simple fare of a local restaurant). Vegetables prepared with special local sauces, and any of the "spicy" dishes offered will quickly reveal why Hunan's food has gained such a wide reputation. The region is also famous for its oranges and kumquats.

SHOPPING

The people of Changsha and Shaoshan produce an array of distinct regional handicrafts. The embroidery is justly famous. Hotel shops display crafts such as miniature sampans made from shells. Pottery and ceramic ware is also recommended (especially the tiny figurines) as are eiderdowns (quilts and pillows filled with duck feathers).

CHENGCHOW

kingdom of Cheng

Pinyin Spelling:
Zhengzhou
("chung-joe")

Chengchow is the capital of Honan Province
and a major city in north-central China. It is
located a few miles south of the Yellow River and is
about 640 km. (400 mi.) due south of Peking.
Geographically, it sits at the western edge of the
agriculturally important North China Plain.

A major railway center that links Kwangchow
and Peking (on the north-south axis) and Sian and
Shanghai (on the east-west axis), Chengchow continues in its traditional role as a major market and
transportation center. Infrequently visited by
tourists in the past, it is becoming an increasingly
more common stop because of its central location
and its exemplification of a well-planned town
with balanced development of agriculture and industry. All told, Chengchow provides a powerful
visual symbol of the rebuilding that has taken
place in new China.

The population of 900,000 enjoys a pleasant
climate in spring and autumn, but midsummer
temperatures soar above 90°F, with heavy rains
occurring in July.

Chengchow in History

Chengchow has a long history, the site having
been continuously settled for more than 3,000
years. It ranked as one of the most populous
regions in China during the Shang Dynasty (ca.
1760-1100 BC), but for a period thereafter waned
in importance because of the proximity of Anyang,
which emerged as the dynastic capital.

The modern development of the city began in
1898 when foreign interests were granted concessions for the construction of major north-south and
east-west rail lines. These were completed in 1910.
In the 1920s, the railway was the focus of several
labor disputes, including a notorious incident on
February 7, 1923, when a strike against the local
warlord was bloodily suppressed. Because of its importance as a major railway center, Chengchow
was a primary objective of Japanese forces during
their push through China in 1937. In an infamous
incident now memorialized locally, the Kuomintang (Nationalist) army breached the dike of the

Yellow River less than 20 miles northeast of the city in order to deny it to the Japanese. The action resulted in devastating floods that cost thousands of lives through drowning or subsequent starvation. The diverted river continued to threaten the city until 1947, when the break was repaired through US assistance. Chengchow was again severely damaged in fighting that took place during the civil war in 1948-49. Labor troubles resurfaced in the 1970s, and local officials speak of the "sabotage carried out by the 'gang of four' and their henchmen,"

Economy and Culture

Chengchow was initially rebuilt during 1949-50, but significant urban expansion did not take place until after 1954 when the city was designated as a site for concerted industrial development. Food-processing and cotton textile industries were given priority. By the 1960s, Chengchow had become an important industrial center as well as a transportation hub.

The textile sector includes five mills that produce both yarn and finished cloth. Associated facilities include a textile printing and dyeing plant and several textile machinery plants. Food and agricultural industries include a meat-processing and by-products plant, flour mills, and a plant that processes cottonseed into edible oil and other products. Chemical fertilizer, insecticides, and tractor repair plants (the region's flat terrain makes it ideal for agricultural mechanization) are also located in Chengchow. Major agricultural products are rice, wheat, and cottonseed.

Chengchow has 175 primary schools, 42 secondary schools, and 13 technical schools. Technical schools specialize in medicine, architecture, commerce, forestry, hydraulic engineering, and agriculture. The city maintains 8 theaters and 13 cinemas.

HIGHLIGHTS FOR TRAVELERS

Although Chengchow's tourist attractions do not rival those of Shanghai, Sian, or Peking, it is nevertheless a city of considerable interest. Most of the city is modern in appearance, reflecting its tremendous growth since 1950 (when its population was 100,000 and had only five factories employing 700 workers). In the new section of town, blocks of governmental, educational, and cultural buildings are intermingled with extensive residential areas. There are broad, tree-lined avenues and a variety of monumental civic structures.

There is also an old town core, with narrow, maze-like streets and traditional houses that serve as a reminder of other times. Some housing foundations and graves from the 3rd century BC have been discovered in this old section, and remnants of the ancient wall still stand.

Cenotaph In the heart of the shopping district of the old section stands a cenotaph built to commemorate the bloody general strike of railroad workers in February 1923.

Honan Provincial Museum Located in the newer section of town, the museum contains exhibitions from the neolithic period, early dynasties, and the modern period, including the railway strikes, the war of resistance against the Japanese, the civil war, and post-1949 developments. Artifacts from early dynasties include tools from Yang and Shang cultures, lacquerware, wooden figurines, bronzes, and textiles from tomb sites dating from the Chou and Six dynasties eras, bronzes from the T'ang Dynasty, and samples of pottery from the Sung. All artifacts were discovered in Honan Province.

Textile Mills To demonstrate the comprehensive development of modern China, factories, communes, and educational institutions are included on the itinerary of most visitors. Chengchow's textile mills are among the most advanced in China. Leading members of factory management committees often remark with pride about how the "old" Chengchow has been transformed.

People's Park Just behind the Opera Theater, this park has pleasant walkways and a lake fed by the Chin-shui River, which is connected by a canal to the Yellow River to the north. The Park serves as a rough dividing line between the old and new towns, with the city's major department store just one block south and workers' residential areas situated immediately to the north.

HOTEL ACCOMMODATIONS

Most visitors will be put up at the Honan Hotel, a grand structure built in Soviet style, with a large fountain in front, a cavernous lobby, and a huge, red-carpeted marble staircase. The massive external scale telescopes into small but comfortable rooms. The hotel has the usual tourist amenities, including a retail shop (with relatively sparse selection), telegraph and post offices, and bank. The building is surrounded on three sides by wheat fields. During harvest times, many of the hotel employees leave to join in the agricultural work.

Since the hotel stands on the outskirts of town, it may give the visitor a feeling of isolation. The cenotaph, marking Chengchow's center, is a good 45-minute (two-mile) walk, as is the People's Park.

SHOPPING

The lapidary shop is a common stop on most itineraries. Jade from several provinces is sold here. Linens and textiles are also a good buy. Handicrafts feature egg-shell painting, feather painting, and stuffed animals. Since the store in the hotel is not well-stocked, a trip to the Chengchow Department Store and local specialty shops is recommended. There is no Friendship Store in Chengchow, although there is an antique store.

Drying peanuts

Chengtu is the capital of Szechwan Province, and an important agricultural and industrial city in southwestern China. The total population is 3.7 million, divided among two city districts, three suburban areas and two outlying prefectures. About 1.4 million persons reside in the city center.

Chengtu was added to the general itinerary in 1978. It is a pleasantly laid-out city with broad streets and many public parks, but is perhaps best known as the headquarters for the famous spicy food of Szechwan Province. The natives are reputed to be as peppery as the food—but are friendly to foreign guests.

By rail, Chengtu is 2,048 km. (1,200 mi.) from Peking. Situated at an elevation of 500 ft. on a vast plain, it has a temperate climate and abundant rainfall.

CHENGTU

capital city

Pinyin Spelling:
Chengdu
("chung-doo")

Chengtu in History

Until 1949, Chengtu's reputation rested more on its ancient history than its modern development. Some 2,000 years ago, during the Chou Dynasty, the kingdom of Shu moved its capital to this site. Later, during the Han Dynasty, the brocade trade brought so much prosperity that a government post was created for the town's management and it earned the nickname "city of brocade." It became the "city of hibiscus" during the Five Dynasties period when a local feudal lord had those colorful flowers planted atop the town wall.

The renowned T'ang Dynasty poet Tu Fu lived in Chengtu for three years, composing over 200 poems before his death. Subsequent centuries saw little change, and Chengtu remained comparatively underdeveloped until 1949 when the new government decided to build it up as a regional industrial base.

Economy and Culture

Traditionally a center for handicrafts and brocades, Chengtu today has a solid industrial base. City officials will tell visitors that industrial output has increased 92 times since the early 1950s, and that the number of factories has increased from the original 10 to over 1,900. The workforce numbers one-half million. Examples of industry are metallurgy, coal mining, machine building, aluminum, and electronics (including computers). Natural gas is abundant in the region.

There are 180,000 hectares (425,000 acres) under cultivation in the area, and the land produces rice, wheat, sweet potatoes, tea, tobacco, and medicinal plants and herbs.

Chengtu is also an important cultural center. Szechwan opera, for example, has a tradition of close to 2,000 years. It is characterized by its combination of music, dance, and acrobatics full of local Szechwan color and flavor. Recently revived, the tradition is now taught at the local Opera Art Institute.

Chengtu has 12 institutions of higher education, 32 technical institutes, and 2,100 middle and elementary schools. Some 50,000 teachers are employed in the city.

HIGHLIGHTS FOR TRAVELERS

One thing that immediately strikes the visitor is that Chengtu is among the most "energy conscious" of China's cities, taking advantage of the nearby natural gas fields which have been widely tapped. Public buses run on natural gas, stored in rubber bags on top. These are refilled twice daily, with one bagful providing a range of more than 180 miles. It costs only about 3 cents for a refill.

Chengtu is also quite proud of its annual lantern festival (January-February) which dates back 1,300 years. The more than 20,000 elaborately designed lanterns for the 1978 festival included birds, an arrangement of swan and fish lanterns floating on a pond amidst lotus blossoms, and an elephant carrying grain.

Tu Fu Cottage The great poet Tu Fu (712-770) lived in Chengtu for three years, and a shrine was built during the Sun Dynasty on the site where his modest house used to stand. The spot is marked by a small stream. Inside the shrine there is a painting which attempts to evoke the poet's moods. Many contemporary figures, including Mao, Chu Teh, and Kuo Mo-jo, have written couplets in praise of Tu Fu.

Chuko Liang Shrine Chuko Liang (also known as Wu Hou) was a renowned military strategist of the third century. This shrine in his memory was built during the T'ang Dynasty, and reconstructed and enlarged during the early Ch'ing Dynasty. Further reconstruction took place in 1952 and it is now one of the "protected treasures" of the state.

River View Pavilion The stately River View Pavilion stands by the East Nine-Arch Bridge in the city's outskirts. A three-story wooden

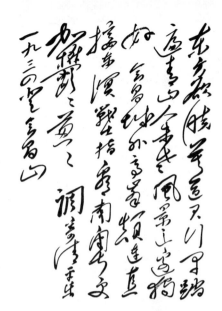

HUICHANG

Soon dawn will break in the east.
Do not say "You start too early";
Crossing these blue hills adds nothing to
    one's years,
The landscape here is beyond compare.

Straight from the walls of Huichang lofty
    peaks,
Range after range, extend to the eastern
    seas.
Our soldiers point southward to Kwangtung
Looming lusher and greener in the distance.

A poem by Mao Tse-Tung in his calligraphy, written in 1934
It is composed in the style of tzu, *a T'ang Dynasty form*
at which Tu Fu excelled.

structure in the architectural style of South China, it is built above the water at the edge of the Chin Chiang (Brocade) River. There is a tea-house in the pavilion, and many bamboos are planted nearby.

Wangchianglou Park Situated on the Chin Chian (Brocade) River on the eastern side of the city, the park is well-known for its pavilions made entirely of cedar wood and for its bamboo forest with 120 varieties of that species. The initial construction of the park dates from the end of the Ming Dynasty but the park did not assume its present form until the reign of Kuang Hsu (1875-1908). It has recently been enlarged.

Clear Awakening Temple Extending over 15 hectares to the north of the city, this park features a Buddhist temple of colossal proportions.

Tuchiangyen Dam and Green City Peak About 40 km. (25 mi.) northwest of Chengtu, this engineering marvel dates back over 2,000 years. Built in 250 BC as a mammoth irrigation project, Tuchiangyen Dam checked the Min River which comes down from Green City Peak. A trunk canal was cut through the mountain, and a water distribution network set up that irrigated 1.3 million hectares of land. Expansion has been undertaken since 1949, and the whole system today irrigates well over 6.67 million hectares.

HOTEL ACCOMMODATIONS

Still awaiting renovation, the Friendship Hotel in Chengtu is a rather somber building in the socialist-realist style. Accommodations are comfortable, and the hotel is located in an interesting area of the city.

LOCAL CUISINE

Although best known abroad for its hot, spicy food, the region's cuisine is just as famous in China for its refined and varied tastes, often enhanced by the use of medicinal herbs and flower petals. Among the well-known dishes are "soft-fried lotus flowers," "orchid-petal chicken strips," "duck cooked with medicinal herbs," "Pock-marked Grandma's beancurd," and "street vendor's noodles."

SHOPPING

Chengtu, which once bore the title of "storehouse of heaven" for its agricultural wealth and handicrafts, still lives up to that name. The local crafts make good souvenirs. Embroidery and brocade make excellent purchases. Among Chengtu's crafts, lacquerware, bamboo or plaited straw ware, cutlery, and pottery are among the best known. In the Han Dynasty tomb of Mawangtui (see under Changsha, Hunan Provincial Museum), hundreds of lacquer-ware pieces were found bearing the mark "made in Chengtu." By way of evidence that these traditions are still being upheld, over 400 Chengtu articles appeared in the recent National Exhibition of Arts and Crafts in Peking.

Chungking is one of China's largest municipalities, the most important industrial city of southwest China, and a key regional transportation hub. Located at the confluence of the Chialing and Yangtse rivers—about 2,400 km. (1,500 mi.) upstream from Shanghai—and at the juncture of important north-south land routes, transportation played a key role in the city's early development and its more recent and rapid urban growth. Although the old city (population 800,000) is physically confined by its site on a narrow peninsula with steep embankments, the city has been progressively enlarged during recent decades by incorporation of new industrial and mining districts and rural agricultural areas within its municipal boundaries. Today's total population is about 6 million.

As it rises on the 500−600 m. (300−400 ft.) slopes of a mountain wedged in between the two rivers, Chungking is said to resemble the superstructure of a gigantic ship. The old section of Chungking is dissected by a maze of narrow lanes that often merge into flights of steps connecting the various levels of the town. The western side of town has more open space, trees, and large buildings.

Unfortunately, Chungking has one of the least appealing climates of China's major cities, as suggested by its local nickname as a "furnace of the Yangtse." Summer temperatures rise into the mid-90s F. and typically are coupled with high humidity. From May to September, heavy and frequent rains occur (commonly for 4 days out of 10). The city also gets about 90 days of fog a year, giving it a dank appearance. Autumn and early spring are the best times to visit Chungking. At least until the early 1980s, the city was not expected to be visited more than occasionally by foreign groups.

CHUNGKING

repeated good luck

Pinyin Spelling:
Chongqing
("chung-ching")

Chungking in History

Little is known of the early history of this ancient trading settlement. Apparently it was not until the 12th century that the name "Chungking" was first used. Although gradually expanding in population and importance over the last six centuries, it was not until recent decades that the city began to expand beyond its western battlements. Chungking became a treaty port in 1891, but even the few foreigners who came to settle on the south shore made little impact.

The modern development of Chungking began in 1928 under a planned program of widening streets and starting up industry. The major spurt of growth came in 1938, however, when Chungking became the wartime capital of Nationalist China. Whole industrial plants, universities, and service facilities were moved from the war zone along the eastern coast into the adjoining municipal districts. Local deposits of coal provided the energy base upon which rapid industrialization could proceed. By the war's end in 1945, nearly 2 million people were jammed into the municipality. Even the Japanese bombing failed to slow city growth, although the city was damaged during the ensuing civil war.

US GIs meet Mao Tse-tung in 1945.

Chungking in the Revolution. Although Chungking was the Nationalists' seat of government during World War II, the Communists were also openly active in the city. The last years of the war witnessed a degree of cooperation in the guise of providing the united front against the Japanese invasion. During the course of the war, figures such as Chou En-lai, Tung Pi-wu, Yeh Chien-ying, and Teng Ying-chao were in Chungking as Communist Party representatives. They had their headquarters in Red Crag Village, now a tourist site.

Local residents particularly remember the activites of Chou En-lai, who directed the *New China Daily* and was engaged in various anti-Kuomintang activities. Chairman Mao himself came to Chungking on August 28, 1945 to negotiate the ill-fated truce with the Nationalists.

Chungking's KMT bastion was defeated one month after the official declaration of the founding of the People's Republic of China, and repair and expansion of Chungking's industrial base began soon thereafter. Growth was accelerated by improvement of navigation on the Yangtse and by the construction of new railroads that linked the region to a national rail network. Although some rebuilding, street-widening, and construction of cable railroads brought some alterations to the eastern and older sections, more dramatic changes during the recent decades have occurred in the western half of the city. A 300-foot hill was leveled to provide space for a new stadium and several major governmental and cultural buildings. Trees were planted and parks laid out to give the new section a more open and brighter appearance.

Economy and Culture

Chungking has built up a comprehensive industrial base embracing steel, machinery, chemicals, power, textiles and light industry. Its machinery plants now produce complete sets of equipment for small and medium-sized factories. Industry now accounts for 90% of the total value of output of industrial and agricultural production. New Chungking's industrial capacity is 22 times that of before 1949.

Situated on the north-south rail lines (some of which are spectacular engineering feats), the city is also an important reshipment center. During the winter of 1977, work began on a one-kilometer-long highway bridge over the Yangtse, the first for this city, which had always had to rely on ferries. Although originally scheduled for completion in 1982, the bridge was likely to be finished by 1980.

Cultural and educational institutions include the Szechwan Academy of Fine Arts, the Chungking Working People's Palace of Culture (where mass sculpture was featured in 1978), and several universities and technical schools.

HIGHLIGHTS FOR TRAVELERS

Chungking lacks many of the attractions offered by other cities in that there are no ancient monuments, and old walls and temples have long since disappeared. But the old city, with its winding stone-step streets and busy riverfront activities, still powerfully evokes the urban China of another age. Visits to examples of modern industry and to nearby coal mines are included in most visits.

Chungking harbor at night

The visitor will surely be taken to Loquat Hill, the highest point in the city, for an overview of Chungking, and there are hot springs north and south of Chungking for relaxation. A building that was formerly the site of the Sino-American Special Cooperation Organization (for military training during the anti-Japanese war and used as a prison by the KMT) is now a martyrs' museum. Cassia Garden, where Chairman Mao stayed during his visit to Chungking, and the Red Crag Revolutionary Museum (housing Chou En-lai's wartime office) are also commonly on the itinerary.

The Yangtse River Gorges Chungking is a starting point for cruises down the Yangtse River gorges, certainly one of the natural wonders of the world. There are three famous gorges of the Yangtse lying in a 189-km. (118-mi.) stretch between Chungking and Wuhan: Chutang Gorge, Wuhsia Gorge, and Hsiling Gorge. Towering mountains drop almost perpendicularly into the river as if hewn by an axe. The spectacular grandeur of these walls and the turgid river that roars through them have long been the subjects of China's romantic poets and painters. To boatmen and navigators, however, they meant dangerous bends, shallows, rapids, and reefs. Adding to the danger are a fast current (prior to recent man-made modifications in the "green shallows," the flow reached 7.9 m. per second) and a river-level swing of as much as 53 m. (175 ft.) between dry and flooded seasons.

Yet, boats have plied this part of the Yangtse since the Western Chou Dynasty (1122-770 BC). Foreigners who traveled this fabled stretch in the early 1900s recount how it took anywhere from 20 to 60 days to traverse the 648-km. (405-mi.) stretch between Yichang at the mouth of the gorges and Chungking. The downstream trip took from 3 to 10 days.

Today, the Yangtse journey takes but three days up and two days down, and the entire stretch between Shanghai and Chungking can be completed in eight days up and five days down. This has been due to the enormous task that has been undertaken to literally rebuild the river bed. Some 107 danger spots have been eliminated by widening the channel, blasting away rocks and reefs, mechanizing the winches that pull boats up the roughest segments of rapids, and the installation of a much improved navigation system for signaling around bends and in heavy weather.

Foreigners are now being allowed to book passage aboard one of the 20 "East Is Red" steamers which traverse the river. These modern white ships are 71 m. (220 ft.) long and 15 m. (50 ft.) wide, with a draft of just over 2.5 m. (8 ft.). The ships are driven by 2,400-hp. twin-diesel engines with twin screws. Maximum speed is 28 km. (17.5 mi.) per hour. The 700-800 passengers are accommodated in five classes, with a total sleeping capacity of about 500. Second class, the one assigned to foreigners, means a cabin with bed, washstand, chest of drawers, small desk, and two chairs. Showers and toilets are in small, separate rooms. Excellent food is served in the dining room by white-jacketed stewards and stewardesses. On lower decks, passengers sleep in two-tiered bunks in cabins as wide as the steamer, and spend the day reading, playing cards or chess, or looking at the magnificent scenery. The second class fare for the 1,370-km. (856-mi.) journey from Chungking to Wuhan is Y57.2 (about US$50).

杭
州

HANGCHOW

city across the river

Pinyin Spelling:
Hangzhou ("hong-joe")

H angchow, one of China's most famous scenic sites, is the capital of Chekiang Province, as well as its political, economic, and cultural center. Situated on the Chentang River at the southern end of the Grand Canal, it has an area of 429 sq.km. (165.6 sq.mi.) and a population of 980,000. It is also a prosperous industrial and agricultural city, with good flight connections from Peking (710 mi.), Kwangchow, Nanking, and Shanghai.

The local scenery is legendary, due largely to the beautiful West Lake (Hsi Hu). The lake was originally a shallow bay adjoining the Chentang River. Gradually, with the silting up of its outlet, it was transformed into an inland lake. Over the centuries, the lake has been repeatedly dredged. Causeways, bridges, and pavilions, subtly adorned with trees and flowers, produced a setting of such striking beauty that it became China's most popular resort.

Hangchow in History

The extension of the Grand Canal southward from the Yangtse River late in the 6th century transformed Hangchow from a sleepy fishing village into a bustling commercial center. Its continued growth was assured as the fertile lower Yangtse valley supplanted the North China Plain as the country's prime agricultural region. Between the 8th and 12th centuries, it was alternately the capital of several kingdoms and dynasties. Although the city was devastated by the Mongol invasion of the late 13th century, Hangchow's importance did not diminish. Its function as a trade center together with the splendor of its religious monuments continued to attract merchants and visitors from all over the world (including Marco Polo).

Hangchow's political and commercial significance was dramatically curtailed in the mid-19th century as a result of the Taiping Rebellion. Much of the city was reduced to ashes, many of its most venerable religious structures were damaged or destroyed, and thousands of its inhabitants were killed in the course of the ensuing turmoil.

The local guides take pride in pointing out that

the city has been virtually rebuilt since 1949. Up until then, it had only a few small factories and one cotton textile mill. After the Great Leap Forward (1958), capital construction began on a massive scale. Today, old, crowded houses are overshadowed by newly constructed apartment buildings. As the Chinese say, the city has taken on "a new look."

Economy and Culture

Industry came relatively late to Hangchow, but the pace of progress has been rapid. Before 1949, the estimated size of the workforce for the 33 small-scale and one large factory was 5,000. Today, nearly one-third of its population are industrial workers. The value of the city's industrial output has doubled since 1965 and is reported to have increased 24-fold since 1949. The city now boasts an iron and steel mill, machine tool factories, petrochemical and oil refining facilities, and an electronics industry. The Hsinan River Hydroelectric Power Station, situated on the upper reaches of the Chengtang River, has a capacity of 650,000 kw. Power generators, light trucks, and small tractors are also manufactured in Hangchow.

Hangchow ceramic masters impart traditions and skills

The silk industry, which dates locally to the 7th century, is another economic feature of Hangchow. Natural silk fabrics, brocades, and parasols produced here are renowned for their design and quality.

The agricultural output of Hangchow is dominated by tea, which is grown by the Tea Production Brigade of the West Lake People's Commune. The commune is located near the heart of the old city of Lungching (Dragon Well), after which this highly prized variety of tea is named.

HIGHLIGHTS FOR TRAVELERS

Areas of interest to the visitor can be divided into three parts: the city itself, local examples of modern industry and agriculture, and West Lake and its surroundings.

The city of Hangchow is endowed with few distinctive features. The crowded, narrow streets of the old section are frequently choked with traffic. However, there are also newly constructed apartment complexes, schools, government buildings, and industrial installations, many of which face broad, tree-lined boulevards. Examples of the modern development of Hangchow often visited include:

Tu Chin Sheng Silk Brocade Factory Famous for its intricate brocade portraits of Chinese scenery and heroic scenes from the revolution, the mill employs 1,700 workers and uses 300 electric looms. Its annual output includes about 3 million meters of silk, including over 1,000 patterns.

West Lake People's Commune is the home of the Lungching (Dragon Well) tea. It is now a year-around operation for the 1,300 members of the Tea Production Brigade. By careful management and intensive agricultural techniques, the tea shrubs now yield 2,100 kg. of tea leaves per hectare (1,848 lbs. per acre).

Hsinan Power Station began generating electricity in 1960. The reservoir covers an area of 580 sq.km. (224 sq.mi.) and has a capacity of 17,800 million cu.m. (23,140 cu.yd.).

Hangchow Zoo Hangchow's new zoo was completed in 1975 and features skillful imitations of natural environments that house more than 100 kinds of animals and birds. Among the featured species are giant pandas, gold-striped monkeys, black-leaf monkeys, and Manchurian tigers.

WEST LAKE

The focal-point of a visit to Hangchow is West Lake. The lake itself has a surface area of 1,235 acres, with a 15 km. (9 mi.) shoreline. There are two dikes built to control the water flow, and the lake has four islands, the largest of which is Ku Shan ("Solitary Hill"), in the northwest.

North Shore

Solitary Hill (Ku Shan) Island Linked to the north shore by a bridge and to the east by the willow and peach-tree lined Pai Chu-yi Causeway, the island was originally landscaped during the T'ang Dynasty (618-907), when its first pavilion was built. Its name is misleading since the island has become a favorite stopover for visitors. Its most famous pavilion is the Autumn Moon and Calm Lake Pavilion, used as a study retreat by the K'ang Hsi Emperor of the Ch'ing Dynasty (r. 1662-1723). It was so named because its appearance is most striking when cast in the clear and silvery moonlight of autumn. Other places of interest on Ku Shan include the Crane Pavilion, the Chekiang Provincial Museum (consisting of a small botanical garden and sections on physical geography, popular arts, and history), the Seal Engravers Club, and the Chekiang Library. Additions since 1949 include the Octagonal Pavilion, Quadrangular Pavilion, and the Terrace on the Lake. Cassia and maple trees grace the site.

Lotus in the Breeze at the Crooked Courtyard This poetic name refers to a modern pavilion and small park situated directly across from the Hangchow Hotel.

West Shore

Su Tung-po Causeway This north-south causeway is the lake's largest. It has six bowed bridges (Crossing the Rainbows, Tung-po, Suppressing Dike, Viewing Hills, Locking Waves, and Reflecting Waves), and was named after the famous poet-governor who ruled Hangchow in the 8th century.

Viewing Fish at Flower Harbor (Hua Kang Kuan Yu) This site is located on the southwestern end of West Lake where a small creek formerly emptied into the lake. During the Ch'ing Dynasty, a pavilion was set up on the south side and fish were stocked in an artificial pond. The area has since been enlarged to 23 hectares (55 acres) and several lotus ponds have been added. A peony garden embraces the old stream.

South Shore

Three Pools that Mirror the Moon (Santan Yinyueh) Also known as Hsia Ying Chou, this is the second largest island in the lake. It is really a series of circular embankments, creating the impression of a "lake within lakes." It is landscaped in typical Chinese style with the Nine-Bend Bridge (actually a series of right angles) linking the islets. There are many small pavilions, terraces, display rocks, and flower beds. Walkways are bounded by circular windows, each providing a different perspective for viewing the scenery.

Eastern Shore

The eastern shore of the lake has a number of parks (Chingpo, Children's, Liu-lang-wen, and Hupin). The China Liberation Memorial is the centerpiece. A hotel for overseas Chinese is located on this side of the lake, and it is from here that boat expeditions embark. Rowboats may be rented.

Sites Surrounding West Lake

Precious Stone Hill (Pao-shu Shan) This is the most prominent hill on the north side of the lake, with an altitude of 200 m. The hill is famous for its oddly shaped boulders, the inspiration for an assortment of legends. There is a prehistoric cave (Chuan Ching) containing stone furniture and a seven-story pagoda originally erected in the 10th century and rebuilt in 1933.

Ko-ling Hill This hill, which rises just behind the Hangchow Hotel, has the Early Sun Terrace at its summit. Excellent for viewing the sunrise, it also affords the best overall view of the lake and the city of Hangchow.

Purple Cloud Cave (Tsuyun Tung) One of the five caves on the "Mountain on Which Clouds Stay" (Chia Hsai Shan), this is a favorite place for picnics. The site is surrounded by peach trees and has a good view of the lake.

Monastery of the Souls Retreat (Lingyin Su) This Buddhist Temple was founded by the monk Wei Li in 326 AD, and is the best-known monastery in Hangchow. Its Hall of Heavenly Kings, restored in 1956, contains a gilded, camphor-wood Buddha 82 ft. high.

Six Harmonies Pagoda (Liuho Ta) This pagoda is located at the top of Yuelu Hill, on the north bank of the Chentang River. Originally built in 970 AD, it was thought that its cosmic forces would deflect the huge waves of the powerful tidal bore brought on by the full moon. It also served a practical purpose as a lighthouse for river traffic. The octagonal structure has 13 stories outside and 7 inside and was uniquely

Six Harmonies Pagoda.

constructed with a combination of brick and wood. It is 60 m. (196 ft.) high.

Nanping Hill Built during the Ch'ing Dynasty, the Chin Chi Temple of Nanping Hill overlooks the south shore of West Lake. On the ceiling, it has elaborate paintings of cranes and the roof top is adorned with flying dragons. Just opposite the main entrance of the temple are the remains of the Lei Feng Pagoda, the scene of a fairy-tale romance of a scholar and a white snake.

Yen Hsia Mountain A number of caves are located on the sides of this hill, including the Yen Hsia Cave, the Shiu Le Cave, and the Shih Hu Cave.

HOTEL ACCOMMODATIONS

There are a number of hotels surrounding West Lake but, for the most part, only three are used by Western visitors—the Hangchow Hotel, the Lakeview Hotel, and the Gardens of Flowers Hotel, which adjoin one another on the north side of the lake. The Hangchow is a luxurious accommodation by PRC standards. It has high-ceilinged rooms, verandas, and gardens. Room rates are Y14 per twin-bedded room. The Lakeview is more modern, with nine stories and verandas for each room facing the lake. The Gardens of Flowers features large, commodious rooms. The hotels are literally steps away from some of the best scenery in Hangchow, and exploration on foot is recommended.

HANGCHOW CUISINE

Given West Lake's prominence as a resort, the chefs of the area have succeeded in elevating the level of the local cuisine to a renowned stature. A local vegetable, *shuen chai*, is one of the noted products of Hangchow. Combined in a soup with lake perch, it becomes a delicacy prized for its nutritious quality. It is said that the ancient emperors received this dish as a special tribute from the local populace. Sweet-and-sour fish, snow-white shrimps cooked with Lungching tea and stewed duck tongues are also specialties of the region, as is the honeyed ham. Plain noodles are served with fried shrimp and eel, and there is an exotic noodle dish called "cat's ears." Other local dishes include steamed rice with lotus leaves, cassia and maize soups, and assorted pastries.

The special feature of all Hangchow dishes is the utter freshness of their ingredients. For example, stewed bamboo shoots or fried fish with spring shoots are prepared immediately after the shoots are dug from the ground and the fish caught from the pond.

For these and other dishes, the scenic Lou Wei-lou Restaurant is recommended. It is located on the Pai-chu Causeway at the southeast corner of Ku Shan Island (from the Hangchow Hotel, cross the street, walk past the Chiu Chin Tomb, and cross the Hsiling bridge to Ku Shan).

SHOPPING

Artisans maintain high standards befitting the reputation of the region, creating items of fine quality. Most famous are renderings of local scenery woven in silk. Bright colors and delicate handwork characterize Hangchow embroidery. When purchased locally, it is remarkably inexpensive (imports to the US have been limited by high duties). Chinese visitors favor the local silk umbrellas and parasols, which resemble a stalk of bamboo when closed, but reveal a painted scene when opened. Fans made in Hangchow are also renowned. Most are made of sandalwood, but other materials include ivory, turtle shell, mahogany, chicken feathers, bamboo, and coral. The overlay is either paper or silk. In keeping with local artisan traditions, even common household items produced in Hangchow carry some distinction, notably the scissors and chopsticks.

Tea lovers will appreciate the green tea (Lungching), as well as the famous chrysanthemum tea which is prized as a digestive aid. Also available for purchase are cooked hams, which are sold at the railway station of Kam Hwa (because of import regulations, these are best consumed while in China).

Harbin is an industrial and rail center situated in the far northeast of China. It sits on salty, semi-arid lands, with winter temperatures falling below −40° C (−40° F). The capital of Heilungkiang Province, it is located 694 miles north of Peking by rail, a journey consuming about 19 hours (4 hours by air). It has a population of over 2 million.

Harbin, founded at the turn of the century, has few sites of historical significance. Its growth is owed largely to its strategic location on the Sungari River near Heilungkiang's southern border. Its early development stemmed from railroad construction by the Russians and Japanese. Before 1949, the city was the major food-processing center for the entire northeast. Since then, economic activity has diversified substantially and the city has become an important producer of steam turbines, boilers, electric motors, bearings, machine tools, measuring and cutting instruments, and cement.

Most foreign visitors to Harbin stay at the Harbin Guest House (telephone: 30-846) or the China International Travel Service Hotel (31-431). The city also has a Friendship Store (33-897).

HARBIN

Pinyin Spelling: Harbin
("hah-er-bin")

INNER MONGOLIA

HUHEHOT

green city

Pinyin Spelling: Huhhot
("hoo-he-how-tuh")

Of all the places in China now open to visitors, Huhehot, capital of the Inner Mongolia Autonomous Region, surely ranks among the most colorful destinations.

Huhehot was founded in 1581, and is situated on a high plateau (1,000 m.) at the edge of the Mongolian grasslands some 425 km. (260 mi.) northwest of Peking. It is just over an hour away from the capital by plane. The more interesting train trip—crossing through the same mountain passes that cradle the Great Wall—consumes about ten hours.

In summer, Huhehot has pleasant weather, but winters last 5-6 months with temperatures dropping to −40°C. There are only about 130 frost-free days. To protect against the bitterly cold northern winds, traditional houses are constructed with a very thick north wall, a flat roof sloping away, and, at the southern end, an entrance adorned with colored glass and carved wooden ornaments.

Inner Mongolia

The Inner Mongolian Autonomous Region was established on May 1, 1947, the first such special region for a minority nationality in China. It has an area of 450,000 sq.km. (173,700 sq.mi.), with a population of 8.6 million. Today, however, Mongolians make up only 20% of the provincial population—most of the remainder are Hans, who were settled there to lead the PRC's drive for modernization. Other minority nationalities include Hui, Hanchu, Tahur, Koreans, and Owenk.

The region stretches along China's northwestern border with the Soviet Union and is considered strategically vital for China. It comprises four administrative regions, divided further into three municipalities and 43 counties (called "banners").

Inner Mongolia is famous for its grasslands which cover about two-thirds of its area; it is one of China's major centers for animal husbandry. A 800-km. stretch of the Yellow River flows through the region, and the Hotao Plain, with relatively fertile soil, has some 43 million *mu* (one *mu* is about 1/6 of an acre) under cultivation. Inner Mongolia also has abundant mineral deposits, including coal, iron, chromium, manganese, copper, aluminum, zinc, gold, silver, rare earth metals, mica, sulfur, and asbestos.

In the past, Inner Mongolia's herdsmen (who now number 340,000) were nomadic, following their livestock in search of grass and water. Recognizing both the need for security in a sensitive border region and the benefits of a more stable grazing pattern for greater productivity, the government in Peking reorganized the herdsmen into people's agricultural communes. Pasturelands were fenced, irrigation systems installed, and permanent settlements constructed.

As the Chinese put it, "these measures rapidly changed the old backward nomadic way of life of the herdsmen who were formerly forced to make their homes wherever there was water and grass, as well as the methods of production which kept livestock-breeding utterly at the mercy of nature." The new settlements also facilitated integration with central political administrations in Huhehot and Peking.

Officials inform visitors that 74% of the herdsmen now have permanent dwellings, and the livestock population is today almost 4 times that of 25 years ago. Grain output has also increased 2.66 times (base figures are not available). From no industry at all, the region today boasts a fairly comprehensive industrial system embracing mining, iron and steel, coal, power, machine-building, chemicals, and light industry. In Paotow, Inner Mongolia's largest city (population 800,000), there is a large iron and steel plant which combines a dozen or so large factories and mines, including ore-extracting, sintering, iron and steel making, and steel rolling.

There are ten universities in the region, and 54 scientific research institutes specializing in subjects such as agriculture, industry, and Mongolian culture. Senior political cadres are trained at institutes of national minorities in Huhehot and Peking. Inner Mongolia has 13,700 primary schools and 3,700 secondary schools. Doctors and trained nurses number 26,700. There are 880 hospitals and large clinics. To help spread culture in the remote regions, 1,000 film projection teams have been organized.

HIGHLIGHTS FOR TRAVELERS

A visit to Huhehot is likely to be an unforgetable experience. Whether landing at the dusty airport—with little on it except a runway, windsock, and control tower—or arriving at the busy train terminal after a ride through the foothills of northern China, the traveler is likely to be whisked off immediately to a traditional Mongolian rodeo.

Settled in a reviewing stand under a set of Turkish domes painted bright blue, the visitor is treated to a display of horsemanship including sharpshooting, trick riding, racing, and a round-up of the small Mongolian ponies (which seem to have stepped directly out of the T'ang Dynasty).

Of more serious concern to the residents of Huhehot is the threat of an invasion by the "polar bear" (Soviet Union). As part of their preparedness, a 7,000-meter (5-mile) tunnel system has been built to aid evacuation of the population to the Taching Mountains. The tunnel is 3.8 m. (12 ft.) deep, and a bus ride through the system reveals evidence of block houses, storage areas, and assiduous maintenance. Even communes in the area have their elaborate underground systems (some with "natural ventilation"), and the Taching Mountains bristle with defense installations.

The military preparedness theme is carried over to industry. Antiaircraft guns, for example, are in place at the city's largest textile mill. In 1977, this mill employed 3,200 people (18% of whom were Mongolian). Its 10,000 looms turn out 2 million meters of gabardine yearly.

The highlight of any visit to Huhehot is a three-hour bus ride across the Taching Mountains to visit the grasslands. The Ulantoke

Commune in the Da Mao Banner, for example, visitors are greeted with a bowl of bracing Mongolian tea and a briefing, and then with an obligatory display of horsemanship—Mongolians in colorful native garb dashing across the vast expanse of grasslands against an endless powder blue sky. Then there is a chance to visit a model of a yurt (the traditional Mongolian tent made from animal hides) and commune facilities.

HOTEL ACCOMMODATIONS

The Huhehot Friendship Hotel is a two-story structure made of grey brick, with more than adequate facilities. The friendly staff is settled in its own compound. The hotel boasts an excellent dining room with skilled chefs. A walk in the neighborhood to meet the friendly curious local children is a must.

MONGOLIAN CUISINE

Mutton is the staple of the Mongolian table. Served in large chunks, it is meant to be carved and eaten with a uniquely shaped knife, the only utensil on the table besides chopsticks. The traditional tea is also worth a try. A rich, warm broth, it is fortified with goat's milk, butter, and grains, and served with various breads including short-bread cakes.

SHOPPING

The local department store doubles as the Friendship Store. This two-story emporium sttracts shoppers from both the city and the grasslands, making the crowds as interesting as the merchandise. Excellent local crafts include blankets, costumes, millinery goods (colorful lace), knives, and artifacts such as reindeer statues made from river shells. Even Mongolia's traditional wooden saddles are offered for sale.

昆明

KUNMING

Pinyin Spelling:
Kunming
("koon-ming")

Kunming, the capital of Yunnan Province, is a regionally important manufacturing center and a major transportation crossroads for southwest China. Although the city traditionally was one of China's more isolated and backward provincial capitals, the growing importance of the southwestern provinces since the late 1930s has spurred rapid growth and the Kunming municipality (including rural areas and satellite towns) has now achieved a population of 1.5 million.

Kunming lies on a flat, fertile plain at an elevation of 6,200 feet in the center of the Yunnan Plateau. The city is encircled by mountains to the north, west, and east; a large lake, the Tien Chih, adjoins the southwestern edge of the city. Kunming is often termed the city of eternal spring because of its temperate weather and perpetually blooming flowers. Its short winters are sunny and dry, with daytime temperatures in the low 60s F., dropping at night to near 40° F. It's occasionally hot and muggy during the summer, but the temperature remains in the 70s with late afternoon thunderstorms occurring during July and August.

Kunming in History

Kunming was founded in 1382 as a traditional walled Chinese city, although an earlier settlement at the approximate site had existed for many centuries. From its founding through the 19th century, the city was an isolated provincial capital and a regionally significant market and transport center. Until this century, Kunming was an archetypal Chinese city characterized by congestion, dirt, and a maze of winding *cul-de-sacs* and crooked lanes lined with one and two-storied wood and mud-brick buildings. The residents were considered "provincial" and Kunming was probably considerd a hardship post by Chinese administrators sent there to govern the province.

Kunming in the Revolution. Although the completion of the French Indochina Line into Kunming in 1910 stimulated the city's commercial development, major changes and sizable growth did not take place until the Japanese invasion of China and the onset of World War II. When the Nationalists moved their capital to Chungking, east coast refugees poured westward, with many reaching Kunming. Moreover, thousands of Yunnanese from the surrounding agricultural countryside migrated to work in the numerous factories that were soon established. In addition to the added population and new construction, the impact of the 1937-45 period was also reflected in a dilution of the city's parochialism and a gradual turn toward more progressive and modern attitudes.

Today, Kunming is undergoing rapid change, and its urban landscape has begun to take on the same appearance as that of other major Chinese cities. Industrial and commercial districts have been established, new wide streets and modern office buildings have been built, and new roads and railroads now connect the city with its hinterland and other parts of China.

Economy and Culture

Kunming is the focus of transportation routes and communications in Yunnan, and it is served by both the "Burma Road" of World War II fame and the former French Indochina Rail Line. Industrialization has been aided by a mineral-rich hinterland (including important deposits of coal, iron ore, and copper) and the city's factories produce a wide range of industrial and consumer goods. Kunming also serves as the military center of Yunnan.

Urban reconstruction has been a major factor in the building of Kunming's economy. Old lanes and alleys are being obliterated in favor of straight, paved thoroughfares. The squat wood and mud-brick buildings that line the major streets are being replaced by five- and six-storied concrete buildings. Sewers and street lights have been installed and silver birch and crabapple trees planted along the major roads. The streets, no longer full of peddlers' conveyances and shop people, are now crowded with buses and trucks, and evidence of construction is widespread.

Kunming residents are especially proud of their city's industrial development. Traditionally a "consumer" city, it is developing into an important production center, producing a wide assortment of steel and other metal products, machinery, mining equipment, chemicals, motor vehicles, textiles, and several consumer items. The rail line heading southwest from the city is flanked by a heavy concentration of industrial plants that produce brick, cement, chemicals, machinery, and electric power.

Culturally, Kunming is today more diverse than in the past. Some of the east coast war refugees and their descendants have remained, numerous minority peoples indigenous to Yunnan live in the city, and youthful workers sent in from other provinces further contribute to the mixture of peoples.

There are some excellent institutions of higher education in Kunming, including the tree-lined campuses of Yunnan University, Kunming Normal College, and the Institute for Nationalities.

HIGHLIGHTS FOR TRAVELERS

Kunming, a relatively new city, does not possess the rich historical and cultural heritage of some of China's older cities. Kunming is a showcase of the present, an example of the kind of transformation that the government is trying to induce for all of China. Kunming's industries and factories are its "living museums" and many are likely to be included on a visitor's itinerary.

The southern half of the city has new office and commercial buildings, although old residential structures remain along the alleyways leading away from the main central thoroughfares. The northern part of the city, devoted primarily to institutional and recreational use, is Kunming's most beautiful section. An excellent view of this area can be had from the remaining section of the old city wall in the northeast, where an elevated, tree-lined promenade passes over a small hill.

Ts'ui Hu (Green Lake) Located on the northeast edge of Kunming, this is a large willow-lined lake with walkways, a temple, and gardened shores nestling at the foot of Yuantung Hill. In the spring this hill is splashed with color from the blossoms of its peach, plum, and crabapple trees.

Takuan Park Southwest of the city, this park has recently been enlarged. It also contains the city zoo which has over 90 species of native animals.

Chiung Chu Monastery West of the city, this monastery is known for its 500 lifelike statues of Buddha's Chinese disciples.

Golden Temple The Golden Temple sits on the summit of a small mountain four miles northeast of the city. The gates, pillars, and roofs of the temple buildings are all highly ornamented and gilded with bronze.

Temple of the Western Hills Perhaps the most beautiful and restful spot in the Kunming area is the Temple of the Western Hills. A Ch'ing Dynasty mason spent nine years cutting a long corridor with many niches and caves into the face of a rocky cliff. A Taoist temple—

the Hall of the Taoist Trinity and its Dragon Gate—is carved out of the highest point of the cliff, overlooking Tien Chih Lake. From the temple, Kunming is visible in the distance, often shining in a mist reflected from the lake.

Forest of Stones Travelers who will be in Kunming for more than a day may be given a longer side trip to an area about 96 km. (60 mi.) southeast of the city where an interesting geologic formation known as "Forest of Stones" is located. This large rock formation consists of a vast area of 96-144 m. (60-90 ft.) high limestone towers and obelisks. From a distance, the area appears to be a stony forest, with the individual towers resembling fir trees.

HOTEL ACCOMMODATIONS

The Kunming Hotel boasts among the cleanest facilities and most pleasant service staff in China. It was built in the typical "heavy socialist" style reminiscent of the Min Dzu in Peking, but is very comfortable. As of 1978, a new hotel was under construction to receive the anticipated increase in tourism in 1979-80.

SHOPPING

A Friendship Store is now under construction in Kunming, but even when that is finished the visitors should not miss Kunming's Store of the Nationalities. Here one can buy colorful costumes, embroidered hats (Y40), excellent blankets (Y10), knives, and a variety of other decorative crafts. Batik is a rare find in China, but the local arts and crafts store has some lovely items. The store in the hotel also has a good selection of local crafts.

LOCAL CUISINE

Yunnan ham is a justly famous local dish, and the steamed chicken prepared in its own crock is tender and flavorful; the process also results in delicious broth. The food in the hotel is excellent.

KWANGCHOW

broad region

Pinyin Spelling:
Guangzhou
("guahng-joe")

K wangchow, the capital of Kwangtung Province, is the most important industrial city in southern China and one of the country's chief trade outlets. While some visitors have found the city ungraceful and cluttered, its lush parks, tree-lined streets, leisurely pace, and distinctive cuisine have lent it a character that is unique among China's large cities.

The municipality of Kwangchow covers an area of some 4,330 sq. km. (1,678 sq.mi.) and has a population of over 3 million—including 2 million in the city itself and 1 million in the surrounding six counties. Known for many years as Canton by Westerners and Chinese alike, Kwangchow is located at the northern edge of the Pearl River Delta, some 182 km. (75 mi.) northeast of Hong Kong by rail and 2,234 km. (1,443 mi.) directly south of Peking.

As China's focal point for foreign trade, the city hosts the semiannual Chinese Export Commodities Fair which attracts more than 30,000 overseas businessmen. It is also the country's principal tourist gateway. During the Chinese New Year, some 200,000 overseas Chinese and Hong Kong residents visit relatives and friends in the area.

A unique facet of Kwangchow in the late 1970s was its rapid integration with Hong Kong—in ease of travel connections, commercial links, and interchange of people. By 1979 there were three different links to the city from Hong Kong. The train is the most time consuming, with the trip broken into two segments—from Hong Kong to the border and from the border to Kwangchow (although direct service was being planned for early 1979). A hydrofoil service was inaugurated on November 17, 1978, bringing Kwangchow within 2 hours, 40 minutes from the ferry piers of Hong Kong's central district to Kwangchow's deep-water harbor at Whampoa (cost, HK$150, or about US$32.00). Departures are at 7:30 AM, 11:30 AM, and 3:30 PM. Finally, a charter air service has been started between the two cities at a

cost of HK$250 (US$54). Flights depart Hong Kong's Kaitak Airport at 9:15 AM and 8 PM, arriving 25 minutes later at Bai Yun Airport in Kwangchow. Return flights leave Kwangchow at 8 AM and 6:45 PM.

Kwangchow in History

According to legend, Kwangchow was founded by five celestial beings riding goats, who arrived bearing grain for the people. The legend has stuck, to the extent that Kwangchow is still referred to in Chinese as "Goat City." "Goat Brand" bicycles are manufactured here, and a modern statue of the five goats still proudly surmounts a hill in Yue Hsi Park.

As early as the 9th century BC, Kwangchow was known as Chu Ting. It received its present name in the 3rd century BC. In 714 AD, the T'ang Dynasty set up a bureau in the city to handle overseas trade, thus designating it as the first officially sanctioned foreign trade port in China. As such, Kwangchow was also the first Chinese city to experience an unsettling influx of Christian, Muslim, and other foreign influences. Although the city was enriched both by periodic migrations from northern China and by influences from abroad, the local culture remained fiercely independent, with its own colorful dialect, literature, music, customs, and sense of identity.

Kwangchow fell most directly under Western influences in the 19th century. Western commercial settlements, with their spacious buildings and large compounds, sharply set off the poor housing and cluttered canals of the main city. Modernization of the city began in the 1920s when canals were filled and rows of buildings demolished to make way for wider boulevards. A police system was set up and public health facilities were expanded. A new wave of construction began under the PRC government, which added parks, industrial sites, and modern harbor facilities. Among other achievements, more than 630,000 trees were said to have been planted by the mid-1970s, both for beautification and as a measure to control air pollution.

Role in the Chinese Revolution In 1757, Kwangchow became the country's only government-sanctioned foreign trade port. Thus, Kwangchow was destined to become a major point of confrontation between Western expansionism of the 19th century and the struggle for national identity within China. During the period 1839-1927, the

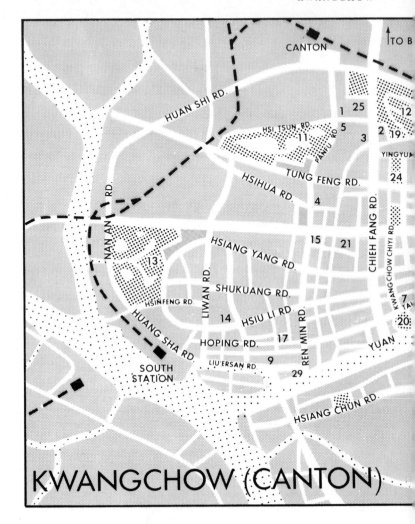

KWANGCHOW (CANTON)

1	Chinese Export Commodities Fair	7	Kwangchow Hotel
2	Civil Aviation Administration of China	8	Hua Chiao Mansion
3	Public Security Bureau	9	Kwangchow Cultural Park
4	Kwangchow No. 1 People's Hospital	10	Kwangchow Zoo
5	Tung Fang Hotel	11	Liu Hua Park
6	Bai Yun Hotel	12	Yue Hsi Park
		13	Pan Hsi Restaurant
		14	Kwangchow Restaurant

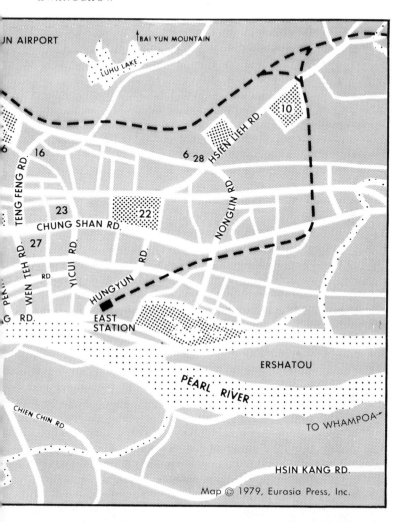

Map © 1979, Eurasia Press, Inc.

Cantonese were at the forefront of several of China's reform movements and revolutionary activities. The city had developed rapidly as China's export center for silks, tea, spices, and other items prized on European markets. To finance these purchases, the British sold opium (produced under their rule in India) to the Chinese. China tried to halt this by imperial decree in 1839. When that device failed, officials ordered the opium confiscated and publicly burned. The British, anxious for a pretext, took this act as just grounds for initiating military action. Britain's victory in the resulting Opium War (1839-42) led to the Treaty of Nanking, which compelled China to open four additional treaty ports along its coast. Coupled with the threat from the West, China was also experiencing a period of social and economic dislocation associated with dynastic decline. The Taiping Rebellion, a movement of the 1860s, was led by a Cantonese (Hung Hsiu-ch'uan). Cantonese were also at the forefront of the national government reform movement of the 1890s.

Sun Yat-sen, a native son of Kwangchow (and still nominally revered in China today), was the father of the revolution of 1911 that succeeded in overthrowing the imperial system. As the seat of China's Republican government in the early 1920s and the site of Sun's founding of the Kuomintang (Nationalist) Party in 1923, Kwangchow became a focal point of political resurgence, with the Communists gaining early strength there. In the spring of 1927, the Kuomintang launched an extermination campaign against the Communists, who responded by fomenting the "Canton Uprising." Although the insurgents succeeded in occupying government offices and leading a general strike, the revolt was put down in three days. Communist activity in the region was not again a factor until the advent of the Sino-Japanese War, when guerrilla forces worked to undermine the invasion. Of Kwangchow's role in the revolution, contemporary PRC accounts relate that the "people of Kwangchow launched one after

another heroic struggle against the invasion and oppression by imperialism, feudalism, and comprador capitalism."

Economy and Culture

The rich alluvial area of the Pearl River Delta provides the Kwangchow region with a highly productive agricultural base. Today, some 92,000 hectares (227,000 acres) are under cultivation. In addition to three yearly rice crops, the area produces wheat, fruit, vegetables, sugarcane, and oil-yielding plants. Within Kwangchow itself there are 33 communes and 16 state farms.

Kwangchow's major industrial products are newsprint, refined sugar, ships, cement, steel, chemicals, automobiles, machinery, textiles, rubber goods, and canned foods. The industrial sector comprises about 2,000 enterprises employing a total of 500,000 workers. The average rate of growth since 1966 has been estimated at 9.5% per year, with the total value of industrial output rising by 213% from 1966 to 1975. Priority has been given to steel (up 198%), automobiles (up 477% since 1971), chemical fibers (up 500%), and shipbuilding. The city is also important for its light industrial products, although this sector has grown more slowly. Among the key products are clothing (about one-third of which is exported), bamboo and rattan products, pottery, ivory, jade, and jewelry.

There are 98 hospitals (2 used by foreigners) with 13,700 beds, supplemented by 1,120 medical and health-care units. Long a center of education, Kwangchow has 11 colleges and research institutes, the most famous of which is Chungshan ("Sun Yat-sen") University. There are 1,169 primary and middle schools attended by 770,000 students. In addition, the city has a nationally renowned museum, a library, and a botanical and orchid garden.

HIGHLIGHTS FOR TRAVELERS

Yue Hsi Park Located just east of the Tung Fang Hotel, this 247-acre park with its hills and artificial lakes is an ideal place to begin a tour of Kwangchow. The most famous landmark within the park is the Chen Hai Tower, rising five stories (28 meters) and presenting a commanding view of the city. Built in 1380 (during the Ming Dynasty) and rebuilt in 1686 as a lookout post (its name means "overlooking the seas"), the tower underwent extensive renovation in the 1950s and now serves as the Kwangchow Municipal Museum.

Start the visit, if you are able, by climbing to the top story. Tea is served on a veranda that looks out over the city. The walk down winds through thousands of years of Chinese pottery, starting with the neolithic period and ending, on the second floor, with the modern products of Kwangtung factories. During the Export Commodities Fair, and sometimes during the summer months, students from the Kwangchow Foreign Languages Institute often act as informal guides, approaching the visitor with a request to practice their English, Spanish, French, or German. The small garden in front of the museum has a pair of 19th-century Krupp cannons.

Also located in Yue Hsi Park are some of Kwangchow's excellent athletic facilities, including a stadium (seating 40,000 and often used for political rallies—and a site of mass daily morning exercises), two Olympic pools (open to foreigners in the early morning), and badminton courts. There are many walkways through the park, a place for renting boats, pavilions for viewing the lake, and a garden restaurant. In late fall, a Chrysanthemum Festival is staged here, with some plants producing over 1,500 individual blossoms.

Liu Hua Park Liu Hua Park flanks the Tung Fang Hotel on the west side, and its artificial lake, palm-lined walkways, bowed bridges, and resting pavilions make it popular for a casual stroll. Sporting activities include boating, badminton, and table tennis. The park is popular in the early morning for joggers (mainly Westerners).

Memorial Garden to the Martyrs of the Canton Uprising (Huang Hua Kuang) This Memorial Park commemorates the Communist-led uprising of workers and farmers of December 11, 1927. Kuomintang reprisals resulted in 5,000 casualties. The garden was laid out in 1954 and officially opened in 1957, on the 30th anniversary of the Uprising. It covers 64 acres, and is entered through a rather impressive gate. It includes pavilions, exhibits and a graceful garden.

Mausoleum of the 72 Martyrs at Huang Hua Kuang The revolution that overthrew the Ch'ing Dynasty was actually a series of uprisings, ten of which failed. This Mausoleum commemorates one abortive attempt, the uprising of March 29, which resulted in the loss of 72 lives. The site was originally constructed in 1918 by funds donated by overseas Chinese.

National Peasant Movement Institute Founded in July 1924 on the site of a former Confucian temple, this school was used by the fledgling Communist Party to train cadres for the revolution. Some of the original parts of the structure remain, including a section of wall from the 16th-century temple. Many leaders of the Communist movement, such as Chou En-lai and Kuo Mo-jo, taught at the Institute. Its most famous headmaster was Mao Tse-tung. Visitors are shown a replica of his room and various memorabilia. The Institute trained 327 students in 1926, but was shut down as part of the reprisals in connection with the Canton Uprising.

Huai Sheng Mosque Dating from 627 AD, this is regarded as the oldest mosque in China, and is still used for religious activities. It was reportedly built by the first person to bring the Koran to China, said to be an uncle of Mohammed. Built in Islamic style, the mosque has an 80-foot minaret and two levels.

Liu Yung Temple Constructed in 479 AD, it is also known as the Temple of the Six Banyan Trees. Partially destroyed by fire in 1098, the present name owes its origins to a famous poet of the time, Su Tung-po, who was struck by the presence of six banyan trees on the grounds. The trees are gone, but there is still an octagonal-based pagoda (Hua Tower) with one of those feats for which Chinese architects were famous: 9 stories on the outside and 17 on the inside. The tower is 57 m. (188 ft.) high.

Cultural Park Just a block from the Pearl River, the Kwangchow Cultural Park is a focal-point for mass culture. Rebuilt in 1952, its 20 acres include an excellent aquarium (the Pearl River Delta display, featuring various local species, is remarkable for its variety), seven exhibition halls, flower gardens, theater, opera house, concert hall, and stadium. There is also a roller-skating rink, a tea house, and facilities for table tennis. The park features some 30 exhibitions annually, including a permanent display called "Labor Created Man." Recent exhibits included 500 artifacts from the Paris Commune (on private loan from the UK) and a natural display, "Wildlife of Australia." Storytelling and chess matches are also popular pastimes in the park. Admission to the park is 5 *fen* during the day and 10 *fen* at night, but cultural events and concerts require separate tickets available only from the host organization.

Kwangchow Zoo The Kwangchow Zoo is one of China's four largest, and rivals that of Peking in its varieties of over 200 species. Most popular, predictably, are the panda bears, but also worth seeing are the displays of monkeys, giraffes, hippopotami, camels, tigers, and an aviary. The zoo has a restaurant, snack bar, and small retail shop. It is open 7:30 AM to 3:30 PM daily. Admission is 10 *fen*.

Sha Mien Although it is not the kind of historical site tour guides are likely to recommend, a walk around Sha Mien island will evoke the spirit of the prerevolutionary days when this was the area of the British and French concessions. Built on an island in the river and accessible only by a narrow bridge, its large buildings—once housing banks, churches, and foreign legations—now present a rather forlorn appearance although the ornate Victorian buildings set amidst lush tropical overgrowth produce an ambiance unique in China. Laundry hangs from the windows of a mid-19th century church, and political slogans garland its steeple. Some structures are presently used to house several municipal bureaus, a Polish shipping office, the Vietnamese Consulate, a seamen's club, and military barracks.

There are two restaurants on the island (Sheng Li and Economical), and the tennis courts can be used by Westerners with the persistence to sign up (regulations are posted). The promenade along the river bank is shaded by large banyan trees and makes a pleasant walk, especially to escape the summer heat.

KWANGCHOW SUBURBS

Foshan City An old city located ten miles southwest of Kwangchow, it is usually visited on a one-day trip. Formerly a religious center (the name means Buddha Hill), it is also famous for its pottery, which is the main industry of Foshan today. Visitors are taken for a tour of the factory, followed by a visit to a shop featuring examples of local pottery (look for the tiny natural clay sampans, or the three-inch glazed pandas). Lunch is usually served in a large old hotel. The afternoon is taken up by a visit to the site of a former Taoist temple, now somewhat gaudily restored but housing a number of statues and artifacts from the Ming Dynasty.

Seven Star Crags The local tour guides will boast that this area combines the lakes of Hangchow with the mountains of Kweilin. Although this might raise expectations a bit high, the several-square-mile area is nevertheless worth the three-hour bus ride (62 miles, including a ferry crossing), especially if there is time to spend the night.

Ghost of Seven Star Crags

The local tea is unusual and the entire area is splendid for photography.

Kwangtung Hot Springs (Tsung Hua) Also several hours from the city, the Kwangtung Hot Springs—with its curative waters (112° F)—are a tonic for those spending time in Kwangchow during the hectic trade fairs. A visit usually entails a weekend excursion.

White Cloud Mountain (Pai Yun Shan) This 1,400-foot hill is the highest point in the region. It affords a panoramic view of Kwangchow, the Pearl River, and the entire delta region. Pavilions and teahouses, situated at the summit, encourage a lingering view. Further down the hill are a number of luxurious hotels—the most extravagant to be seen in China. Large villas are appointed with sitting rooms, sunken baths, private gardens, streams, ponds, and bamboo groves. These hotels are used both by high-ranking foreigners and by government officials. Since the hill also bristles with defense installations, walkers need to follow well-marked paths. A hike from the Tung Fang Hotel to the top of the mountain will take about six hours.

WALKING TOURS

Kwangchow offers splendid opportunities for the walker, whether for shopping, strolling through parks, or observing the everyday life of the city and its people.

A good place to begin a walk is Yue Hsi Park. To get there, turn right out of the main gate of the Tung Fang Hotel, and walk one block to the intersection of Chieh Fang Road (easily identified by the traffic circle). Turn left, and the park entrance is just a half block down on the east side of the street, easily identified by its large gate.

Once in the gate, a left turn will lead to the lake, pavilions, flower displays, and, just up the hill, a building for flower exhibitions and, still farther up, tea houses and athletic facilities.

Turning right at the entrance will lead the visitor to the swimming pools and up the hill to Chen Hai Tower (gravestones are now used as steps on the smaller paths).

A side entrance to the park, which leads more directly to the Chen Hai Tower, can be found by turning right at the traffic circle (i.e.,

147

south instead of north to the main entrance). A long block later (past what has been nicknamed the "bicycle restaurant" owing to its popularity with commuters) is another traffic circle, where one turns sharply left up the hill. A hundred yards past the entrance, a set of steps leads up a hill on the left; this leads directly to the statue of the five goats. Retrace these steps back down the hill and turn left again up the main road into the park. At the top of the hill, the Chen Hai Tower is on the left, the Kwangchow Stadium immediately in front. To the right, a path leads to a cenotaph affording another good view of the city.

Liu Hua Park offers less variation, but is ideal for a pleasant stroll. Turn left out of the main gate of the Tung Fang Hotel and cross the first intersection. The entrance is another 300 yards to the left. The park's circular paths make it impossible to get lost.

Also within a half-hour to 45-minute walk from the Tung Fang Hotel (round trip) are the Kwangchow Railway Station, the Gymnasium, and the botanical (orchid) garden.

HOTEL ACCOMMODATIONS

Kwangchow has 55 hotels with some 12,000 guest rooms. Five are especially set aside for foreigners. For the overseas Chinese, it is the Hua Chiao, located on Haichu Square, just by the Pearl River. Japanese are generally accommodated at the Kwangchow Hotel, also on Haichu Square, while Americans and Europeans usually stay at the Tung Fang or Bai Yun hotels.

Tung Fang Hotel Built in 1954, the Tung Fang was the first introduction to China for many businessmen and thus carries a certain nostalgia. The old wing, undergoing renovations in mid-1979 for air-conditioning and general sprucing up, has 400 rooms connected by vast stretches of corridor, with an architecture reminiscent of Eastern Europe. Some rooms have balconies, and all have a desk, two easy chairs, dresser with mirror, nightstand, electric fan, mosquito netting, and a telephone. A new 11-story wing, completed in 1974, has 700 rooms. Although its has a "cleaner" look, some guests find it a bit antiseptic, preferring the red carpets and spaciousness of the old wing to the cement terrazzo floors and plain wood trim of the new.

The Tung Fang has some of the best service facilities in China, including three restaurants (the dining room on the 8th floor of the old wing is best, but is often reserved for special delegations), four retail shops, a bank, a post office, and telegraph and telex facilities. A "snack room"—affectionately known among China traders as the "Top of the Fang"—serves Chinese beer, wine, and spirits. Unabashedly joining the recent "accommodate the tourist" syndrome, the hotel has added

Bai Yun Hotel

a lobby café which serves hamburgers (Y1.40), hot dogs (Y1.00) and coffee (45 *fen*), at least during the periods of the semi-annual Kwangchow Fair.

Service counters are located on each floor, and the helpful staff will take care of laundry, dry-cleaning, and long-distance telephone bookings. They will even do small sewing jobs or other miscellaneous repair work. Beer, soft drinks, mineral water, ice, and cigarettes are available.

At the main service desk, located on the ground floor of each wing, one can book restaurants, have business cards printed, and order film developed. Recreation facilities at the hotel include badminton, ping-pong, and billiards.

The Tung Fang is located on Ren Min Road, North, directly opposite the Trade Fair complex (telephone: 69900). Its rates per night are Y22-26 (US$12.50-15.10) for a single or double room, Y40 (US$23.25) for a two-room suite, and Y150 (US$87.09) for a deluxe apartment.

Bai Yun Hotel Opened in January 1977, the Bai Yun (White Cloud) Hotel is Kwangchow's newest, and was built both to ease the housing pressure on the Tung Fang and to accommodate the new wave of tourists expected in the city. Although many prefer the Tung Fang for its proximity to the Trade Fair complex, the 33-story, 776-room Bai Yun is handsome, with comfortable rooms and a restaurant that overlooks a pleasant inner courtyard. The service staff is good, and the hotel has complete service facilities, including a beauty shop and bank.

Its relatively remote location (in the northwest section of town, halfway between Yue Hsi Park and the Kwangchow Zoo) affords a view of neighboring farmland and foothills, but it also requires a Y2 taxi ride to the Fair (buses are provided free of charge). Kwangchow's new Friendship Store opened in early 1978 across the street.

The Bai Yun is located on Huan Shi Road, East, about 3 mi. from the Trade Fair complex (telephone: 67700). Its rates per night are Y22-26 (US$12.50-15.10) for a single or double room and Y40 (US$23.25) for a suite.

KWANGCHOW (CANTONESE) CUISINE

If there is one thing in Kwangchow that threatens the preoccupation with business, it is eating. Local statisticians avow that there are some 22,000 seats available for eating in the city, and it seems there are at least that many dishes and variations in how they are prepared.

Chinese chefs from Kwangtung Province have fanned out across the world over the years and have had to put up with ersatz varieties of local vegetables, meats, and spices. Not surprisingly, the dishes that have resulted bear little resemblance to the Kwangchow originals. In addition, Cantonese food has lately gained an undeserved "second rate" reputation since Hunan, Szechwan, and Peking cuisines have become part of the international gourmet's vocabulary. But even people from other parts of China will admit that Cantonese cooking, with its appeal to the eye and the vast subtleties of its flavors, is one of the gastronomic wonders of the world.

As elsewhere in China, in Kwangchow the dishes vary noticeably with the seasons, with casseroles and soups prevalent in the chilly, damp winters, and light soups and less oily dishes favored during the hot summer months. In general, Cantonese cuisine is characterized by its variety, the freshness of its ingredients, and its delicate sauces and seasonings.

Compared to the local restaurants, food at the hotels is adequate at best, and there is no better way to spend an evening in Kwangchow than to muster a group and head off to a new find or an old favorite.

The procedure is simple: giving as much notice as possible, go to the main service desk of the hotel and fill out a "restaurant booking form." The hotel will make the reservation, advise of the suggested cost per person, and convey any special requests. Reservations at the restaurant will be listed on a blackboard according to hotel room number. Guests are escorted to the private dining room where tea is served and moist washcloths passed around. Additional food requests are discussed, beverages decided upon (beer and wine are *de rigeur*—seasoned visitors stay away from the fiery spirits called *mao t'ai*), and the dinner proceeds apace. It should be noted that restaurants close about 9 PM, and lingering diners are frowned upon.

Local guides list some 34 restaurants that have special sections set aside for foreign visitors.

Pan Hsi The Pan Hsi is one of Kwangchow's loveliest restaurants, as well as its largest. A staff of 400 can accommodate up to 1,000 people. Dining rooms overlook the lake and gardens that surround the restaurant. The specialty here is dumplings, but that simple term does not do justice to their variety of sizes, tastes, and fillings, all elegantly presented in the shape of little animals and birds. Also try the winter-melon soup (in season), or the squash soup with tiny shrimp.

The Pan Hsi is located at Liwan Park (telephone: 20350).

Pei Yuan This is another restaurant whose internal setting matches the food. Unpretentious from the outside, its courtyard surprises the visitor with its small brook, bamboo trees, leaded glass windows, and private dining rooms. Chicken, vegetables, and soups are memorable here, and the Pei Yuan is less expensive than the Pan Hsi or Ta Tung.

The Pei Yuan is located on Tengfeng Road, North (telephone: 32471).

Ta Tung The Ta Tung has become a favorite among foreign traders who attend the Fair. Set in a bustling part of the city, the top floors are reserved for foreigners and overlook the Pearl River, whose sounds, lights, and water traffic provide a unique setting. Specialties of the house include roast pig (the skin is the delicacy; roasted to crisp per-fection, it is dipped in bean sauce, salt, and sugar and combined with a scallion in a piece of steamed dough).

The Ta Tung is one of the more expensive eating places in Kwangchow, charging Y15 and up per person. It is located at Hsihao Kou (telephone: 88697).

Some other restaurants worth noting: **The Kwangchow Restau-rant** (Wen Chang Street; telephone: 87136) stays open a bit later than most (until 9:30 or so), and serves a good variety of local dishes. For those who simply must have Western food, try the **Economical Restaurant** (Sha Mien; telephone: 88784), where the portions are large. Western as well as Chinese dishes are served at the **Tai P'ing** (Peking Road North; telephone: 32599), although the clientele is mostly Chinese. For the exotic, try the **Snake Restaurant** (Changlan Road; telephone: 24679), where the snakes are skinned in full view of the diners (to demonstrate freshness). The **Yeh Wei Shang Restaurant** (Peking Road; telephone: 30977) is euphemistically called the "Wild Flavor Fragrance Restaurant" but can be more appropriately trans-lated as the "Wild Game Restaurant," since it serves every kind of game imaginable, and then some. Turtle is a Cantonese specialty, and may be found at the **San Chu Restaurant** (Nan Hua Road; telephone: 50844). Noodles—plain, sweet, spicy, crispy, and so on— are served at the **Sha Ho** (Sha Ho Road; telephone: 70965), located in a northeast suburb of Kwangchow. There are also Moslem (vegetarian), Hakka, and Mongolian restaurants.

Other dishes not mentioned above but worth trying include stuffed crab claws (in season), deep-fried fish balls, chicken—with ginger, or steamed in tea leaves—and roast goose served with plum sauce.

🏮 SHOPPING

The Friendship Store is a standard stop on the tourist itinerary. Since Kwangchow is also a major area for antiques, browsing in local stores is well recommended. ———

Friendship Store In early 1978, a new, three-story Friendship Store opened adjacent to the Bai Yun Hotel, replacing the more cramped (if less antiseptic) quarters on Yuang Kiang Road. Its range of mass-produced offerings, however ample, lacks the artistry and charm of its Friendship counterparts in Peking or Shanghai. The ground floor features produce, canned goods, beverages, stationery, appliances, bicycles, and sewing machines. The second floor is given over to clothing and fabric, including a good selection of silks. Men's silk shirts are a good buy here at Y11.50 (US $7.00). The top floor focuses on handicrafts, ranging from ashtrays with pandas on them (Y1.15) to double embroideries from Soochow at Y2,250 (US$1,400). There are also scrolls and the usual range of knick-knacks. The store is open 9 AM to 9 PM. Suitcases are a useful purchase for those with bags already bulging from souvenirs. Ivory and linen are the only items not to be found elsewhere in the city. The store is open from 9 AM to 9 PM, and has a banking office to facilitate currency exchange.

Kwangchow Antique Shop and Kwangchow Antique Warehouse Although both places are recommended for antique hunting, bargains are now a rarity. The Antique Shop (146 Wen Tah Road; telephone: 34229) is an amalgamation of several smaller shops and caters exclusively to foreigners. A spacious center gallery has glass cases displaying jade, seals, and ink stones; its walls are decorated by scrolls. Two other rooms feature wooden carvings, screens, vases, and porcelains. The staff is helpful. The store has a certain orderliness that suggests nothing unusual is likely to be found there. The Antique Warehouse (Hung Shu Road) provides a less pleasant atmosphere for shopping, although its four back rooms house hundreds of items, some yet to be cleaned or prepared for sale (i.e., without the obligatory red wax seals certifying them for export).

During Fair times, antiques are sold in the arts and crafts section of the Light Industry Products Exhibition Hall. In 1976 there were reports of a new warehouse 20 km. outside of the city (in Cheung Pin Tsun Commune) specializing in items costing US$300 or more. The Fair also has six full-time retail shops: a curios and food shop, a bookshop, two textiles shops (one for garments, the other for piece goods), a fur goods shop, a down and feathers shop, and a newly opened arts and crafts shop that features such things as a Mona Lisa needlepoint.

Shopping Tours

In addition to the specialty stores there are a variety of other shops concentrated in the two main shopping districts of Kwangchow: Peking Road and Ren Min Road.

Peking Road This area can be reached in a 30-minute walk from either the Bai Yun or Tung Fang hotels. The following excursion begins at the intersection of Peking Road and Chung Shan Road;

Street Number	Specialty
2	**Department Store** Reopened in 1978 following renovations, its selection rivals that of the Nan Fang (see Ren Min Road).
10	**Music Shop** To the east of the department store (on the north side of the street), this is the largest musical shop in Kwangchow. A large drum can be had for Y30, a traditional Chinese lute for about Y35. Also available is a large selection of flutes (the membranes give Chinese flutes their distinctive "reedy" sound). *Wushu* (martial arts) paraphernalia are also sold here.
11	**Herbalist** Crossing over to the south side, the aromas coming from this traditional herbal medicine store will pinpoint its location.
7	**Dress patterns** Walking a few doors west (towards the intersection), this appears at first glance to be a dress and shirt shop, but its main feature is a large counter for sewing patterns.

Crossing over Peking Road and continuing east on Chung Shan Road (past the bank on the intersection) are the aquarium store (415) and the Cantonese sausage store (189).

393	**Decorative ornaments and housewares** Signs in English advertising cloisonné and jade lead into a narrow store with counters flanking each side. By walking towards the back, up the stairs, past the bamboo furniture, and through the swinging doors, visitors come upon a small room for "foreigners only." There the staff serves tea while showing their wares.

Returning once again to the intersection, turn right (north) on Peking Road.

335	**Sporting goods** A good selection, from ping-pong balls to warm-up outfits.
336	**Fu Wu Shih Tien Bookstore** Specializing in technical books (all in Chinese).
344	**Taiping Restaurant** The dining area for foreigners is a few flights up and to the back of the restaurant; portions are large.
363	**General merchandise** Around the curve to the left, this store

sells everything from door hinges to toilet paper. It is a good place to look for hand-made items such as brooms, baskets, crockery, and leather bags.

Returning once again to the intersection of Peking Road and Chung Shan Road, continue south. While looking at the stores, walkers should take note of the buildings and their roof-lines which present an interesting mélange of styles.

326 **Bookstore** Specializes in political and ideological works.

322 **Art supplies** Formally called the First Cultural and Antique Supplies Store, this shop also has a "back room" frequented by Japanese buyers looking for ink stones and Chinese brushes. It also sells scrolls.

319 **Hardware store** In China, such stores carry everything from bicycle wheel rims (stacked high in the center of the floor) to television sets and radio parts.

314 **Poster shop** One of the two places to buy political posters, an important mass art in China. Subjects include the calligraphy of Mao, the countenance of Hua Kuo-feng, anti-imperialist slogans, and diagrams teaching children how to brush their teeth.

303 **Beauty parlor** The most "chic" in Kwangchow. The maximum charge is Y5 (US$3.15). No tipping.

301 **Stationery and school supplies.**

291 **Crockery** Everyday cookware is quite attractive in China. One can buy sets as well as odd-lot pieces. The store also carries straw items, including hats (although peasant hats are ubiquitous in China, they are rarely sold through normal outlets; in the cities they are nearly impossible to find).

276 **Bookstore** Specializes in high-school texts and literature.

273 **Produce store** The most popular shop in the area for fresh fruit or a quenching soft drink (all fruit should be peeled before eating).

246 **"General" store** This is as close to an "odd-lot" shop as one can find in China, with merchandise including used clothes, plastic flashlights, and pen knives.

Ren Min Road This commercial area, near the Pearl River, is popular among local people of the city as well as visitors from other parts of the country who can be seen buying maps and wandering around like tourists anywhere coming from the countryside to the city. Ren Min Road is a good 50-minute walk from the Tung Fang Hotel and is best reached by taxi. For the return trip, a taxi can be hired at the stand in front of 10-12 Ren Min Road. For the more adventurous, the three-wheeled vehicles available across the street charge about half the rate of a regular taxi (they are not permitted to enter the gate of the hotel).

The tour starts at the Nan Fang Department Store which is just a few doors east of the Friendship Store, on the same side of the street (south).

36 **Nan Fang Department Store** This is the largest retail outlet in Kwangchow. It's an ideal place to mix with the local people and get an idea of the range of commodities available in the local economy.

35 **Dumpling Restaurant** Across the street from the Nan Fang, this is the most popular dumpling house in town; the system is to pay in advance for your order, collect a receipt, and hand it to the person serving from the huge wok.

Continue east a few steps to the intersection of Ren Min Road. This is a natural gathering place where "big-character posters" and slogans appear during political campaigns. The best way to explore Ren Min Road itself is to go up one side of the street and back down the other. Thus, starting on the west side and proceeding north, there are:

9 **Bookstore** This is a good place to buy a map of Kwangchow (8 *fen*). Although the legend is in Chinese, the street plan is clear and correlates easily with the map in this book.

While walking along the street, note the young girls and boys selling small items on the pavement—these range from hairpins to seasonal nuts and spices.

23 **Aquarium Store** In China, aquarium stores sell not only fish, but plants, flowers, vases, and lanterns.

27 **Film Shop** This place sells Kodak film (minus the canisters). A roll of C135-36 Kodacolor II costs Y2.30 (US$1.80).

47 **Bookstore** Specializing in theoretical journals.

65   **Lantern Shop** A good place to buy round Chinese lanterns, ranging in size from 6 in. to 6 ft. All are collapsible for easy packing.

Cross over to the east side and head south towards the river.

60   **Barber Shop** Curiously resembling the set for a cowboy film with its swinging wooden doors, old chairs, and barber pole.

44   **Dried fruits** A popular commodity in China, their taste is unmarred by chemical treatment.

40   **Stationery and School Supplies** Includes an item of old "Americana"—hand-held school bells (Y3.42 or US$1.90).

20   **Housewares** A good place to buy common crockery. Restraint is advised, however; some items are heavy and their lead content exceeds US health maximum standards.

14   **Tea Shop** A wide variety of local teas.

10   **Hotel** This is an old guest house used by visiting Chinese. Set in the pavement in front of the door is a Star of David.

8   **Poster Shop** Posters and memorabilia.

The streets and lanes behind the Ren Min Road area are also worth perusal since they offer a wealth of vignettes of everyday life in Kwangchow. The visitor will pass cinemas, neighborhood factories, coal presses, restaurants, and vegetable markets.

Approached by air, Kweilin's scenery suddenly changes from flat agricultural lands and rounded hills to a forest of sharp, jutting peaks set amidst the blue-gray of lakes and rivers. This, then, is the most famous scenic spot in China, long memorialized in painting and poetry. As the classical poet Han Yu described it: "The river forms a green gauze belt, the mountains are like blue jade hairpins." Kweilin is becoming increasingly accessible to visitors. Today, the whole area is prized not only for its scenery but also for its increasing role as a regional manufacturing center.

Kweilin is in a subtropical region of China, situated in the northeastern corner of Kwangsi Autonomous Region. In prehistoric times, the area was covered by an expanse of sea. The karst landscape was created by the erosion of the limestone surface, forming steep, isolated hills, caverns, and underground channels.

Kweilin has a population of 320,000, with the municipal area covering 780 sq.km. (300 sq.mi.). The urban center itself is only 160 sq.km. (60 sq. mi.). Kweilin is located on the west bank of the Li River and is a stop on the rail line between Nanning and Changsha, thus making it an important link in the transportation network of southern China. The subtropical climate results in long summers that are wet and hot. Spring and fall seasons are notably pleasant.

Kweilin in History

Kweilin was founded in 214 BC as a way-station on the Li River. It gained in importance when the emperor completed a two-and-a-half mile canal as part of a link between the Yangtse River in central China and the Pearl River to the south, thereby bypassing the arduous mountain trails. Today, the canal is used as an irrigation aqueduct. Under the Ming Dynasty, Kweilin was designated a provincial capital and remained so until 1914 (when it was superseded by Nanning). Kweilin was again named a capital in 1936 and, during the anti-Japanese war, it was a stronghold of resistance (the location of some caves was not discovered by the

KWEILIN

cassia woods

Pinyin Spelling: Guilin ("gway-lin")

157

present government until the late 1950s). During the war, printing plants, newspapers, and theatrical companies took refuge here, and the population grew rapidly. Much of the city was heavily damaged or destroyed by bombing raids during this period.

Kweilin's most notable expansion took place after 1949. The city has since doubled its size, the industrial base growing from 4 factories to 260. Farming has been enhanced by the construction of some 2,000 water-control projects—reservoirs, ponds, and irrigation canals. Today the city is neatly laid out, with two- and three-storied stucco buildings replacing the blocks of older mud homes on the river banks. Each fall, hundreds of cassia trees (*osmanthus*)—planted during the last 20 years—fill the air with the fragrance of their yellow, white, and red blossoms. The trees yield tea, herbal medicine, fragrant oil, and a flavorful local wine.

Economy and Culture

In 1949, Kweilin had only one printing plant and a few small factories and handicrafts industries. Since then, numerous factories have been built and the city now employs a workforce of about 100,000. Kweilin produces nitrogen fertilizers, spun silk, cotton cloth, tires, medicines, rubber, machinery, and a wide range of other products. Machine-tool manufacturing gained prominently during the Cultural Revolution and today the city also produces electronic components, semi-conductor apparatus, and transistor radios. Traditional commodities include wine, bean products, candy, pepper sauce, bamboo chopsticks, umbrellas, and perfumes.

The agricultural sector has also been expanded by means of planned development. Major products include grain, rice, bamboo, pomelos, persimmons, and cassia by-products. Fishing is an important activity, as is river commerce.

HIGHLIGHTS FOR TRAVELERS

Time spent in Kweilin is invariably too short. The scenery is magnetic: the crags and rivers seem to take on a new aspect with every change in light. Clouds, sunlight, mist, and rain all have dramatic effects on the mood. Equally distinctive are the region's caves; the unearthly beauty of stalactite and stalagmite formations rivals that of scenes on the surface.

Banyan Lake (Jung Hu) Completely relandscaped in recent years, this lake is the focus of an attractive park with gardens, pavilions, and walkways. Under the T'ang Dynasty, the lake formed part of a moat that protected the town walls. It is now flanked by two hotels and a new city auditorium.

Along the Li River

Seven Star Park (Chi Hsing Shan) This park, located just across a bridge in the eastern section of the city, consists of a large expanse of lawns and cassia trees. Its most noted attraction is Seven Star Hill, whose peaks are arranged more or less in the shape of the Big Dipper (*Ursa Major*). The hill also contains six legendary caves. Their entrances are marked by steles and inscriptions dating from the T'ang, Sung, and Ming dynasties. A 1,000-meter-long path winds through the main cave passing many stalacitite formations that have been floodlit in color and (with a little prompting from local guides) conjure up fruits, animals, and human figures.

Fu Po Hill This is probably the most interesting of the several hills situated within the city limits of Kweilin. The steps and walkways en route to the top are surrounded with interesting sights, among them an enormous cooking pot formerly used in a temple; a south-facing temple surrounded by viewing pavilions, and a cave with many famous engravings. The top of the hill affords a magnificent view in all directions. Taking a different way down, the visitor passes Returned Pearl Cave. Here, legend has it, a fisherman once stole a gleaming pearl used by a dragon to light the cave, but he was so filled with shame that he returned it. Near the cave is Thousand Buddha Cliff, noted for over 300 statues, some dating from the T'ang and

159

*Elephant
Trunk Hill*

Sung dynasties. At the end of the visit, tea is served in a pavilion overlooking the river.

Reed Flute (Luti) Cave Of the many caves around the city, Reed Flute Cave (also known as Reed Pipe Cave) is the most famous. The reeds in question still grow at the cave entrance, and were used to make flutes as well as to conceal the opening. Thought to have been first discovered during the T'ang Dynasty (over 1,100 years ago), the cave became a frequent shelter for the local populace seeking to escape the ravages of wars and bandits. Since 1959, it has gradually been transformed into a tourist attraction. A trail extends 500 m. through the cave to an adjoining tea house that affords a grand panorama of mountains, farmland, and the distant Li River.

The chief attraction in the cave itself is its stalactite formations which, with the aid of somewhat contrived colored spotlights, cast shadows that resemble everything from bumper harvests to a big-city skyline. Chickens and ferocious lions are all part of the internal landscape of Reed Flute Cave, whose stalactites and stalagmites are still growing at a rate of one inch every 100 years.

Li River The highlight of a trip to Kweilin is the 6-hour, 50-mile journey down the winding Li River to Yangshou. Visitors are taken aboard a launch, which is pulled and poled over rapids and shallows and along crags, valleys, and bamboo groves. The excursion passes fishermen on bamboo rafts using trained cormorants—their necks tied to prevent swallowing all but the smallest fish. River craft traveling upstream are towed in a convoy by tugs. Some are still pulled by men and women in harnesses. Along the way, some of the famous rock formations passed include Elephant Trunk Hill—just outside Kweilin proper, this rock suggests an elephant drinking from the river; Lohon Rock—profile of a man with shaven head and long neck; Old Man Peak—trees and shrubs form eyebrows and whiskers on a man's face; Crown Hill—a colossal crown; Ram's Horn Hill; Painting Hill (also

*Camel
Mountains*

known as Nine Horse Hill)—the light has to be particularly good and the imagination vivid to see them all; Ehrlang Gorge; Brocade Hill—vegetation of different colors; Moon Hill (in Yangshou)—this hill has a flat top with a cave in the shape of a half-moon.

Although Yangshou itself is a colorful and distinctive town, schedules do not permit a lingering look. The bus ride back takes about two hours and is equally spectacular, especially during rice harvesting season when the golden stalks, bathed in evening light, offer a sharp contrast to the black hills etched on the horizon.

WALKING TOURS

Because of its small size and well laid-out streets, Kweilin is an ideal city to explore on foot. The Kweilin Hotel looms nearly everywhere on the skyline, making it easy to check one's bearings. Using Banyan Lake Bridge as a base point (a spot equidistant from the Banyan Tree Lake Hotel and the Kweilin Hotel), walk south along the main road (leading out of town). There are some large stores here, including the best souvenir shop in the city (which functions in lieu of a Friendship Store). Further down the street, on the right, is an antiques store, with some items marked for foreigners and others exclusively for Chinese.

To the north of the bridge the main shopping district begins with the department store on the east side of the street. On the same side are some shops featuring cigarette-holders said to be good for (or less bad for?) asthma. A covered market area is one block west of the main street and runs parallel to it. To the east, one can walk along a section of an old palace wall (built in 1393) and among modern residential buildings. Walk up to Chieh Fang Road, the major east-west thoroughfare, until reaching the bridge (two blocks). Winding south again along the shaded river bank, the walkway returns the visitor to the Kweilin Hotel.

HOTEL ACCOMMODATIONS

Until 1976, only a few hundred visitors a year—mostly overseas Chinese—visited Kweilin. But by 1979, with the completion of a 20-story hotel and the expansion of the airport, larger numbers could be accommodated.

Kweilin Hotel This hotel was completed in 1976 and dominates the center of the city. Guests on either side have an unrivaled view of the surrounding city and mountains. Services include a post office, bank, retail shop (with some excellent local crafts for sale), food store, and a large Western dining room. The hotel has steam heat and, in colder months, provides comforters. Even though superstitions are ostensibly eschewed in today's China, the number 13 does not appear on the premises.

Banyan Tree Lake Hotel Because of its size, this establishment falls more in the category of a guest house. It offers comparatively luxurious accommodations for visiting dignitaries and official delegations. A four-story structure with 100 rooms, its dining room serves many colorful local specialties, including rice birds and snake-bile wine.

SHOPPING

The best buys in Kweilin include local bamboo products (the plaited miniature suitcases make sturdy cosmetic cases or overnight bags), carved and painted stones, and local food specialties, including cassia wine, cassia tea, snake-bile wine (recognizable by its green-colored contents), fruit (oranges from Kwangsi provided the seed stock for California oranges). Another product known in the area is embroidered linens, available at very reasonable prices.

Now chiefly an agricultural center, Loyang was the capital of China during the Han and Chou dynasties. It is located about 120 km. (75 mi.) east of Sian, at the confluence of the Wei and Yellow rivers. It has a population of 700,000.

The site of Loyang has been inhabited since Chinese history began, with neolithic remains dating from the Yang and Shang cultures. Parts of the wall built during the Han Dynasty still stand. During the Sui Dynasty (606 AD), the city became known as an artistic and cultural center.

Modern Loyang is famous for its tractor plant — the first to be built in China. In addition, there are machinery works, a ball-bearing factory, and glass works. In 1949, the city had only 100 industrial workers; presently there are 150,000, including 25,000 at the tractor plant. Chief agricultural products of the region include corn, wheat, cotton, and livestock.

LOYANG

north of the Lo River

Pinyin Spelling:
Luoyang ("law-yahng")

The most famous tourist site in Loyang is the Lungmen Cave, a monument to Buddhist influence in China during the 6th century. The cave has a number of carvings, dominated by a 45-ft. statue of Buddha sitting in the lotus position. The torso and hands have been eroded by time and weather, but the chest and head are in fine condition and very imposing. A nearby cave has some 10,000 bodhisattvas carved into the wall.

Other highlights of the itinerary include the tractor plant, Wang Cheng Park (the site of two Han Dynasty tombs), White Horse Temple (one of the first Buddhist temples in China), and the Loyang Municipal Museum (featuring artifacts discovered since 1949).

163

NANKING

southern capital

Pinyin Spelling: Nanjing
("nan-jing")

Nanking is situated amidst one of China's most splendid natural settings. It sits in a basin formed by the Yangtse River on the north and the Tsechin (purple) Mountains on the other sides. The image suggested to ancient writers was one of "dragon curling and tiger crouching." The city has several times served as the capital of China. Today, it is the capital of Kiangsu Province. Located about 300 km. (186 mi.) up river from Shanghai, it has an area of 778.6 sq. km. (300 sq. mi.), with a population of 2.5 million.

After its natural scenery, the dominant feature of Nanking is the Yangtse River Bridge. Built in 1968, it serves as a key link in the country's north-south transportation system, with Peking lying 1,157 km. (719 mi.) by rail to the north and Kwangchow 2,127 km. (1,322 mi.) to the south.

Nanking's climate is marked by intense dry heat during the summer months—the origin of its reputation as one of the "five furnaces of the Yangtse." Scheduled summer stopovers in the city have occasionally been cancelled due to the heat. The city remains temperate throughout the remainder of the year, with a rainy season in late spring.

Nanking in History

Although archeological relics indicate the area was first settled some 6,000 years ago, the city of Nanking itself dates from the 8th century BC. Its importance grew when it became the capital of the Six Dynasties Period (229-589 AD). Records show that it was an active river port, sustained a variety of crops, and had established China's first iron foundries (working iron found in the nearby mountains).

Nanking served as a capital again during the Southern T'ang period (937-75) when, in addition to being a center of commerce, it also had a notable reputation for its intellectual, cultural, and artistic achievements. Buddhism flourished here and it was the home of the poetic master Li Po.

Nanking owes its present character and dimensions largely to the founders of the Ming Dynasty, who built their first capital there. To ensure the city's growth, the emperor ordered 20,000 wealthy families to move there and bestowed honors on those who underwrote new construction and economic expansion. This policy lasted for only one generation, as the succeeding Ming emperor moved the capital to Peking.

As an "adjunct capital," Nanking retained importance. Under the succeeding Ch'ing Dynasty, the development of the city advanced on many levels. Its silk and cotton industries achieved wide repute. *The Scholars*, perhaps the most noteworthy work of fiction from this period (and still widely read in the PRC), is set in Nanking and vividly recreates its 18th-century society. Nanking was also a center for astronomy.

The Opium War (1842) was formally terminated with the signing of the Treaty of Nanking (opening up five treaty ports to Westerners) aboard a British gun boat in the city's harbor. In 1911, the town took part in the revolution that established the Republic of China. Afterwards, delegates of the then 17 provinces of China met in Nanking to elect Sun Yat-sen as president of the Republic. Within a year, however, China's capital was once again moved to Peking. During the civil war period, Nanking was used as a capital by the Kuomintang.

Role in the Chinese Revolution PRC historians consider the rebellions of the 18th and 19th centuries to be antecedents of their own revolutionary struggles in the 1920s, '30s, and '40s. They cite Nanking's capture during the Taiping Rebellion in 1853 as a key event in that process. The Taipings established their own government there. Palaces were built and new coins were struck. Their rule lasted for 11 years (until 1864), whereupon Chinese armies (led by the British General "Chinese" Gordon) recaptured the city, inflicting considerable damage. During the early part of the 20th century, it was an important political and strategic area controlled by the Kuomintang. PRC narratives point to repeated uprisings, strikes, boycotts, and demonstrations of this period—mounted against the prevailing conditions of hunger, civil war, and persecution. Thousands of Nanking's citizens are said to have given their lives to the revolutionary cause.

In April 1949, the People's Liberation Army—whose forces had swelled to over a million—captured Nanking. The campaign was directed by Mao Tse-tung and personally led by Liu Po-cheng and Teng Hsiao-p'ing. In a poem, Mao wrote: "The city, a tiger crouching, a dragon curling, outshines its ancient glories; in heroic triumph, heaven and earth have been overturned."

Economy and Culture

Since 1950, Nanking's industrial sector has been greatly expanded. There are now about 1,500 industrial and mining enterprises employing 300,000 workers (before the revolution, the work force was estimated at only 10,000). Industry in Nanking includes coal mining, metallurgy, petroleum refining, machine-tool manufacturing, and auto and shipbuilding enterprises. The city also manufactures chemical equipment, telecommunication instruments, optical devices, and synthetic fibers. Nanking still serves as an important Yangtse River port.

There are 63 agricultural communes distributed among the five suburban districts and two counties under Nanking's administration. Together, these units farm 110,000 hectares (271,810 acres) of land producing grain, tea, vegetables, apples, cherries, and watermelons. Today's per-hectare grain yield of 7,100 kg. (15,656 lbs.) is 3.5 times greater than that of the early 1950s. Nanking is also proud of its afforestation programs—over 28 million trees have been planted since 1949.

There has been a correspondingly rapid growth in the city's cultural, educational, and medical facilities. Nanking now has 14 institutions of higher learning, 340 middle schools, and over 1,500 primary schools, with a combined student population of about 550,000. The most famous learning institution is Nanking University, founded in 1902. It has 12 departments with 41 specialties and, in 1978, managed three small factories and a farm. Following the educational reforms of 1977, Nanking University emerged as one of the most prestigious learning institutions in China. The Nanking Normal School, sometimes visited by foreigners, trains teachers.

There are some 18,000 medical workers in the Nanking area, serving in 107 hospitals and 740 public health institutions. Over 10,000 hospital beds are available.

 HIGHLIGHTS FOR TRAVELERS

Yangtse River Bridge It is hard to overstate the symbolic importance of the Yangtse River Bridge and the pride which all Chinese take in it. Until its completion in 1968, there was no direct overland link between the important lower Yangtse Valley (encompassing Nanking and Shanghai) and Peking. But even more significant, perhaps, is the bridge's symbolic value: the 70-ft. depths of swirling, silt-laden waters—covering a bedrock floor—had proved too much of a challenge to Western and Soviet engineers. Relying completely on their own efforts, the Chinese undertook the building of the bridge in 1960. An average of 7,000 workers were engaged daily in its construction. On October 1, 1968, the "Mao Tse-tung Locomotive" crossed the span, marking its completion. The bridge is 1,577 m. (5,171 ft.) long

Yangtse River Bridge

between bridge heads. It has two levels, with a wide roadway on the upper level and a dual-track railway on the lower.

Sun Yat-sen Mausoleum Sun Yat-sen, the leader of the 1911 Revolution that overthrew the old dynastic system, founded the first national government in Nanking in 1912. Although a native of Kwangchow, Sun expressed a desire to be interred here and, upon his death in 1925, construction of this imposing monument was begun. The mausoleum is situated on the southern slopes of the Tsechin Mountains in the city's eastern suburbs. The grounds cover 80,000 sq. m. (95,680 sq. yd. or 20 acres), and the memorial hall itself is approached by climbing 392 steps made of Soochow granite.

Within the domed circular hall is a white statue of Sun. An exhibition includes replicas of his will and an inscription of his Three Principles for leading China's people into a new age: "nationalism, democracy, and livelihood." The vault itself contains his coffin (the ashes were moved there from Peking in 1929 when the monument was completed) and is surmounted by a reclining statue of Sun.

Ling Ku Park This park is regarded by local residents as one of the "famous 40 scenic spots" of Nanking, and is located just south of the Mausoleum of Sun Yat-sen, at the foothills of the Tsechin Mountains. The park has several well-kept gardens and is particularly favored in summer for its dense pine forest. The main feature is the Wu Liang Temple, built in 1381 but rebuilt several times since. The park also has a 61-m. (200-ft.) pagoda.

Kiangsu Provincial Museum On the eastern outskirts of the city, just inside the Sun Yat-sen (Chung Shan Men) Gate, is the Kiangsu Provincial Museum, with a collection spanning 5,000 years of Chinese history. There are six exhibition rooms displaying prehistoric artifacts; Shang Dynasty pottery, bronzes, jewelry, and tortoise shells;

iron agricultural tools; printed works; handicrafts from the Ming and Ch'ing dynasties; furniture; and a display on the Taiping Rebellion.

Tsechin Mountain Observatory The observatory, the third largest in China (after Peking and Shanghai), was begun in 1934. A staff of 250 is engaged in research under auspices of the Chinese Academy of Sciences. The main interest for visitors is the museum of astronomy. The Chinese were the first civilization to develop this science. On display is a replica of the original armillary sphere (a set of circles and rings showing the relative position of heavenly bodies), invented over 1,800 years ago. There is also an ancient celestial globe and a device used to detect movement of the stars.

Ming Tomb T'ai Tzu (1327-98), founder of the Ming Dynasty, was buried in Nanking in a magnificent tomb, constructed in 1381. Violence fomented during the Taiping Rebellion laid the tomb to waste and today there remains only a stone gate and courtyard. The primary feature is a sacred path leading to the site, which is lined with 12 pairs of stone animals.

Hsuan Wu Lake Also known as Yuan Wu Lake, it is located in People's Park just outside the city's Hsuan Wu Gate. The park is roughly 15 km. (9.3 mi.) in circumference and was formerly a private imperial preserve. It was first opened to the public in 1911 but was not restored to its present condition until the early 1950s. The lake contains five islets, linked by embankments and classic bowed bridges (Huang Island has a pagoda). The lake itself is noted for its fish and magnificent lotus blossoms in summer. Amenities include a zoo, children's playground, skating rink, and open-air theater.

Mo Chou Lake Another "Chinling scenic spot" (Chinling is the former name of Nanking), the area was first developed in the 5th century AD as a garden retreat for a female member of the royal household. The Pavilion of Victory at Chess survives from the Ming Dynasty, although most of this park's attractions date from the 1950s. New additions include the Lotus Water Terrace, the cherry-apple garden, and an open-air theater. Guides will also point out the collections of fine redwood furniture and some famous examples of calligraphy and painting.

T'ang Shan Hot Springs For those with ample time, an excursion to the neighboring T'ang Mountains (40 km.—24.8 mi.) is recommended. The hot springs here have curative waters that maintain a constant temperature of 40° C (104° F) and contain potassium, sulphur, and calcium. Long immersions are said to be an aid to skin ailments.

Yu Hua Tsai Park Formerly known as Yu Hua T'ai Gardens, legend dates its origins to the 6th century AD when a Buddhist priest so impressed heaven with his sermonizing that the skies opened and flowers fell like rain. The more prosaic will note that it is the colorful, finely-grained pebbles of the area that lend it its rainbow-like hues.

Today, the park serves as a memorial to over 100,000 persons said to have been executed in Nanking during its 22 years of Nationalist rule. Thus, the site is also known as Martyrs' Park. The Taiping Museum is also located in the park.

 # WALKING TOURS

Nanking does not lend itself to ready exploration by foot. The main business district, parks, and historic sites are quite a distance from the hotel. Most visitors are content to walk along the broad boulevard outside the hotel grounds which includes many buildings erected during the era of Western presence in Nanking.

Shan Hsi Lu Square (1 hour) Shan Hsi Lu Square can be reached in a straight 15-minute walk after turning right from the hotel gate. Although some distance from downtown, this market area is always quite busy. A department store is located on the southeast corner of the square and a neighborhood medical clinic just to the southwest (on the north side of Hunan Road). There are also some "store front" factories. Vendors—ranging from shoe repairers to vegetable sellers—line the street around the square itself.

Hsuan Wu Park; Drum Tower (2 hours) Hsuan Wu Park is too vast to explore in a short time, but a two-hour roundtrip walk will enable one to explore highlights of the park. Turn right outside the hotel gate. At Shan Hsi Lu Square bear left, heading directly east along Hunan Road. Hunan Road ends at Taching Road. Turn left and, after a short block, right at the first intersection. This leads directly to the main entrance of the park.

HOTEL ACCOMMODATIONS

Nanking Hotel The Nanking Hotel is known for its tranquil setting. Surrounded by gardens and a high wall (with a soldier standing guard), it is located on Sun Yat-sen Boulevard, a street lined with plane trees brought from France in the 1930s. Even the large political billboard located directly across from the front entrance does not detract from the peacefulness of the setting.

Although some rooms are air-conditioned, they are not particularly luxurious or cheerful by Western standards. The rates are Y10 per day (US$6.00). The kitchen is excellent—serving everything from regional specialties to what has become renowned as the best chocolate soufflé in China (orders should be placed well in advance).

The main disadvantage of the hotel is its relatively remote location—about an hour's walk from the central shopping district. A new hotel was expected to be completed in early 1979.

NANKING CUISINE

Each region of China boasts its local delicacies, and Nanking is no exception. Autumn is the season for plump lake crabs. Other specialties are pickled vegetables, Nanking "flat duck," duck kidneys, and fish. Cherries, watermelon, and other fresh fruits are in abundance. The tea from the nearby hills has renowned aroma and flavor.

SHOPPING

The shopper will find the craftsmen of Nanking skilled at making reproductions of old relics such as tomb figurines. Chinese tourists often collect pebbles from the Yu Hua Terrace (Martyrs' Park), which will reflect an array of colors when placed in water.

N anning is the capital of Kwangsi Autonomous Region and is the southernmost of China's major cities. It lies some 300 mi. due west of Kwangchow and has a population of 350,000. Closed off to visitors until 1977, it is now being included in shorter itineraries that originate from Hong Kong (and include Kwangchow and Kweilin).

The town was founded during the Yuan Dynasty, serving as a market center on the trade routes that extended west to the Himalayan plateau and south to Annam (Vietnam) and elsewhere in southeast Asia. Nanning began to develop industrially in the 20th century and now has food-processing factories, flour mills, sugar refineries, tanneries, printing works, chemical fertilizer plants, and bauxite and coal mines. The predominant crops are rice and sugarcane. The region is also China's leading producer of tung oil.

Among the popular cultural attractions in Nanning is the annual dragon boat regatta. Traditionally held on the fifth day of the fifth moon (usually falling in early June), this 2,000-year-old festival was revived in 1978. Winners are determined both by the speed of the oarsman as well as by the design of the dragon-shaped boats. The 1978 race attracted 200,000 onlookers and a field of 17 crews comprising both men's and women's teams. There are few sites of major interest in Nanning proper other than a Drum Tower and a Bell Tower. In describing the city, Chinese publications note that it was an "important center during the Vietnam War"; i.e., it served as a major staging base for Soviet and Chinese war materiel and other assistance.

南宁

NANNING

tranquil south

Pinyin Spelling:
Nanning ("nah-ning")

A young urban woman, resettled in the countryside, works in Kwangsi's forests.

HIGHLIGHTS FOR TRAVELERS

Among activities for tourists in Nanning is a visit to the Yiling Stalactite Cave. Located a pleasant hour's ride north of the city, this huge cave boasts artificially lighted formations bearing the sobriquets "bumper harvest," "fruit bowl," and "city skyline," as well as suggestions of human and animal forms. Nan Hu ("south lake") Gardens are also on the itinerary, as is a visit to the Nanning Arts Institute.

HOTEL ACCOMMODATIONS

Of the two hotels in Nanning, the Ming Yuan is the preferred choice. It is a three-story "L"-shaped structure with private terraces that overlook a pond and a park. Nearby is the Friendship Hotel, built in the 1960s. Both hotels are located about a 15-minute walk from downtown Nanning.

KWANGSI CUISINE

Similar to Cantonese, Kwangsi food consists on the one hand of exotic dishes such as suckling pig, turtle, lizard, and snake, and of simpler but elegantly prepared vegetable dishes on the other.

SHOPPING

Nanning has both a department store and an arts and crafts store. Examples of local crafts include bamboo ware, lacquer-ware, and wood and stone carvings.

PEKING

northern capital

Pinyin Spelling: Beijing
("bay-jing")

Although Peking has been the capital of China for the better part of the past 700 years, its role has never been as dominant as it is today. It is at once the seat of the strongest central government in China's history, and the political, administrative, communications, and cultural hub of the People's Republic of China. The city is one of China's three centrally administered municipalities (Shanghai and Tientsin are the other two).

Peking occupies 17,800 sq.km. (6,870 sq.mi.) at the northwest edge of the great North China Plain. Its latitude is approximately that of Philadelphia or Madrid. The municipality as a whole has a population of about 7,570,000, ranking it among the world's ten largest cities. Nearly half of the population resides outside of the urban nucleus in the several thousand square miles of rural area that have been annexed to the municipality.

Peking today has retained many facets of its antiquity, but has subordinated them to intensive urban development. Most of the old walled town in the heart of the city (including its basic street plan) dates to before the 16th century, but today the venerable Gate of Heavenly Peace faces the Monument to the People's Heroes and the Mao Tse-tung Memorial Hall. The old city walls have been torn down, their lines now traced by a circumferential subway surmounted by 15-story apartment buildings.

Peking has no central business district, just a series of market areas and squares connected by wide boulevards. As a result, there is no center-oriented rush hour. Modern factories have been built to the southwest to avoid adding industrial fumes to the prevailing dust-bearing northwesterly winds. Government office buildings are scattered in various sections of town. Thus, the center of Peking tends to convey a rather empty feeling. The impression is heightened by the old-style residential areas (called *hu-tungs*) where grey stone dwellings huddle inside long walls that blankly frame the narrow streets and alleyways. Yet there is no mistaking the central impor-

*Ch'ien Men
Gate*

tance of Peking: even clocks in the most remote corners of the country
set their time to Peking's. The key national Party and government
newspapers are printed here, the national political congresses take
place here, and all of China's major railway lines and air routes radiate
from the city. Unquestionably, standing at the Gate of Heavenly
Peace and facing Tien An Men Square, the visitor senses proximity to
the heart of China.

An ideal time of year to visit Peking is late September and early
October, after the summer rains have lost their intensity. During this
short period, Peking remains green and cool. It then undergoes an
abrupt transition into a cold winter when temperatures often drop
below freezing. By late winter, the dry earth is fanned by brisk
northern winds that swirl dust everywhere. Most summers are characterized by spells of oppressive heat, interrupted by periods of heavy
rainfall; temperatures may occasionally exceed 38° C (100° F). July is
the rainy season, when almost 40% of the total annual precipitation
occurs, often in the form of violent thunderstorms.

Peking in History

A skull of "Peking man" said to be over 500,000 years old gives
evidence that the Peking region had been occupied in prehistoric

times, indeed as far back as the very dawn of human evolution. Archeological records of a town date to 3,000 years ago. At that time, during the Chou Dynasty, Peking was a small village on the edge of the Yang Tung River (12 miles southwest of Tien An Men). It served as a commercial link between the mountains of the north and the fertile plains to the south.

During the Warring States period, Peking was known as "Chi" (meaning "reed"). With the building of the Great Wall under the Ch'in Dynasty in the 3rd century BC, the town began to grow and prosper, and continued to expand under both the Han and T'ang dynasties. In 608 AD, the Emperor Yang Ti constructed a canal from the Yellow River to the Peking area in order to supply his armies in their campaigns against Korea; this was the start of the Grand Canal. During a period of turmoil in the 10th century, when northern tribes held power over China (Five Dynasties), the town lost its strategic importance. In fact, it at one point served as the southern capital of the Khitan people (Khitan, or Khitai, is the origin of "Cathay," the name for China used in Medieval Europe).

The Mongols captured the town in 1122 AD. They renamed it Chung Tu (Central Capital) and enlarged it, retaining the square layout but adding walls and gates. During the early 13th century, the city was destroyed in a struggle between warring factions. It was not until the Mongol ruler Kublai Khan established himself there in 1267 —renaming it Ta Tu (Great Capital)— that the town was rebuilt and the basic plan that still dominates present-day Peking laid out. Life in the city during its Mongol renaissance (Yuan Dynasty, 1260-1365) was grandiloquently described by Marco Polo, who visited Peking in 1275.

When the Mongols gave way to the Ming Dynasty, they left behind a ruined capital city. The first Ming emperor established his capital in Nanking, but Emperor Yung Lo (1403-24) re-established the imperial capital at Peking in 1421. New city walls were constructed, extending to a height of 40 feet and forming a 14-mile battlement around the city. There were four main gates, each protected by an outer portal. (At present, only the north and south gates remain standing; urban renewal under the present government has necessitated removal of the others.) The Imperial Palace was built during the Ming era, adding an element of architectural grandeur to an otherwise bleak, unprepossessing setting.

At the end of the Ming Dynasty (1644), Peking fell under the control of peasant insurgents (prompting the last emperor to hang himself). The invading Manchus, actually abetted by panicked Ming officials, inflicted further havoc on the city, looting and burning. During their subsequent long rule (Ch'ing Dynasty, 1644-1912), these non-Han conquerors undertook to rebuild the monuments to Chinese imperial power that their linear predecessors had sought to destroy.

The Manchus began to allow foreigners to travel north of Kwangchow (Canton) to visit the emperor's court. By the 19th century, a sizable community of non-Chinese were living in Peking. Ultimately, foreigners became a factor in the city's deterioration. At the end of the Opium War, Western troops forced the emperor to flee, burning part of the city and wresting residential concessions (the old French legation was just south of the present-day location of the Peking Hotel).

In 1900, the Boxers (a Chinese secret society) tried to expel the foreigners, but to no avail. During the subsequent two decades, Peking remained the focal point of nationalist sentiment (see below). In 1928, it was renamed Peip'ing (Northern Peace) by the Kuomintang government, which in turn established its capital at Nanking.

On July 7, 1937, a clash between Japanese and Chinese troops led to the "North China Incident," signaling the start of a general state of war in China that lasted until 1949. During much of this period, Peking was occupied by Japanese forces, although its strategic and political importance had been largely drained by domestic events of the previous three decades.

Peking's Role in the Revolution The roots of the modern revolutionary movement in Peking can be traced to the invasion of the city by 17,000 British and French troops in 1860, an event that ushered in five decades of Western expansionism and hastened the erosion of the imperial dynastic system. Russians, British, French, Americans, and Japanese all vied for influence at the imperial court, which they alternately sought to prop up and force terms upon.

Various reform movements were adopted by the Chinese government to try to recapture its lost strength. The most notable effort came in 1898 when a group of ministers tried to forestall China's rapid deterioration by modernizing the government, forming a parliament, and building up the armed forces. This utopian reform movement failed, however, bringing to power more extreme factions, whose rallying cry became "Expel the barbarian!" The opposition found an effective political and military ally in the Boxers, a secret society founded in the late 18th century on the premise of fomenting popular rebellion against imperial reign. But the Boxers quickly narrowed their emphasis to an anti-foreign thrust and entered into a dubious alliance with the imperial government. The Boxer rebellion of 1900 ended disastrously, signaling the final death-throes of the old society.

The overthrow of the dynastic system by Sun Yat-sen's revolution of 1911 led to the first attempts to lay the foundations for a modern nation. A new government was subsequently established in Peking by

Yuan Shih-k'ai (who had usurped Sun's position). But chaos continued to reign. Factionalism, the rise of warlords in different regions of China, and the continuing threat posed by foreign powers led to greater instability. Lingering traditional values could no longer cope with the new forces of social and political change that were welling up. The clearest and most compelling response to this state of confusion was provided by students whose strident calls for nationalism quickly won wide attention and support. On May 4, 1919, some 300,000 youths rallied in the capital to denounce the weakness of the central government's response to the Japanese seizure of Shantung in 1914 and to Japan's "21 Demands" of 1915. The students endorsed a manifesto that concluded:

> China's territory may be conquered but it cannot be given away. The Chinese people may be massacred but they will not surrender. Our country is about to be annihilated. Rise up, brethren!

The May 4th demonstration was among the most important political events in China in the first part of this century, as it signaled the emergence of modern nationalism as a dominant force in Chinese politics. The student movement in Peking gained support from newspapers, intellectuals, political leaders, and peasants. The next 30 years of Chinese political life were largely caught up in a search for the most effective means of enacting the nationalist sentiments first expressed in 1919. China's abject weakness, as evidenced by its economic subjugation by foreigners, its inability to control the rise of the warlords, and its occupation by Japan, could ultimately find remedy only in nationally derived strength and self-reliance.

An answer was given on October 1, 1949 as Mao Tse-tung (who had been an assistant librarian at Peking University during the May 4th Movement) stood on the rostrum of the Gate of Heavenly Peace facing Tien An Men Square. Standing literally before thousands of years of Chinese history, Mao proclaimed the founding of the People's Republic of China, declaring that "the Chinese people have stood up!"

Economy and Culture

Since 1949, Peking's industrial development has been rapid and diverse. Although the city still ranks behind Shanghai and Shenyang as a manufacturing center, Peking has become a major producer of textiles and synthetic fibers, petrochemicals, automotive and agricultural equipment, and light and heavy machinery. Recent growth has emphasized manufacture of communications and electronics equipment, as well as advanced military weapons. Peking's factories also produce railroad cars, newsprint, and machine tools.

Expansion is itself an important industry in Peking. Since 1960, new construction has enlarged the original area by one-third, with over 150 major new residential complexes built since 1949. In 1977 alone, new housing projects completed or under construction had a total floor space of 2 million sq. m., the highest annual residential construction rate since the founding of the People's Republic. The new dwellings could house 40,000 families (or 200,000 people).

Large public works projects include the subway, a vast underground network of air-raid shelters, and monumental structures such as the Great Hall of the People, several national museums, and the Mao Tse-tung Memorial Hall. Major projects—and their maintenance—continue to employ large segments of the workforce. In 1978, expansion of the airport included the addition of a 3,200-m. (10,496-ft.) runway.

Peking's artisans are famous for their handicraft work. Carpets, embroidery, silks, ivory carving, paintings (both new styles and classical reproductions), jade, cloisonné, and lacquerware are of the highest quality. A crafts museum has been established to display the best of these artisan skills.

The city's thousands of fruit and vegetable stands are nearly all supplied by the surrounding region, where some 111,300 hectares (275,000 acres) are under cultivation. The area southwest of Peking is extremely fertile, and the creation of reservoirs and irrigation systems has assured a continuous food supply. There is an eight-month growing season in this part of China. Cereals grown include wheat, rice, maize, sorghum, barley, and kaoliang. Local vegetables are also important. These include cabbage, turnips, spinach, tomatoes, cucumbers, eggplant, sweet potatoes, beans, soybeans, peas, lotus root, onions, and garlic. There is also a wide variety of fruits—peaches, apricots, apples, pears, and persimmons (which can be seen drying on the slate roofs in the October sun). A variety of farm animals and poultry (Peking ducks!) are raised on neighboring communes.

There are many institutes of higher learning in Peking. Several help to support the capital's large and growing skilled labor force through excellent technical research facilities. The prestigious Peking and Tsing Hua universities are here, as are several language institutes, theater and drama companies, and the Institute for National Minorities (where minority representatives receive academic and political training prior to their return to leadership positions within their native groups). The cultural life of Peking is further enhanced by 25 theaters and numerous cinemas.

1 Summer Palace
2 Peking University
3 Capital Gymnasium
4 Peking Zoo
5 Peking Planetarium
6 Min Dzu (Nationalities) Hotel
7 Hsi Tan Market
8 Cultural Palace for the National
  Minorities
9 Peking Telegraph Building
10 Pei Hai Park
11 Coal Hill (Ching Shan)
12 Imperial Palace (Forbidden City)
13 Tien An Men
14 Great Hall of the People
15 Tien An Men Square
16 Museums of History and Revolution
17 Mao Tse-tung Memorial Hall
18 South Gate (Chien Men)
19 Shopping Area for Antiques
20 Peking Department Store
21 Peking Hotel
22 Temple of Heaven
23 Capital Hospital
24 Hsin Chiao Hotel
25 US Embassy
26 Worker's Stadium
27 Friendship Store
28 Friendship Hotel

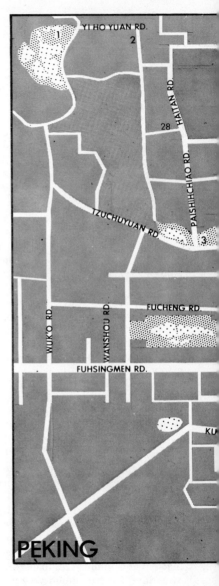

PEKING

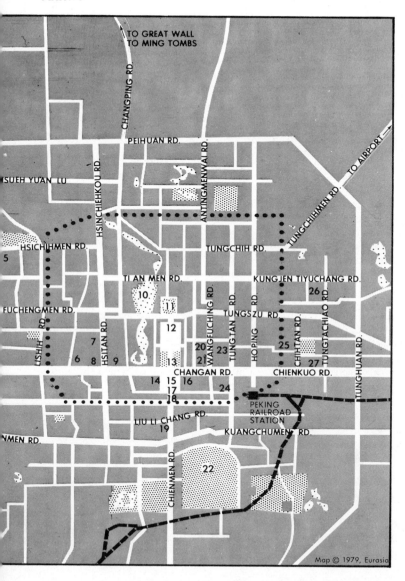

TO GREAT WALL
TO MING TOMBS

CHANGPING RD.

PEIHUAN RD.

SUEH YUAN LU

HSINCHIEHKOU RD.

ANTINGMENWAI RD.

TUNGCHIHMEN RD.

TO AIRPORT

HSICHIHMEN RD.

5

TUNGCHIH RD.

TI AN MEN RD.

10

11

KUNGJEN TIYUCHANG RD.

26

FUCHENGMEN RD.

WANGFUCHING RD.

TUNGSZU RD.

TUNGTAN RD.

HOPING RD.

CHIHTAN RD.

TUNGTACHIAO RD.

TUNGHUAN RD.

12

7

LISHIH RD.

HSITAN RD.

20 23

21

25

6 8 9

13

27

14 15 16

CHANGAN RD.

CHIENKUO RD.

17

24

18

PEKING
RAILROAD
STATION

LIU LI CHANG RD.

19

KUANGCHUMEN RD.

NMEN RD.

CHIENMEN RD.

22

Map © 1979, Eurasia

HIGHLIGHTS FOR TRAVELERS

Mao Tse-tung Memorial Hall Few men in world history have had the impact of Mao Tse-tung. His stature as an international figure and as the preeminent leader of the People's Republic of China is symbolized by the Chairman Mao Tse-tung Memorial Hall on the south end of Tien An Men Square. In the past, emperors chose their own monuments and built them away from the cities where they lived. Quite appropriately, perhaps, Mao Tse-tung has been interred in the heart of Peking, close to the masses he served until his death on September 8, 1976. The cornerstone for the Memorial Hall was laid by Mao's successor, Chairman Hua Kuo-feng, on November 24, 1976. It was completed on September 8, 1977, a year after Mao's death.

Located just south of the Monument to the People's Heroes and just north of Peking's South Gate, the Memorial Hall is a structure measuring 105 m. (344.4 ft.) square. The flat, low-tiered roof with its golden-yellow glazed tile cornices is supported by 44 granite pillars. In the north hall, facing Tien An Men, is a white marble statue of Mao Tse-tung. Inside the mausoleum itself, Mao's remains recline in a crystal sarcophagus, the red flag of the Communist Party of China draped over his body.

Groups may visit the Memorial Hall by prior arrangement with their host organization. Decorous attire is encouraged (e.g., no shorts, jeans, sneakers, or bright colors) and photographs inside the building are prohibited.

In the southern hall is a huge marble scroll on which the following poem is engraved in Chairman Mao's handwriting:

Reply to Comrade Kuo Mo-jo—
To the Tune of Man Chiang Hung

On this tiny globe
A few flies dash themselves against the wall,
Humming without cease,
Sometimes shrilling,
Sometimes moaning.
Ants on the locust tree assume a great nation swagger
And mayflies lightly plot to topple the giant tree.
The west wind scatters leaves over Changan,
And the arrows are flying, twanging.

So many deeds cry out to be done,
And always urgently;
The world rolls on,
Time presses.
Ten thousand years are too long,
Seize the day, seize the hour!
The Four Seas are rising, clouds and waters raging,
The Five Continents are rocking, wind and thunder roaring.
Our force is irresistible,
Away with all pests!

January 9, 1963

Tien An Men Square: at the center is the Chairman Mao Memorial Hall, completed in September 1977. To the rear is Ch'ien Men. The obelisk to the right is the Monument to the People's Heroes.

TIEN AN MEN

This name is applied generally to the central square of Peking (it was so named in 1651). The square encompasses Tien An Men Gate, Tien An Men Square, and several important monuments and buildings. Just as the Imperial Palace represents the "closed in" trappings of the past, Tien An Men today explicitly declares China's "open" future.

Gate of Heavenly Peace (Tien An Men) This massive stone gate with its wooden roof was built in 1412 and restored in 1651. A stream flows at the foot of the gate, spanned by five sculptured white marble bridges. A central portal is dominated by an immense portrait of Mao Tse-tung. On top is a rostrum where, on special occasions, China's leaders present themselves to the people. Inscribed on each side of the portal are two durable political slogans: on the left, "Long Life to the People's Republic of China!"; on the right, "Long Live the Unity of the Peoples of the World!" The grandstands below have a capacity of 20,000, usually filled by official guests reviewing parades and partaking in celebrations.

Tien An Men Square Tien An Men Gate overlooks the largest public square in the world. Originally covering 27 acres, the site was rebuilt in 1958 (during a massive, city-wide face-lifting campaign) and extended to 98 acres. Each flagstone is numbered so that parade units can line up in the appropriate sequence.

Monument to the People's Heroes In the center of the square is an obelisk 36 m. (118 ft.) high, a tribute to the heroes who died in the cause of the revolution. The cornerstone was laid by Chairman Mao and the structure completed on May 1, 1958. A bas-relief of soldiers, peasants, and workers depicts key episodes in the revolution (the sequence begins from the east side). The obelisk carries two inscriptions. One, in Chairman Mao's calligraphy, states, "The People's Heroes Are Immortal." A second, longer text, by Chou En-lai, is one of the rare public examples of his calligraphy.

South Gate (Chien Men) The Gate, recently refurbished to better complement the Mao Tse-tung Memorial Hall, was originally built in the 15th century. It once connected the north and south towns, but recently the surrounding area has been cleared so as to accommodate the subway and the widened east-west street to the south.

Great Hall of the People On the eastern side of the square is the Great Hall of the People, referred to in some older guides as the National People's Congress Building.

This great hall, built over a course of just ten months during 1958-59, can accommodate a meeting of 10,000 delegates. On the occasion of Richard Nixon's visit to China in 1972, it held 5,000 dinner guests. There are also a number of reception rooms of various sizes where top-ranking leaders conduct interviews with foreigners. The building occupies 51,520 sq. m. (61,600 sq. yd.) and extends 310 m. (1,017 ft.) from north to south.

Museum of the Revolution and Museum of History Two large buildings dominate the eastern side of Tien An Men Square. These are the Museum of History (covering periods up to 1840) and the Museum of the Chinese Revolution (after 1840). The former, closed during the Cultural Revolution, reopened in 1976; the Museum of the Revolution has recently reopened with a display on the life of Chou En-lai.

Cultural Palace of the Minorities Less than a mile and a half west of Tien An Men stands a large rectangular structure with a 13-story (195-ft.) tower. This is the Cultural Palace of the Minorities, dedicated to the cultural contributions of China's minority peoples. The building is a gay array of yellow stucco with green trim and a turquoise tile roof, giving the impression of a traditional Chinese design draped over a Western frame. Completed in 1959, it has four sections: a cultural center, a theater, a library, and a museum with 18 exhibition halls.

China's national minorities are credited with important status by the PRC government. While the Han (Chinese) people make up 94% of China's population, the remaining 6% inhabit nearly 60% of China's territory, giving them political significance well beyond their numbers.

*Museum of the
Chinese Revolution*

THE IMPERIAL PALACE
(KU KUNG)

River of Golden Water (Jinshuihe) between Wu Men and Tai Ho Men

Also known as the "Forbidden City" and the "Palace Museum," as well as the "Former Imperial Palace," this complex is both a mecca for tourists and an abiding symbol of traditional China. The entire complex has over 9,000 rooms and comprises the largest and most complete group of ancient buildings that has survived to the present age. Although it is old China's most imposing complex, its simple architectural lines play down its grand scale and lend a feeling of peaceful, harmonious solidity.

The present structures were built largely during the period 1406-20, under the reign of the Ming Emperor Yung Lo, and were inhabited by each of the remaining 12 Ming emperors. Sacked and looted by the Manchus during the Ming Dynasty's overthrow, the complex was restored to its orginial splendor under later Ch'ing rulers (mainly by Emperor Ch'ien Lung, 1736-96). It acquired its "Forbidden" name because entry by common citizens (and foreigners) was regarded as a capital offense. Under the People's Republic of China, the area has been converted into a public museum, open to all.

Nearly all of the buildings are two stories high, flanked by courtyards whose proportions vary with the importance of the palaces to which they were attached. Overall, the Imperial Palace covers an area of 250 acres, and is surrounded by a moat and a 35-ft. wall with towers on each corner.

The palace grounds are divided into two sections. The foregrounds consist of three large public halls from which the Ming and Ch'ing emperors issued edicts and decrees and conducted important state ceremonies. The rear part of the complex is made up of three main palaces, a few smaller "east" and "west" palaces, and the Imperial Gardens. In this setting, emperors divided their time between the affairs of state and their families.

The Palace Foregrounds

Meridian Gate (Wu Men) Wu Men demarcates the main entrance to the Forbidden City. It was first built in 1420 and restored in 1647. It was here that the emperor presided over military ceremonies and announced each year's new calendar (even the months and days were the province of the emperor). The imposing doors are festooned with wooden carvings and a set of lion-head knockers.

Hall of Supreme Harmony (T'ai Ho Tien) The Meridian Gate opens onto a large paved courtyard traversed by a small river. Opposite, the courtyard is guarded by a smaller gate, the T'ai Ho Men (Hall of Supreme Harmony Gate), fronted by two stylized bronze lions.

The Hall, built in 1420 and restored in 1697 during Emperor K'ang Hsi's reign, is 35 m. (115 ft.) high, and has an area of 2,377 sq. m. (2,843 sq. yd.). It is the tallest and most expansive of the palace buildings, and was used by the emperor on special occasions. The emperor's original throne is preserved here, surrounded by screens, four cloisonné incense burners, and a setting of ornate furniture.

In its more current history, the courtyard was the scene of a ceremony held by Western and Chinese military troops to celebrate the end of World War I.

Hall of Perfect Harmony (Chung Ho Tien) Passing through the Hall of Supreme Harmony, one descends 28 steps into the largest courtyard of the Palace, beyond which is the Hall of Perfect Harmony. The hall was built in 1420, restored in 1627, and further renovated in 1690. Used by the emperor to don formal regalia before entering the Hall of Supreme Harmony, it was also where he performed such ceremonies as examining seeds for the new planting.

Hall of Preserving Harmony (Pao Ho Tien) This Hall was built in 1420, rebuilt in 1625, and repaired in 1765. In 1789, it became the site of the "Palace Examinations," the highest stage of the Imperial Examination System and ostensibly the origin of all modern meritocracies. Successful candidates won the title of Chin Shih (loosely, "scholars"). Graduates of the system passed into high positions in government and administration throughout the empire, and their future wealth and status was assured. Although frequently undermined by corruption, the system did provide a modicum of upward mobility in traditional Chinese society.

187

The Imperial Palace

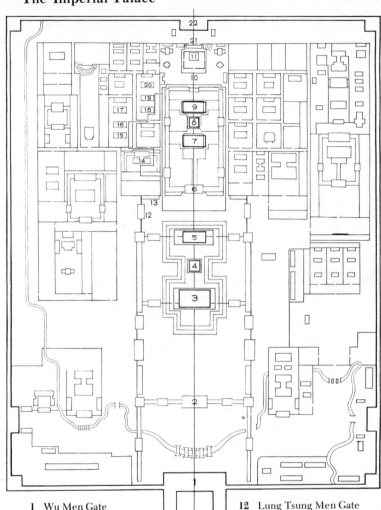

1	Wu Men Gate	12	Lung Tsung Men Gate
2	T'ai Ho Men Gate	13	Office of the Grand Council
3	T'ai Ho Tien Hall	14	Yang Hsin Tien Hall
4	Chung Ho Tien Hall	15	T'ai Chi Tien Hall
5	Pao Ho Tien Hall	16	T'i Yuan Tien Hall
6	Ch'ien Ch'ing Men Gate	17	Ch'ang Ch'un Kung Palace
7	Ch'ien Ch'ing Kung Palace	18	Yi K'un Kung Palace
8	Chiao T'ai Tien Hall	19	T'i Ho Tien Hall
9	K'un Ning Kung Palace	20	Ch'u Hsiu Kung Palace
10	Imperial Garden	21	Shun Chen Men Gate
11	Ch'in An Tien Hall	22	Shen Wu Men Gate

The original throne remains in this room, and is surrounded by some fine bronzes. The Hall's anterooms have been converted to museum galleries that display relics of the imperial households.

The flight of steps behind this Hall is called the "dragon pavement." The largest stone carving in the Imperial Palace, it is a work of the Ming period.

Rear Section of the Palace Grounds

Palace of Heavenly Purity (Ch'ien Ch'ing Kung) Entering the courtyard of this hall, the visitor passes through the Gate of Heavenly Purity, the longest-standing original structure in the compound. (The Palace of Heavenly Purity itself was burned and restored three times since its original construction in 1420.)

From the Ming to the early Ch'ing Dynasty, emperors resided and handled routine affairs of state in these quarters. The terrace surrounding the palace has gilt incense burners, bronze tortoises and cranes, a sundial, and a few miniature temples. The palace was last used for an "imperial" occasion in 1922 when the former child emperor, P'u Yi, last of the Ch'ing Dynasty imperial line, was married.

Hall of Union (Chiao T'ai Tien) Used by the Ch'ing emperors for birthday celebrations, this hall was built in 1420 and rebuilt in 1655. On display is one of ancient China's most remarkable scientific inventions, a clepsydra (water clock)—a mechanism that dates back 2,500 years. On the west side of the hall is a mechanical clock made by the Works Department of the Imperial Board in 1797.

Palace of Earthly Tranquility (K'un Ning Kung) The Ming empress lived in this palace which was built in 1420. Later, Ch'ing rulers used it as a place to offer sacrifices. An eastern side-room was used as a bridal chamber.

East and West Palaces To the sides of these main halls are a series of six eastern and six western palaces used for libraries, ceremonies, living quarters, and so on. Today, they house exhibitions that include furniture, jewelry, and other household items. Usually, only one or two rooms are opened for inspection.

Imperial Gardens At the rear of the Palaces are the Imperial Gardens, which cover 7,000 sq. m. (8,400 sq. yd.) and were originally built during the Ming Dynasty. The pines and cypresses growing here are several hundred years old. The grounds are arrayed with statues, rock gardens, pebble walkways laid out in intricate designs, and an artificial mountain (built in 1538) adorned with a cave, waterfall, and pavilion.

A visit to the Imperial Palace usually consumes a full morning or afternoon. Visitors leave through the rear gate (Cheng Kuang Men), a simple portal guarded by two gilded bronze elephants. The grounds are exited through the massive Gate of Divine Pride (Shen Wu Men), where buses wait for the return trip to the hotel.

Areas Surrounding the Imperial Palace

Within the compound and on its flanks are some worthwhile sites not normally included in tours.

The Chinese History Museum A museum complex on the eastern side of the Ku Kung features a special archeological exhibition that traces the path of Chinese history. It can be reached by walking east on the road that runs between Wu Men and T'ai Ho T'ien. The collection includes a remarkable jade burial garment and an assortment of carved stone horses and warriors unearthed in 1976 near Sian. Advance permission must be obtained for visits to this museum.

Sun Yat-sen (Chung Shan) Park Just inside the Tien An Men Gate, there are two large public gardens. On the west is Sun Yat-sen Park, situated on a site laid out in 1421. It affords a convenient place to relax from the rigors of sightseeing, and to walk slowly among the trees, sip tea, and watch Peking's citizens at their leisure.

People's Cultural Park The People's Park may be found by turning east after entering the Tien An Men Gate. With a tree-lined boulevard in the shadow of the old imperial walls, this is a popular place for morning exercise, music practice, badminton, or just a leisurely stroll along the moat.

Coal Hill (Mei Shan or Ching Shan) Coal Hill is situated directly opposite the exit gate of the Imperial Gardens. Now more commonly called Ching Shan (Prospect Hill), it is entirely artificial and was used by the emperors to bring a little of the countryside into the flat plain of Peking. They stocked the area with hares and other small game. The park was built in the 13th century and covers 23 hectares. The hill was formed from earth excavated from the moat around the Imperial Palace.

Closed for "renovations" during the Cultural Revolution, it was reopened to the public in March 1978. Sites in the park include the Beautiful View Tower (Chi Wang Lou) and the Pavilion of Everlasting Springs (Wan Chun Ting), which commands a breathtaking view of the Imperial Palace and the full expanse of the capital.

Chung Nan Hai This is the combined name for "middle and southern lake," which flanks the Imperial Palace to the west. As it is the area where China's present leaders live and work, it is closed off to visitors. The entrance to this compound is about a half-mile east from the center of Tien An Men. A flag pole and soldiers standing guard mark the gate.

Pei Hai (North Lake) Closed for "renovations" until March 1978 (as a result of the Cultural Revolution), this park is one of the loveliest in Peking. It was originally built about 300 AD and is a favorite spot for the local population. Its beauty is subtle and can best be appreciated on a weekday when it tends to be less crowded. The Bridge of Perfect Wisdom (Chih Chu Chiao) is one of the park's more famous landmarks. The park's White Pagoda (Pai Tai) was built in 1651. Damaged by the 1976 earthquake, it has been reinforced, and the covered corridors, pavilions and terraces in the park have all been repainted. Views from the Pagoda include: to the north, North Lake, with the Ministry of Defense building to the left, and a portion of the Peking University campus on the right. In the distance is the Bell Tower and the Drum Tower. To the south, the magnificent panorama of the Ku Kung, and, beyond that, the line of high-rise apartment blocks that trace the line of Peking's former wall. Also restored to its original splendor is the famous Nine Dragon Wall (Chiu Lung Pi), a 5-m. high and 27-m. wide screen with nine dragons formed of variegated glazed bricks on each side. The entire park is said to have been the former palace of Kublai Khan, as romantized in the Samuel Coleridge poem "In Xanadu."

The Great Wall Rising and falling with the ridges of the northern hills and undulating far off into the distance, the Great Wall consistently exceeds the expectations of visitors. The only man-made object visible from earth orbit, the wall remains one of the most astonishing feats of human endeavor. The amount of brick and stone employed to construct the Great Wall could be used to surround the earth with a dike eight feet high.

Once, the Great Wall stretched from the Po Hai Sea in the east to the Chiayukuan in Kansu Province to the west, winding its way over a length of 10,000 ancient Chinese *li* (about 5,000 km. or 3,100 mi.). Construction began during the Warring States (480-422 BC) period, when different sections were built in scattered areas.

Following China's unification under the first Ch'in Emperor (221-207 BC), 300,000 men (many of them political prisoners) were put to work connecting the segments into one huge rampart of stone and earth. From the end of the 16th century AD until the Ming Dynasty, the Great Wall was frequently overrun and became obsolete as an

effective barrier against determined invaders (for whom bribes became the most effective weapons). The Ming emperors, successors to the Mongols, again tried to make it into a useful fortification, adding cement, bricks, and blocks of stone. The wall was made wide enough to accommodate six horses running abreast. Overall, it averages 6.6 m. (22 ft.) in height and 5.8 m. (19 ft.) in width. Battlements, built at intervals of 140 m. (459 ft.), were used as signal towers.

Formerly all tourists took a two-hour bus or car ride to the Great Wall, winding rather precariously up to the restored section at a mountain pass north of Peking. In April 1978, however, daily train service was inaugurated to augment road transport. By either means, the routes pass agricultural communes, market towns, extensive rock quarries, and, finally, lead into the rugged, rock-strewn foothills that once formed China's northern frontier. Here, at Pataling Pass, a section of the wall has been restored, and one can climb either left or right—for 500 yards or so—to the top of the closest hill.

The Ming Tombs In keeping with an imperial tradition that dated back to the Chou Dynasty, the Ming emperors selected the location and design of their tombs while they were still alive. Construction of the tomb site began in 1584 and was completed in four years at a cost of 4 million oz. of silver. All but one Ming emperor (T'ai Tzu, buried in Nanking) chose to be buried in this beautiful valley 48 km. (30 mi.) north of Peking.

The road to the tombs, which branches off from the route to the Great Wall, was once a four-mile-long sacred way, forbidden to all but the emperor's retinue. Today, the bus first drives through a great marble gate (built in 1540) with five arches. About a mile further up the road is the Great Red Gate (Ta Hung Men), a massive 36.6 m. (120 ft.) portal on which were formerly hung three huge wooden doors. Just beyond the gate sits a stone tortoise with a stele inscribed by the fourth Ming emperor (1426). Thirty feet high, it is the largest stone tablet of this type in China. Here begins the famous "Avenue of the Animals" (tours will stop here after a visit to the Tomb itself, but only if time allows). Lions, camels, elephants, horses, and two sets of mythical beasts, totaling 12 statues, line each side of the road, alternately standing and kneeling. Following are a series of stone statues of 12 imperial ministers, all dating from the 15th century.

Of the tombs themselves, only two have been excavated, those of Chang Ling and Ting Ling. The sepulchre of the first has not been opened, however. Visitors are taken to the tomb of Ting Ling, who was buried here with two wives in 1620 in a marble vault some four stories underground (apart from the remarkable feats of engineering and architecture that characterize the vault, its depth makes it one of the coolest spots in China during the summer). The entrance to the grounds is marked by a large gate with a magnificent bronze lion. Through the gate several museum buildings house tomb objects. Thereafter, the walkway leads up the hill to the tomb itself.

Temple of Heaven The Temple of Heaven is one of traditional China's most striking monuments. Its 15th-century planners used the most advanced principles of architecture, mechanics, and geometry known at the time. The aesthetic goal was to create a structure that blended harmoniously with sky and earth.

The temple and its accompanying buildings are set in a large park (6.1 sq. km.—2.4 sq. mi.) to the south of Peking. The grounds are expansive enough so that the everyday sounds of Peking do not intrude. Indeed, silence adds to the aura.

The Temple of Heaven was built in 1420. It was first restored in 1751 and, after a fire begun by lightning, rebuilt in 1889. After 1949, scientists carefully studied the paint pigments and wooden structure so as to recreate precisely its original splendor. The temple had been used by emperors as a personal altar to pray for better harvests and to seek heaven's blessing on events of the coming year.

The building is set on a triple-tiered round marble terrace, each layer surrounded by a balustrade 11 m. (36 ft.) high. The base of the temple is 96 ft. in diameter, and is topped by a triple cone-shaped roof of blue-glazed tiles (representing the sky), culminating in a gilded ball. Not a single nail was used in the construction. The interlaced wooden frame is supported by 28 columns hewn from trees brought from Yunnan. There are four large support pillars in the interior, each 18.3 m. (60 ft.) high. The roof, covered by some 50,000 glazed tiles, is

193

Stele before tomb of Emperor Wan Li (1563-1620)

supported on an articulated skeleton, without the use of ceiling joists.

Nearby, in the courtyard of the main temple, are two auxiliary buildings. Their cone-shaped roofs are miniature versions of the main temple. The point of interest here is the "Echo Wall." Two people standing on opposite sides of the courtyard near the wall can hear each other's speech without raising their voices. Moreover, three large stones that lie in the central walkway leading to the main temple, known as the "Three Echoing Stones," display further acoustic oddities. A single shout or hand-clap from the first stone produces a single echo; a double echo is produced on the second stone; and on the third, three echoes. (The effect is due to the different distances of the stones from the walls, producing measured variations in the distance for sound reflection.)

In 1978, a 600,000-*yuan* (US$353,000) renovation project was completed, which included the setting in place of an ensemble of three pavilions and a long covered corridor brought to this site from Chungnanhai (Peking's government compound). These structures originally formed part of an imperial garden and were built by the Emperor Ch'ien Lung to celebrate his mother's birthday.

The southern part of the complex has the equally fascinating Round Mound, consisting of three round white marble terraces first built in 1539 and enlarged in 1749. When standing on the center stone, a voice will appear to come back louder and fuller than the original spoken word, giving the effect of an echo chamber. (Sound waves are amplified by reverberating across the round walls and stone fences before being reflected back.)

The Animal Way leads to Ming tombs.

Of final note are the numerological patterns built into the architectural features of the Temple of Heaven complex. The main temple has 28 pillars: the four main pillars holding up the temple represent the four seasons, and the 12 interior posts the months of the year. In ancient days, the Chinese divided the day into 12-hour periods, represented by the outer ring of 12 pillars. The symbolic number nine, signifying the sky (or heaven) and the emperor, recurs in the design of the Round Mound. Thus, the flagstones on the upper terrace are arranged in concentric circles in multiples of nine; i.e., the first circle has 9 stones, the second 18, and so on to a final total of 243 in the 27th and outermost ring.

Gate of the Summer Palace

Summer Palace The Summer Palace lies seven miles northwest of Peking, and is a favorite of Peking residents for a cool, breezy picnic in summer, and for skating on Kunming Lake in winter.

There have actually been two Summer Palaces. The original was built by the Jurchen Tartars during the Chin Kingdom (1115-1234 AD) where the rear gate of Tsinghua University now stands, and maintained until the late Ch'ing Dynasty when, in 1860, the British burned it in an effort to compel the imperial court to "see reason."

The present Summer Palace is largely the work of the Ch'ing emperors, and is set on 283 hectares (700 acres) of land on the shores of Kunming Lake. The Emperor Ch'ien Lung built the Pai Yun (White Cloud) Palace on top of Longevity Hill in 1791 as a tribute to his 60-year-old mother. The Empress Tsu Hsi extended the palaces and the lovely "Painted Gallery," a wooden walkway 728 m. (2,388 ft.) long that girds the north shore of the lake. Its wooden beams are painted with exquisite landscapes. Tsu Hsi is also responsible for a now famous curiosity, the Marble Barge, built by funds diverted from their intended use in creating China's first modern navy.

A complete tour of the Summer Palace requires a full day. Unfortunately, most visits are allotted only half that time. The best view is provided from the top of Longevity Hill, which affords a panorama of the lake, with its traditional humpbacked (17-arched) bridges, the exotic Jade Belt Bridge, a lovely pagoda, and the Garden of Harmonious Interests (Hsieh Ch'ou Yuan). Shimmering in the summer sun, the glazed golden tiles of the palaces impart the feeling of a traditional Chinese landscape painting.

Marco Polo Bridge (Lu Kuo Chiao) Although not a stop on most itineraries, the bridge is usually crossed when traveling to the western and southern suburbs (en route to Peking Petrochemical Factory, for example). The bridge lies about 16 km. (10 mi.) southwest of the city, spanning the Yungting River. The Chinese name for the bridge is Lu Kuo Chiao (Reedy Moat Bridge), and it dates back some 780 years. Marco Polo visited the area in 1290, later describing the bridge in expansive terms, and thus giving it its nickname.

The original bridge was washed away by a flood in 1698, but a faithful replica was built in its place. It is constructed of white marble and is 235 m. (770 ft.) long, supported by 11 arches. It was widened in 1969, but the original balustrades, containing some 280 parapets adorned with miniature stone lions, were retained.

The bridge is famous as the site of the "Marco Polo Incident," a 1937 clash between Chinese and Japanese troops that helped spark the anti-Japanese war.

Peking Zoo If seen at all, the zoo is usually tacked onto visitors' itineraries as part of a long day of sightseeing. This practice is unfortunate, since the zoo is worth more than the standard, cursory visit to its most famous inhabitants, the pandas.

The Peking Zoo dates from the Ming Dynasty when it was the site of an imperial park. A zoological garden was established on the site during the Ch'ing Dynasty, but only a dozen or so animals had survived by 1949. Much expansion has gone on since, and now the Peking Zoo boasts more than 2,000 animals of 300 species. Some of the more prized species are the giraffes, lions, polar bears, roe deer, and gibbon apes. Another major highlight is the zoo's superb outdoor bird sanctuary. One of the two musk oxen given to China by President Nixon (in exchange for the two pandas now in Washington) is still alive. The best known panda variety is the giant panda, native to China. A smaller, rust-colored species is more directly related to the raccoon, and suffers in the shadow of its more glamorous cousin. A map of the zoo is sold at concession stands on the grounds.

The large domed building across the street is the Peking Planetarium. Entrance fees to both the planetarium and zoo are 10 *fen*.

Peking Petrochemical Plant Peking has more of interest than its historical monuments, and a visit to China's capital is likely to include at least one tour of a modern factory or other industrial site. China is justly proud of its petroleum industry, and visitors are sometimes taken to the Peking Petrochemical Plant, about a two-hour drive past the Marco Polo Bridge. The complex is Chinese in design and execution (although some Romanian technical equipment has been added). It consists of ten major plants. It has an annual capacity of 7 million tons and processes 50 varieties of fuels and lubricants. It also makes synthetic fibers and rubber products. Some of the crude oil comes from the famous Taching Oil Field near Harbin, some 1,600 km. (994 mi.) to the north.

Management personnel told visitors that 1977 saw a 42% increase in oil-processing capacity, and that the state target was fulfilled by December 26 (Mao's birthday). There were some 30,000 workers in 1978 (35% women), but the complex is being expanded to employ 100,000. The average wage is Y60 per month (US$35.30). Capital investment has totaled over Y4 billion (US$2.35 billion). Typical of most large state-owned enterprises in China, the plant has its own schools (including six high schools), nurseries, a hospital, and a large expanse of modern workers' housing.

Peking University Since Peking is also a center of education, tours are likely to include one of the city's famous universities. Peking University was founded in 1898 as Yenching University, a US-sponsored institution. Many of its students partook in the May 4th Movement of 1919. And it was here that the debates giving rise to the Cultural Revolution (1966-69) began. During that period, many of its most noted professors, under attack by the Red Guards, publicly confessed their guilt for putting academic pursuits ahead of revolutionary ideals. By 1977, however, most were restored to their former posts and the promotion of research and academic achievement was receiving support from the highest echelons of China's new leadership. In 1978, its 3,000 students were augmented by several thousand more who, in the fall of 1977, took the first nationwide university-entrance examinations held in China since 1966.

Emperor Ch'ien Lung's Tomb The 18th-century tomb of the Ch'ing Emperor Ch'ien Lung (1736-96), located about 100 km. east of Peking in Tsunhua County, Hopei Province, was opened to the public in 1978.

The tomb, known as Yu Ling, is on a grander scale and of higher artistic quality than most others in an assemblage of 15 tombs of the Ching Dynasty that cover an area of some 2,500 sq. km. Construction of Ch'ien Lung's tomb began in 1743 and cost 90 tons of silver. It covers and area of 462,000 sq.m. tres. The wood used was durable fragrant close-grained nanmu, with some logs weighing up to 20 tons.

The tomb is, in effect, an underground palace, based on the architectural style of the imperial tombs of the Ming Dynasty (1368-1644). Nevertheless, Yu Ling has distinctive architectural features. Flanking the roadway leading to the tomb are eight pairs of stone sculptures depicting civil officials, military officers, horses, *chi-lin* (a mythical animal of good omen), elephants, camels, *suan ni* (mythical monsters), and lions. Each sculpture was carved from a complete stone block. The largest is 30 cu.m. and weighs about 43 tons.

The underground palace of Yu Ling covers 327 sq.m. and is 54 m. long. It has three stone halls and four pairs of stone gates, all arched. The overhanging eaves, tile gutters and ridges, and animal-shaped ornaments on the gate corners were worked in white marble. Each gate weighs about two tons and contains a Bodhisattva, each with a different mien. The inner walls and arched ceilings of the gateways and halls are decorated with four celestial guardians (also called Deva kings), seated statues of gods and Buddhas, and carvings of potted flowers and small three-legged tables for placing incense burners and Buddhist scriptures.

The coffin of Ch'ien Lung is in the innermost part of the underground palace, placed over a well which never runs dry.

WALKING TOURS

There is no better place in China for a walk than Peking. The symmetry of the city's layout facilitates wandering through the varied matrix of dusty alleyways and broad boulevards. (Since city streets in China tend to change names every several blocks, a good map should be brought along for back-up.) Because Peking is so spread out, walkers should not expect to "do the town" in one afternoon or even in one day. It is better advised to set out in a taxi to a particular area of town (e.g., the Temple of Heaven) and then walk back, saving valuable time and energy.

The best period for walking is in the early morning, as near to sunrise as one can manage. In the early morning light, the sun glistens on

the yellow roofs of the Palace Museum. Mornings are times for recreation in China and outside its red ochre walls can be heard the strains of the flute or violin, a Peking Opera aria, the recitation of a poem, or the blare of a bugle. Individuals or groups fill the open spaces to practice *t'ai chi ch'uan* ("shadow boxing") and *wu shu* (traditional martial arts) or to play badminton, basketball, or other sports.

But the main thing is to take to the streets and look at the people of Peking—their neighborhoods, their stores, their places of work, and the quiet, earnest industry that marks all aspects of their lives.

The two suggested walking tours that follow begin at the Peking Hotel.

A Market Walk: Wang Fu Ching (40 minutes or more—round trip distance, 2.2 mi.)

Although Wang Fu Ching is best known as the busiest shopping district in Peking, it is also one of Peking's more venerable neighborhoods. Wang Fu Ching is the street immediately to the east of the Peking Hotel. To reach it, one should proceed north. Three blocks to the right down San T'iao Hu Tung is the Capital Hospital, a pre-1949 structure built with grants from the Rockefeller Foundation. On the next block (Shuai Fu Yuan) is the China Art Gallery, followed by the Tung Feng people's market. This is the crossroads of Tung An Men and at this point shops begin to thin out. Two and a half blocks further is the Eastern Church. Three blocks further is the Capital Theater, and two blocks beyond that, on the left, is the Academia Sinica Institute of History and its library.

The main hotel for overseas Chinese is on the corner of the next major intersection of Han Hua Yuan Ta Chieh, to the left, and Chu Shih Ta Chieh, to the right. The Museum of Fine Arts, on the northwest corner, often carries exhibitions of both foreign and Chinese art.

A Sunrise Walk: Tien An Men (1 hour, 4.2 km—2.6 mi.)

This excursion is designed to let the visitor observe morning exercises and commuting activity in Peking. The walk begins by turning right out the main door of the Peking Hotel and following Chang An

Boulevard toward Tien An Men. Enter the Tien An Men Gate and walk north towards the Wu Men Gate of the main Imperial Palace. To the left there will be an entrance to Sun Yat-sen Park; to the right, the Working People's Park. Either is worth walking through.

Or, one can proceed straight on, turning right (east) just before Wu Men, passing through a relatively small gate and following the road along the wall. The area astride the moat is a favorite for *wu shu* artists and badminton players. Continuing along the wall as the road turns left, head east again at the first chance—across a large bridge that spans the moat (the only one in the vicinity). The walker has now reached Tung An Men Ta Chieh. This should be followed past two large intersections, until it crosses Wang Fu Ching. The Peking Hotel (and breakfast) are four short blocks away on the right.

 HOTEL ACCOMMODATIONS

Peking Hotel Completed in 1975, the Peking Hotel is among the country's most modern, and boasts architectural and service features found in no other PRC hotels. Its location is excellent: around the corner is Wang Fu Ching, Peking's main shopping district. Tien An Men is two long blocks away.

The hotel consists of three wings. The western wing was built in the early 1950s in grand Soviet style, with an ornate lobby and wood-paneled rooms. Now rarely used by foreigners, it is retained for high-ranking PRC officials and citizens. The middle wing is used for tour groups, and is now being added to.

The centrally air-conditioned new wing—by far the tallest building in Peking—is used exclusively by foreign guests. It has 141,000 sq. m. (168,636 sq. yd.) of floor space spread over 17 stories (with no 13th floor). Eight elevators serve 900 rooms with 1,800 beds. There is a large (almost cavernous) waiting room with a refreshment bar (serving both liquor and dishes of delicious—if somewhat soupy—vanilla ice cream) and retail shop, a red-carpeted lobby (with a map of the world displaying times around the globe), a billiards room, post and telegraph office (open 8 AM-6:30 PM), a bank (8-11 AM; 2-5 PM), chess rooms, and a bookshop. The central building in the old wing has a grocery store. A barbershop and hairdresser are located on the second floor.

The kitchen serves Szechwan, Cantonese, Huaiyang, Tanchie, Japanese, and Western dishes, although the selections both on the Chinese and Western menus have been cut back. The dining room is open 7:00-8:30 AM for breakfast; noon-2:00 PM for lunch; and 6:00-8:30 PM for dinner. Although both food and service have sharply deteriorated in recent years, a rotation of service workers in 1977 improved the situation somewhat.

Delegations and tour groups are assigned tables, usually towards the back of the room beneath a huge mosaic of scenes from Kweilin. Businessmen usually occupy the front tables, often engaging in "tourist watching" to help relieve long weeks of negotiations. The touches of home found on different tables—instant coffee, jams, honey—usually belong to these "regulars."

Rooms are comfortable, fairly clean, and good-sized, and feature drapes that are electrically controlled. Balconies on some rooms offer a spectacular view of Peking, particularly those that look west over the Forbidden City and the hills beyond (rooms whose numbers end in 44, 43, 41, 39, 38, 37, or 36). The service desks provide laundry and dry-cleaning services, and sell refreshments (including beer, wine, and soda), cigarettes, and other sundries. The hotel staff is available to polish shoes and carry out minor repairs.

The Peking Hotel is located on Chang An Chieh (telephone: 552231). Its rates per night are Y55 (US$32.35) for a twin room, and Y155 (US$67.65) for a suite including a refrigerator and radio.

Hsin Chiao (New Citizen) Hotel This six-story hotel, built in the Soviet style and located to the southeast of Tien An Men in the old legation quarter, used to be an exclusive haunt for foreign journalists, businessmen, and other "new China hands." The new wing of the Peking Hotel (where the prices are suitably higher) has taken away some of the Hsin Chiao's clientele, although there remains a warm familiarity about the place.

Rooms are just large enough to accommodate twin beds, a desk, and two easy chairs. A dining room on the lobby floor serves some of Peking's best Chinese dishes, but many foreign guests prefer the Western dining room on the sixth floor, which provides a lovely view of the city. For some foreigners, the hotel's main attraction is a bar (until the opening of the Peking Hotel, the only one in town) and a roof garden that stays open late into the evenings during the warm summer months. The usual range of services is available. A new amenity in late 1978 was a massage service: Y6 for a complete rubdown. A martini cocktail is available at the hotel's bar for 40 *fen*.

The Hsin Chiao Hotel is located on Chung Wen Men (telephone: 557731). Its rates per night are Y9 (US$5.30) without bath, and Y14 (US$8.24) with bath.

Min Dzu (Nationalities) Hotel The 11-story Min Dzu is in most ways the most old-fashioned and basic of the hotels reserved for foreign guests in Peking. Nevertheless, it is clean, has an adequate-to-good dining room, and provides excellent services.

The hotel is located almost two miles due west along Chang An Boulevard from Tien An Men, and is thus not convenient to Peking's central sites. Nearby, however, is the Hsi-tan market area, a colorful district almost as well-stocked as Wang Fu Ching across town.

Rooms are plain, with brown coverlets adorning straw-mattressed beds. There are the customary two chairs, dresser, and desk. As in most other hotels, bathrooms are old-fashioned (e.g., hand-showers) but adequate. They are supplied with soap, towels, and—surprisingly —combs. A thermos with hot water is provided for making tea (also supplied in little wooden boxes) and there is a carafe filled with drinking water. Most rooms are equipped with adjustable fans (the Min Dzu is not air-conditioned).

The Min Dzu is located on Chang An Boulevard (telephone: 668541). Its rates per night are Y17 (US$10) for a single twin-bedded room and Y34 (US$20) for a double room.

Chien Men Hotel The Chien Men is situated by the South Gate and the Mao Tse-tung Memorial Hall. Although an older structure, it is situated in an excellent neighborhood for walking. Within one square mile are antique shops, old-style houses, and many interesting small stores. Telephone: 338731.

Friendship Hotel In the western suburbs, beyond the zoo and the capital gymnasium, lies the Friendship Hotel, long the home of foreign residents in China. One wing has now been freed for tourist use. New paint and some refurbishing, plus a good dining room, still do not make up for its long distance from the center of the city. Telephone: 890621.

Hsi Yuan (Western Garden) Hotel. Opened to foreign guests only since October 1978, this hotel, too, was pressed into service to try to accommodate the new wave of foreigners. The setting is pleasant enough, and it's a five-minute walk from the zoo and the planetarium. There are the usual tourist facilities (a shop, post office, barber shop, stamp and telegraph office are in the building behind #10, where most guests stay). There is new paint on the walls and floors and the facilities are clean, but many rooms do not have private baths (the only shower available is in the ladies' room—but the door locks). The Hsi Yuan has a good dining room, and features such dishes as lamb shish-kabob (Chinese style). Some rooms also do not have a telephone. Telephone: 890721.

PEKING'S CUISINE

Of course, there is Peking duck. But there is also a wide range of other specialties to try. Peking cuisine is really a mixture of many styles from northern China, including Mongolia, Shantung, and even Szechwan. Highly recommended dishes include hot-and-sour soup (with emphasis usually on the hot), the cold preliminary dishes, dumplings, fried prawns, and sea slugs. A memorable dessert is apples covered with molten toffee (and then solidified in ice water).

All of this can be washed down with some excellent local beers: Peking or Tsingtao brands. There are some good local wines (made from kaoliang grains); the most highly regarded is the slightly sweet Shaohsing, usually warmed before serving.

Peking has 656 restaurants catering to over one million people a day. This actually represents a smaller volume than a decade ago, but urban reconstruction and damage by earthquakes have taken their toll. The situation is being remedied, however, with ten new restaurants scheduled to be opened in 1978-79. In any event, from the traveler's viewpoint, there certainly is no shortage of fine restaurants to choose from.

Peiching Kaoya Tien (Peking Duck Restaurant) Two branches of Peiching Kaoya Tien specialize in this justifiably famous local delicacy. The first one listed suffers the indignity of being referred to as the "sick duck"—because of its proximity to the Capital Hospital. It is located on a little lane found on the east side of Wang Fu Ching between numbers 170 and 180 (telephone: 553310). The other "duck" is located near the South Gate and Chien Men Street (751379). Reservations for both are advised since they are often crowded with banquet parties. Diners should be prepared for two things: the cost (a "medium quality" dinner for five, including drinks, was Y150 [US$95] in October 1978); to get so much as a glimpse of the duck, and the occasional disappointment in the food. A new Peking duck restaurant was to open in 1979.

Min Tsu Fan Chuang Peking has a host of minority-nationality restaurants, including several that feature hearty Mongolian cuisine. The Min Tsu offers the advantage of being close to the Peking Hotel. It is off Wang Fu Ching, at the north entrance of the East Wind market. From the hotel, go up Wang Fu Ching, turn right at the traffic light into Tung Hua Men, and follow a long block up the street to No. 160 (telephone: 550069). The dining section for foreigners is upstairs. Other recommended minority-nationality restaurants are the Hung Pin Lo (Hopei, Muslim) and the Sinkiang Tsan Ting.

Feng Tse Yuan Expensive, but worth it, since the Feng Tse (Horn of Plenty) is one of the famous restaurants of long standing in Peking. Given the proper budget and imagination, diners will be treated to a masterful, subtle meal. Feng Tse Yuan is located at 83 Zhu Shi Kou (telephone: 332828).

Szechwan Restaurant Formerly known as the Chengtu, this restaurant is notable for its feisty Szechwan food (i.e., hot and spicy) and colorful atmosphere; several single-floor buildings are linked by cobblestone courtyards in the style of traditional China (telephone: 336356). Try the warm Shaohsing wine, and be prepared to spend Y30 and up per person for dinner.

Fang Shan ("imitation imperial") Restaurant Now the most favored dining spot in Peking, this restaurant is picturesquely located in Pei Hai Park at the edge of the lake. Here they recreate the food of the emperors and empresses (the last empress' dream about a certain dish led to minced pork stuffed in biscuits). Japanese tour groups have come for three days of nonstop dining on the most exotic foods imaginable. In the event that reservations are secured, count on spending Y50 per person for the ersatz "imperial" treatment. Telephone: 442573.

T'ing Li Kuan This restaurant is located on the grounds of the Summer Palace and has recently become a favorite of visitors to Peking, both because of its surrounding scenery and a good menu (try the fish dishes).

Kao Jou Chi This is a true "neighborhood" eating place and is among several excellent Mongolian-style restaurants in the city. Specializing in barbecued meats, it is located near South Lake (Nan Hai).

Those who crave a hot dog will find a reasonable facsimile at the Jitan Park Restaurant (open to foreigners only), which also serves good dumplings, the everyday dish of Peking.

SHOPPING

In addition to Peking's Friendship Store there are five main shopping areas: Wang Fu Ching and Liu Li Ch'ang—the two largest, and Sung Tang, Hsi Tan, and Chien Men. For those who have more time, fruitful bargain-hunting can be conducted at second-hand furniture shops.

Friendship Store Peking's is the largest Friendship Store in China; three floors are well-stocked with everything from jade jewelry to a wide variety of wines and spirits. It has a complete range of local goods, Chinese export products, and handicrafts. Even if Peking is the first stop in China, it may be wise to indulge shopping impulses here since many items may not be available anywhere else (except quite possibly in Hong Kong). It is also the only place in Peking (and for that matter, one of the few in all of China) that will provide packaging, customs clearance, and shipping of items—including those purchased elsewhere in Peking. There are no bargains in shipping charges, however, which may run as high as Y300 (US$176.50) per cu.m. (35 cu. ft.).

The Friendship Store is open from 9AM to 9PM daily (subject to seasonal variations); its Bank of China branch is open 9AM to 7PM to exchange money.

Wang Fu Ching

Peking's major general shopping area is Wang Fu Ching, a street adjoining the Peking Hotel. Turn left out of the hotel driveway and left again up the flagstone pavement.

The following shops are found on the west (left) side of Wang Fu Ching, heading north:

Street Number	Specialty
299	**Film shop** Chinese and (sometimes) foreign films, photographic supplies, albums, and so on. Most Chinese color film is not of the same standard as Western varieties, although the quality of black-and-white film (Seagull brand) is good.
295	**Hi-fi shop** A good way to see what Chinese record players, radios, and televisions look like. Prices are relatively high for larger equipment, which is rarely purchased by individuals in China.
265	**Arts store** Previously a jewelry store, it has recently been converted to an outlet for scrolls and rubbings, with prices ranging from 80 *fen* for a woodblock print of the famous flying horse from Kansu to Y750 for a scroll.
261	**Chop (signature seal) shop** Outside of Liu Li Chang, this chop store offers the best variety. A small but well-chosen collection, especially in the lower price ranges.
255	**Pai Huo Ta Lou** The large, five-story building, set back from the street, is Peking's biggest department store. Everyone from

chauffeured army commanders to out-of-town Chinese shop here. A good selection of most common items, including sundries, tools, and housewares.

235 **Foreign Languages Bookstore** Probably the best selection of Chinese books in English (and other languages) in China. Interesting items include opera libretti, tourist maps of Peking, and postcards from all over the country.

229 **Jewelry Store** On the southwest corner of the intersection, this unprepossessing shop carries necklaces made from precious stones (including pearls), jade objects, and vases.

Having now arrived at the first major intersection (marked by a traffic light), turn left. On the left-hand (south) side of the street are:

16 **Record shop.**

28 **China Stamp Export Company** As the name indicates, a large selection of Chinese stamps are available, many arranged in bound sets. Chinese stamps make colorful, informative souvenirs, even for non-collectors.

Although the stores tend to thin out north of the intersection, it is worth ducking into #217, just north on the west side of the street. This is a hardware store and features bamboo baby carriages, baby chaise longues, and a wide variety of kitchen utensils, including the Mongolian hot pot.

Returning back down Wang Fu Ching, and across the intersection, are the following shops (walking south):

142 **Tea shop** A large variety of good teas.

156 **Shoe and hat store** Includes a wide selection of inexpensive fur garments, including hats for both children and adults.

Next to 156, set in from the other store fronts and directly across from the department store, is a "covered market" called the East Wind Market (just follow the crowds). A popular place for everything from clocks to ice cream, it combines many shops and stalls grouped together under one roof.

172 Children's store Includes clothing, shoes, and toys.

174 Clock shop Peking's largest collection of clocks and watches.

192 Fur and leather shop Fur, suede (an especially good purchase in China), gloves, hats; most items can be made to order, although this may require too much time for most visitors.

200 Peking Handicrafts Exhibition Center Two floors display a full range of handicrafts and supplies, from cloisonne to brushes and ink.

210 Odd-hour bookstore Caters to those who have to work during the day. It is open only from 7 to 9:30 AM and from 7:30 to 9:30 PM, and hence earns the name "Early-Late Bookstore."

214 New China Book Store The largest in Peking, carrying a large collection of literature and technical and scientific books, as well as art books and posters on the second floor.

Liu Li Ch'ang

This narrow street, synonymous with antiques, is located in the heart of the old city of Peking, about a mile southwest of the Gate of Heavenly Peace. It is a cross street of Hsin Hua Road South, set in the middle of small lanes, old housing compounds (*hu-tungs*), and a bustling residential district.

Tour buses or taxis park directly in front of the bookstore on the northeast corner of Liu Li Ch'ang and Hsin Hua roads. The following shops line the east side of Liu Li Ch'ang:

136 Rubbing and Figurine Shop Directly across the parking lot from the bookstore, this shop carries inexpensive but often exquisite Han funerary-tile rubbings, both black and white and in color (US$.60-6.00), as well as reproductions of Han and T'ang

Dynasty funerary figures such as ceramic horses and figurines. (Most items now fall in the range of US$20-150.)

Bookstore A tiny, unnumbered shop featuring old Chinese books, including outsized art books with reproductions.

92 **Scroll and Lantern Shop** This store expanded its inventory considerably in 1978 and now features scrolls of good quality. There is also a woodblock print of the famous flying horse from Kansu, not found in #136. Also lamps, and lampshades to fit any lamp.

89 **Art Supplies shop** Peking's best selection of quality brushes, ink stones, and other art supplies.

80 **Peking Antiquity Shop** Specializing in old porcelains, its stock has been well picked-over by connoisseurs, although it still carries one of the best selections in China. Poking through the jumbled cases at least provides the illusion of discovery.

70 **Peking Antiquity Shop** This is more an "odds and ends" store, but offers curiosities such as old jewelry, leather boxes, and cloisonne.

63 **Scroll shop** Sells both old and new scrolls and paintings. Also has painted fans, books of paintings, and antique clothing and brocades.

60 **Chop store** Prices often mystify first-time shoppers. Although the aesthetic criteria may seem obscure, some stones are simply deemed rarer than others. No sentimentality is lost on their former owners and chops can be re-engraved on request. The store has a glossary of common Western surnames with their equivalents in Chinese characters. Samples of different styles of calligraphy are also available. Stones may also be engraved in combinations of Chinese and Romanized script. It usually requires two days or more to prepare custom-engraved chops.

58 **Contemporary Artists Shop** Contrasted with #63 and #92, this store sells originals and copies of scrolls by famous contemporary artists, including one of China's best known painters, Wu Tso-jen, whose works command about Y15,000 (US$9,000).

Doubling back and crossing to the west side of Liu Li Ch'ang, there are three shops of interest:

20 **Chop and rubbing shop** Features excellent-quality old rubbings and chops. While most chops and some rubbings are out in the display cases, the walls are lined with shelves carrying thousands of old rubbings. The problem is that one must know what one wants (e.g., particular calligraphers, styles of calligraphy, certain historical figures), since the shop staff is reluctant to expend their time in aimless searches. Inkstones and silver cigarette boxes are also sold here.

17   **Porcelain and Pottery shop** Newly opened in 1978, this store is similar to the shop at number 80, but its display cases are less jumbled (in both stores, it's a good idea to explore cupboards and drawers beneath the glass cases). A giant vase about 100 years old in blue and white commanded the highest price for any shopping item ever seen in China: Y40,000 (US$25,000).

19   **Jung Pao-chai** China's foremost workshop and outlet for art reproductions, this store also carries everything from blank cards with peasant paintings on them to inkstones and brushes. Oil paintings (many not for sale) and reproductions line the walls. The shop's most fascinating aspect is what it "hides." Behind the store is a labyrinth of workshops that turn out the reproductions, original paintings, and fine crafts displayed in front. Even if a special trip is required, a visit here is especially recommended.

24   **Bank of China Foreign Currency Exchange Bank** For travelers who have not yet converted their US$25,000 into RMB, this branch of the People's Bank will oblige between the hours of 9-12:30 AM and 2:30-6:30 PM.

31   **Scroll-making shop** Workers here will mount a favorite painting or rubbing on a scroll (costs vary greatly depending on the style and materials chosen). The shop also offers a good selection of reproductions, art supplies, and prints. Be sure not to miss the "back room" behind the curtain to the right of the entrance. Behind the shop are the workshops which turn out its artifacts.

In September 1978, it was reported that Liu Li Ch'ang was to be reconstructed. The project called for a "facelift" of the 2,400-ft.-long street, including a decorated entrance and exit. Temples on the street will be converted into museums displaying the history of the area. Whether this will enhance the old-time charm of the area or cover it with modern plaster as happened with the shop at #19 remains to be seen.

The famous Weiwei

Morning exercises along Shanghai's Bund

Shanghai is China's most populous city and its largest in area, covering 6,100 sq.km. (2,355 sq.mi.) overall and supporting a population of some 10.8 million. About 5.47 million people live in the congested urban core, which covers an area of 140 sq.km. (54 sq.mi.).

Shanghai is one of three large cities administered directly by the central government (Tientsin and Peking are the other two). Its political importance is underscored by the traditionally high proportion of its citizens in chief government and Party posts in Peking. It is divided into 10 districts, which are in turn divided into 80 neighborhood units.

Shanghai is the center of China's trade and industry. Almost half of the country's entire internal and external commerce passes through the city, conveyed by ocean vessels, river craft, airplanes, and railroads. Situated on the Whangpoo River, it lies 12 miles upstream from the mighty Yangtse River. The Yangtse in turn links Shanghai to the Pacific Ocean on the east and to the interior cities of Nanking, Wuhan, and Chengtu. Shanghai is served by four airports, two of which are civil. Hung Chiao Airport is the principal link for international and domestic travel. The main railway station, with its huge freight yards, is in the north-central section of the city.

Shanghai has the most Western European look of any Chinese city. Its urban and industrial growth occurred while under the domination of Western powers. The famous Bund—Shanghai's bustling boulevard along the west bank of the Whangpoo—presents an impressive skyline of tall buildings. Once hotels, clubs, banks, and offices for foreigners, they now house municipal offices, branches of PRC foreign trade corporations, a customs house, and two hotels.

South and west of the downtown area the architecture is more typically Chinese, with low-lying, close-quartered buildings, small shops, and busy markets. The architecture of the north section of the city still bears evidence of the former

SHANGHAI

up from the sea

Pinyin Spelling:
Shanghai
("shahng-high")

Japanese concession. Along much of the waterfront in the outlying areas are sizable industrial districts, with many of the newer developments surrounded by workers' apartment blocks. The newest section of Shanghai is in its southwest corner. Here, an impressive indoor stadium has been built along with several high-rise apartment buildings.

The climate of Shanghai is temperate, with hot and humid summers (usually with considerable rain), and winters that can be chilly and grey. Spring and autumn are the most comfortable seasons, with pleasant temperatures and infrequent precipitation.

Shanghai in History

Compared to most other major cities of China, Shanghai's history has been short and, until the last century, relatively uneventful. In the 11th century, it was a fishing village built atop some isolated mud flats. During the 17th and 18th centuries, with the development of silk and cotton production in the surrounding areas, it became more of a trading center. By the early 1800s, it was a flourishing domestic port of some 50,000 people.

Significant growth did not occur until the arrival of Europeans in the mid-19th century. In 1842, near the end of the Opium War, Shanghai's garrison surrendered to the British fleet. From that point until 1949 the city developed largely as an enclave for Western commercial interests in China. Lying off the sea and just upstream from the Yangtse—a river that could be navigated several hundred miles into the interior on oceangoing vessels—Shanghai provided a gateway to a vast internal market. Each of the major foreign powers claimed a section of the city. Residents of these infamous "international concessions" were exempt from the laws of China, and Chinese were subjected to the added humiliation of being barred from free access to portions of their own territory. Shanghai soon surpassed Kwangchow as China's most important foreign trade center. Numerous traders and speculators—French, US, and Japanese—soon joined the British. By 1936, the Western population of Shanghai had reached 60,000.

Shanghai in the Revolution While Western merchants prospered and Shanghai's export-oriented industry and commerce flourished, the city spawned vast urban slums. Gradually, these conditions prompted growing discontent, strikes, and revolts against foreign rule and influence. On July 1, 1921, the Chinese Communist Party was founded in Shanghai. In 1925, the Party helped carry out the demonstrations and strikes known as the May 30th Movement. A year later, workers organized an armed uprising, but it was bloodily suppressed by Chiang Kai-shek's Nationalist troops in 1927. During

the 1930s, Shanghai was relatively quiet as the revolutionary movement changed its focus to the countryside. By the 1940s, it had earned
the reputation as an "adventurer's paradise." Under its glittering surface festered opium dens, brothels, crime syndicates, and rampant
corruption. During World War II, the city was occupied by the Japanese. In May 1949, following a brief revival of Nationalist rule, the
Red Army triumphantly entered the city.

Economy and Culture

The Chinese are quick to point out that since 1949 Shanghai has shed
its identity as a center of consumption. No longer a drain on the national economy, it is now one of its chief sources of production. Before
1949, Shanghai's economy was fueled largely by commerce, with
some light industry and textiles. Today, it supports more than 8,000
factories. Industrial output in 1977 was reported to be 19.2 times
greater than that of 1949 and the city's share of heavy industry in the
gross national product rose from 13.6% to over 53%. Shanghai now
produces significant quantities of iron and steel (some 1,000 types of
specialty steel for 20,000 different products), heavy machinery,
chemicals, electrical equipment, motor vehicles, ships (up to 10,000
tons), tires, paper, and glassware. Petrochemical plants and oil refineries line the Whangpoo River. In the first half of 1977, Shanghai han-

Workers check quality of satin bedding cover, Shanghai.

213

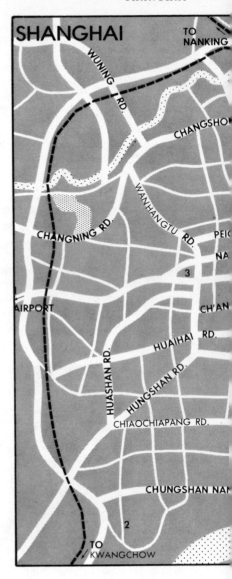

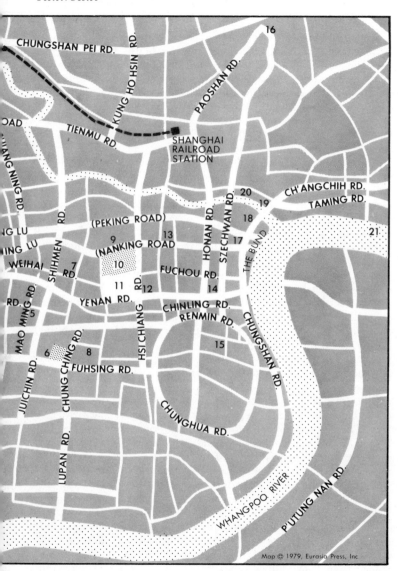

CHUNGSHAN PEI RD.

KUNG HO HSIN RD.

PAOSHAN RD.

16

TIENMU RD.

OAD

ANG NING RD.

SHANGHAI
RAILROAD
STATION

20

19

CH'ANGCHIH RD.

TAMING RD.

NG LU

NING LU

SHIHMEN RD.

(PEKING ROAD)

9

(NANKING ROAD

13

HONAN RD.

SZECHWAN RD.

18

17

THE BUND

21

WEIHAI

7 RD.

10

FUCHOU RD.

11

12

HSI CHIANG RD.

14

MAO MING RD.

RD.

5

YENAN RD.

CHINLING RD.

RENMIN RD.

CHUNGSHAN RD.

6

8

CHUNG CHING RD.

FUHSING RD.

15

JUICHIN RD.

LUPAN RD.

CHUNGHUA RD.

WHANGPOO RIVER

PUTUNG NAN RD.

Map © 1979, Eurasia Press, Inc.

dled 34% of the country's seagoing freight. The port has recently been expanded and is now capable of handling containerized cargo. Since 1973, 16 new or reconstructed deep-water berths for 10,000-ton freighters have been added to bring the port's total number of berths to 52. Six new docks and oil storage tanks have also been constructed.

About 2.5 million people are employed in the industrial sector, earning an average monthly wage of about Y65 (US $38.25), which includes the pay raise given to 60% of China's workforce in late 1977. Family income averages Y100-150 (US $58-88) per month, of which about 5% is taken by rent and 8-15% by food.

Improvements in living standards include new housing projects that have increased residential floorspace by 15 million sq. m. (18 million sq. yd.). There are two elevated railways with a subway nearing completion (the harbor tunnels have already been set in place). Shanghai's inhabitants own 1.1 million bicycles—a figure second only to Peking's.

Although agriculture plays a less prominent role in Shanghai's economy, output from surrounding farmlands meets the municipality's requirements for vegetables and cooking oil and has made it nearly self-sufficient in total food needs. Some 360,000 hectares (889,560 acres) are cultivated, yielding four times the output of the early 1950s. Suburbs of Shanghai boast 198 communes, producing crops such as rice, wheat, barley, cotton, vegetables, grain, poultry, livestock, and fish. The region now supports three grain crops each year. It is a model area for farm mechanization, with 90% of the land now under mechanized ploughing and 98% irrigated by electric pumps.

Shanghai also considers itself the leading cultural and educational center of China and in this regard carries on a friendly rivalry with Peking. The city supports 16 professional performing arts troupes, including several outstanding ballet and opera companies, symphonies, puppet troupes, acrobats, and a circus. There are four film studios. Its reputation as a literary center has been enhanced by famous writers such as Lu Hsun, whose powerful accounts of misery and corruption in Shanghai during the 1930s are now regarded as classics of modern Chinese fiction.

Shanghai has 23 institutions of higher learning. Primary and secondary education is now universal, with some 5,300 schools operating at various levels. Futan and Chiaotung universities are among Shanghai's leading higher institutions. The city pioneered in the creation of part-time schools at factories where workers are trained in technical skills. At the Shanghai Science and Technical Exchange, industrial workers from different sectors meet to exchange scientific and technical information (as of late 1977, it had 1,500 members

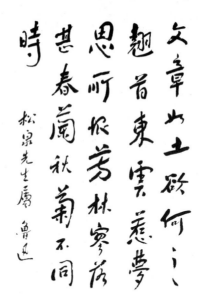

A poem by Lu Hsun in his calligraphy

working in 22 teams). Shanghai is also important for medical training. The city now maintains 380 hospitals staffed by some 80,000 medical personnel. A world-famous team of doctors at the Number 6 Hospital specializes in the reattachment of severed limbs. Shanghai also has a teaching hospital for foreign doctors seeking to learn acupuncture.

HIGHLIGHTS FOR TRAVELERS

While Shanghai is one of the most fascinating cities in the world, it is not particularly endowed with historical attractions—there are no great architectural landmarks or archeological sites. Rather, Shanghai has become a place where visitors may vividly come to grips with the ways in which China functions today. Shanghai's new housing projects for workers offer insight into how China is organized politically and socially at the neighborhood level; factories demonstrate the role of management teams. The local agricultural communes have achieved impressive levels of diversity (and prosperity).

People's Square and People's Park Occupying an area of about 1 sq. mi. in the heart of the city are the People's Square and the adjoining People's Park. The area was originally laid out in 1861 by a foreigner who traced a large oval on horseback with a sword and then bought up everything within it (including farmland and buildings) to build a park and a race course. The racetrack has now been replaced by a pleasant park with lawns, ponds, and tree-shaded walkways. The

217

large, 35-hectare (86-acre) square to the south is used for celebrations, processions, and political rallies. An interesting historical museum is located within the park grounds. It houses ceramic figures, bronzes, jade objects, and some tortoise plastrons (in ancient times, heat was applied to the shells, producing cracks that were used to divine the future).

Fu Hsing Park This 8.77-hectare (21.7-acre) park, located in the south-central section of the city, was built in 1909. It is notable for its massive trees with foliage so dense that the hot summer sun hardly penetrates, and for a small zoo (Shanghai's main zoo is in Hsi Chao Park). The park offers a convenient airing for residents of the nearby Chin Chiang Hotel. It is often filled with older people playing Chinese chess and minding the grandchildren. Nearby is the former residence of Sun Yat-sen. It is maintained as a small museum.

Hsi Chiao (Western Suburbs) Park Although it is rarely part of the tourist's formal itinerary, this park is delightful to explore on one's own (if there is a half-day's free time). As its name implies, it is located on the western edge of the city and is near Hung Chiao Airport. The park contains a number of small lakes (e.g., Swan Lake), small pavilions, a children's playground, an open-air theater, and a skating rink. The Shanghai Zoo is also located here, boasting 400 species of animals living in as natural an environment as possible.

Hung Kou (Rainbow's End) Public Park Lu Hsun (1881-1936), one of China's most famous modern writers, used to walk through this park, located in the northeastern section of the city. His grave is in the park, marked by a steel statue erected in 1961. In the garden surrounding the grave are two trees: one planted by Madame Lu, the other by Chou En-lai. The calligraphy at the site is by Mao Tse-tung. A Lu Hsun Museum contains photographs, letters, manuscripts, furniture, and other memorabilia.

Shanghai Museum of Art and History Less well known than the Municipal Museum (perhaps because it is less accessible), this museum houses the best art works in Shanghai, if not in all of central China. The museum's third floor features paintings from the Sung and T'ang dynasties, tomb paintings, and two warriors and a horse excavated at Sian (many of the paintings are reproductions; signs indicating that it is forbidden to take pictures of a particular object serve as a partial guide). The second floor features a ceramics exhibition, tracing Chinese craftsmanship from the Neolithic period through to the present. Especially noteworthy are the Ming blue and whites,. On the first floor are bronze artifacts including a huge *ting* (three-legged cauldron) and a rich collection of ritual vessels, tools, and mirrors. Other exhibits rotate. Hours are 8:30 AM-Noon and 1:00 PM to 5:00

In a Shanghai park

PM. Admission is 10 *fen*. The third floor has a newly opened store selling reproductions.

Lung Hua Temple District This scenic district in the southwestern suburbs of Shanghai is renowned for its peach blossoms, pagoda, and temple. The seven-tiered Lung Hua Pagoda was first built in 247 AD and reconstructed during the Sung Dynasty. The pagoda was a popular site for foreigners during the first half of this century. The source of fascination was its slight tilt. It was fully restored in 1954, with small bronze bells hung from its numerous eaves. The temple features a 10-ft. statue of a laughing Buddha and others of Buddha's disciples. A neighboring palace features a 3,300-lb. bronze clock built in 1382.

Garden of the Mandarin Yu (Yu Yuan) The old section of Shanghai, which is just south of the central shopping and business district, is demarcated on the map by the ring road. It used to have an unsavory reputation among foreigners living in Shanghai, since only Chinese could wander through in safety. These days it is perfectly safe, although the visitor is likely to be followed at a discreet distance by curious school children, who find great humor in visitors' frequent turns into blind alleys.

It was here that a city official named Yu built a garden in the late 16th century (Ming Dynasty). A small lake has a zig-zag bridge, and the elaborate garden features 15 teahouses, hills, rock gardens, and terraces. A huge stone dragon decorates the wall. This site was the headquarters of the Small Sword Society, which led an uprising in 1853 against the foreign presence in Shanghai. The park opens at 8 AM and entry is 10 *fen*.

Workers Cultural Palace Pre-1949 guide books wistfully refer to the Ta Shih Chieh (Great World) entertainment center, which once comprised ten theaters, a circus, and other forms of amusement. Today, the site is occupied by the Workers Cultural Palace. It is closed to foreigners except during the yearly commemoration of Chairman Mao's "Talks on Art and Literature at the Yenan Forum," when all theaters in Shanghai burst forth with plays, operas, ballets, dance dramas, and other forms of entertainment for the people.

Shanghai Industrial Exhibition This large exhibition hall is often included on the visitor's itinerary. Built by the Soviets in the early 1950s, it was formerly called the Palace of Sino-Soviet Friendship. Over 5,000 industrial and consumer products are on display, from mechanical rice harvesters to precision grinding machines, from heavy construction equipment to small toys that intone a song usually associated with Disneyland, "It's a Small World Everywhere." Handicrafts and spectacular examples of embroidery are also on display. A small store is usually visited on the way out.

Children's Palace Children between the ages of 7 and 17 who show particular skills in subjects such as dance, music, mechanics, and mathematics have an opportunity to receive part-time specialized training at "children's palaces." These schools have excellent facilities, with instruction often provided by leading professional artists. There are 11 such palaces in Shanghai. The largest, called the Shanghai Municipal Children's Palace, is on Yenan Road near the Industrial Exhibition. It is also the city's first such institution, converted in 1949 from a mansion that belonged to a foreign businessman. The concept (with roots in the Soviet Union) was promoted in China by Soong Ching-ling, Sun Yat-sen's widow, who has held honorific positions in the government since 1949.

Workers' New Residential Areas Eleven new housing districts on the outskirts of Shanghai are readily identified on Chinese maps. Visitors are usually taken to one of three. Such visits are important facets of any visit to China since they serve to demonstrate the impact of political, social, and economic changes on the lives of ordinary citizens.

Most of these areas were built around large factory sites on the outskirts of the city so as to alleviate crowding in central Shanghai and to avoid putting additional strains on the transportation system for commuters. Politically, these units operate at the "neighborhood" level of Shanghai's administration, with each local unit's committee exercising authority over the building of schools, shops, and nurseries, as well as recreation and medical services.

The Chao Yang residential area, Shanghai's first, was built in 1951. It has been expanded several times and now occupies some 200 hectares (494 acres). Housing consists mainly of 2- to 5-story apartment buildings. In 1977, Chao Yang had 72,000 residents distributed among 17,800 households. The area has 8 middle schools, 9 elemen-

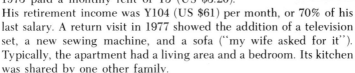

tary schools, 7 kindergartens, and 8 nurseries. There are 2 hospitals and 12 cooperative public health stations. Other amenities include a cinema, park, bookstore, shopping center, post office, public baths, and a department store.

Visitors are usually taken to see a worker's apartment. A retired worker (aged 60) visited in 1973 paid a monthly rent of Y5 (US $3.20). His retirement income was Y104 (US $61) per month, or 70% of his last salary. A return visit in 1977 showed the addition of a television set, a new sewing machine, and a sofa ("my wife asked for it"). Typically, the apartment had a living area and a bedroom. Its kitchen was shared by one other family.

Futan University Educational policies implemented after Mao's death and the demise of the "gang of four" have included the first administration of university entrance examinations since the Cultural Revolution (1966). In 1978, broad reforms were still taking place. Futan University, often identified with "radical" educational policies in the past, was expected to undergo dramatic changes as a result of these new policies.

The university was founded in 1905 and now has 14 departments, including foreign languages, international politics, history, chemistry, physics, mathematics, genetics, and atomic energy. In early 1977, it had 4,100 students and a teaching staff of 2,000. Overall, about two-thirds of the students specialized in the sciences, the remainder in the arts and humanities.

Factories Factories included on the visitor's itinerary are frequently those producing electrical turbines, buses, diesel engines, and toys. Shanghai Machine Tool Plant No. 1 is among the most famous units in China, having been designated as a model factory by Chairman Mao himself in the 1960s. Its output typifies the progress China has been making in building automated and semi-automated precision tools. The plant employs 6,000 workers who earn an average of Y68 (US$40) per month, with the highest worker's wage set at Y124 and the lowest, Y42. Technical and administrative personnel receive up to Y250 (US$147) per month. In addition, all employees receive subsidies for health care, commuting, and other items.

Of special pride to the Machine Tools Factory are its three schools for training technicians from among the workers. The system developed here is regarded as a national model. Workers who reach a certain level of skill and political status may enroll in these schools. Afterwards, they are often transferred to factories in different parts of China so as to pass on their skills in regions where they are most needed.

221

🀫 WALKING TOURS

Shanghai's outgoing residents love to take long walks, especially along the riverfront. For those up on their PRC geography, a simple guideline for getting around is to remember that the east-west streets in the center of town are named after Chinese cities (e.g., Nanking, Peking); north-south streets are named after provinces. The walks that follow originate at the Peace Hotel.

The Bund (30 minutes or more) It may seem unnecessary to note that a street has two sides; yet, Chung Shan Road—the name now given to the Bund—acts much as a boundary between two separate worlds. On the eastern side is the river, fronted by a long, narrow park. Here, Shanghai residents relax, walk along the river, perform *t'ai chi ch'uan* (in the early mornings), and hold hands and whisper quietly (in the evenings). The western side is all business. People hurry along, darting in and out of the office buildings that line the road.

Proceeding left from the Peace Hotel along Chung Shan Road, one passes buildings that formerly housed Japanese and US banks, now the office of branches of China's foreign trade corporations. As you cross Peking Road, still heading north, a low wall marks the grounds of the Friendship Store and the Seamen's Club (not open to visitors). This was formerly the compound of the British Consulate. The Friendship Store, once occupying three buildings, has been consolidated to make way for new construction.

Just before Soochow Creek and the Garden Bridge is a small park favored for morning exercises and evening gossip. After walking to the middle of the bridge (for a view of the river traffic), return (walking south) along the western side of the street. Just by the edge of Soochow Creek is a lovely park (entrance fee, 10 *fen*) with rock gardens, comfortable benches, small flower beds, and shade trees. Along the river is a concrete wall—perfect for reclining, taking pictures, and watching the changing river scenery. Follow the river bank south to the old weather station at Yenan Road; the guy wires formerly used for hoisting different colored flags to indicate changes in the weather are still there. Cross the street and return northward.

There is another seamen's club at the corner of Kwangtung Road, just before the famous Customs House, with its bell tower that used to chime out "The East Is Red." At the northern corner of Foochow Road, two bronze lions still stand astride an immense doorway to the old headquarters of the Hong Kong and Shanghai Banking Corporation. The building has been renovated and its use radically transformed to house the municipal headquarters of Shanghai. The Peace Hotel is two short blocks up the street.

The Old Chinese City (2 hours or more) South along the Bund past Yenan Road lies a part of the city with a totally different look. The colonnaded buildings give way to block offices and low-slung dwellings, and the orderliness of the Bund gives way to more typical waterfront disorder, with its ware-houses and small cobblestone streets.

After Yenan Road the first main street is Chinling Lu, followed by Ren Min Road. Continue two more blocks until reaching Fuyu Lu, and turn right (west) into Shanghai's old Chinese quarter. This street first crosses Ren Min Road (which is circular) and then, a short block later, Tan Feng Lu. It veers slightly right and then crosses An Jen Chieh. Here is the Yu Garden, marked by a white wall with temple roofs protruding above it. For the entrance, continue along Fuyu Lu (i.e., westward) until just past the wall; there is a covered bazaar on the left. Walk through these colorful stores, turning left again at the end of a short block. Here is the pond and the old quarter's main entrance.

One can either continue exploring the area (the many small lanes at odd angles make it easy to lose one's way) or retrace the same route back. Alternatively, continue one block further west to Szechwan (also spelled Ssu Ch'uan) Road and turn right (north). This street crosses Ren Min Road again, passes by the Shanghai Museum (leave enough time!) and then leads directly to Nanking Road where, turning right, the Peace Hotel is only one block away.

Shanghai skyline

223

HOTEL ACCOMMODATIONS

Shanghai's hotels were originally built by Westerners in the 1930s and still recall the indulgences of that era. Although lacking in modern amenities, they are still among the most comfortable hotels in China. They maintain hand-operated elevators, rooftop dining rooms, and parquet floors. Their service is without parallel in China. Businessmen usually stay at the Peace Hotel, located directly on the waterfront and near the branch offices of the foreign trade corporations. Tourists and general delegations are also put up at the International Hotel, Shanghai Mansions or the Chin Chiang, outside the central district. Another hotel recently opened for tourists is the Jin Kiang, in the southwest section of the city.

Peace Hotel Despite a faded facade, worn carpets, and a rather gloomy lobby, the Peace Hotel (formerly the Cathay Hotel Mansions) is Shanghai's most popular hostelry for foreign guests. It is located at 20 Nan Jing Lu (telephone: 211244), just at the corner of Chung Shan Road, which lines the Whangpoo River.

Rates in the 14-story, 180-room hotel range from Y28 (US$16.50) for a basic twin to Y48 (US$28.24) for a suite. In winter there is a 15% surcharge for heat. Rooms are comfortable. The dining room, which occupies the eighth floor of the hotel and commands a beautiful view of the Whangpoo River, boasts a menu that includes Chinese cuisine from five regions. Western dishes feature T-bone steaks and the best soufflés and creampuffs in China.

Since Shanghai is a terminus for trans-Pacific telephone lines, international communications links are excellent. The hotel, like all others in Shanghai, has telephone, cable, and post office facilities on the premises.

Unlike taxis in Peking and Kwangchow, Shanghai's taxis do not line up at the major hotels, but they are easily summoned with the help of the main service desk in the lobby of the hotel.

International Hotel The International (formerly the Park Hotel) is an 18-story structure that overlooks People's Park. It is situated at 170 Nanking Road (telephone: 291010). Rates are among the cheapest in Shanghai, ranging from Y22 (US$13.00) to Y38 (US$23.35). Like other hotels in the city, the restaurant (on the 12th floor) offers a good view of the surroundings and serves both Chinese and Western food. The hotel has the advantage of being located near the No. 1 Department Store—just two blocks east of the front door.

Shanghai Mansions Foreign visitors to Shanghai are regularly taken to Shanghai Mansions at 20 North Soochow Road (telephone: 244186) for its "bird's-eye view" of the city. Its ordinary guest rooms are a bit more spartan than those of its downtown counterparts, although its suites are nothing short of spectacular. Called the Broadway Mansions before 1949, it was then mainly a residential hotel used by the British. Some of the rooms still have ice boxes, grand pianos, and private balconies. Suites cost Y38 (US$23.35), with other rooms priced accordingly.

The main restaurant is on the third floor, with the top floor reserved for banquets. Some of the service staff have been with the hotel since the 1940s, and the kitchen turns out everything from bird's nest soup to lemon meringue pie.

The hotel's main asset—its picturesque location (it sits on the northern bank of Soochow Creek at the confluence of the Whangpoo)—becomes a drawback in the evening. The sonorous horns of river barges go on all night, posing a constant challenge to sleep (one of the charges against the disgraced Chiang Ch'ing was that she ordered all river traffic to cease when she slept in the city).

Chin Chiang Hotel What this hotel lacks in convenience of location it more than makes up for in elegance. Formerly a mansion used by the French as an apartment hotel, it boasts leaded-glass windows, a parquet-floored dining room, a billiards table, and central air-conditioning. In an anachronistic touch, the elevator operators wear white gloves. The Chin Chiang is situated in a tree-lined residential neighborhood with a wide variety of department stores (along Huaihai Road—a half block to the left of the hotel entrance), shops, and parks. The site of the founding of the Chinese Communist Party is a few blocks away, off Chung Ching Road. A walk to the central part of the town (say, the Peace Hotel) will take about 45 minutes; public buses make the trip in about ten minutes.

The Chin Chiang is located at 189 Chang Tung Road, near Huaihai Road, in the west-central section of Shanghai. Rooms here are in the Y30 (US$17.64) range. Communication facilities include several telex machines, located in the adjacent post office annex. On a visit in October 1978, several new features were noted: there are now three retail shops in the hotel (including one sandwiched in between the front steps) and a "café" has been added with eight tables, serving wines, spirits, and light snacks (5 PM to 12 PM). The modern-style building across the courtyard was where President Nixon and Premier Chou En-lai concluded the Shanghai Communiqué on February 28, 1972.

The restaurant is on the 11th floor, at the site of the former ballroom. It serves excellent Western and Chinese food and the staff will attempt special dishes on request. Service has remained excellent, despite a more harried dining room staff (specialty in October is Soochow crabs, Y4 a pair for this delicacy).

SHANGHAI CUISINE

Two characteristics dominate Shanghai's cuisine: elegant presentation and an abundance of seafood. Particularly at banquets, great attention is paid to making even the most mundane dishes appear colorful and appetizing. Carrots, turnips, beancurd, and other foods are fastidiously shaped to resemble miniature animals and flowers. Among the most famous seafood dishes is steamed freshwater crab (in season from October through December). Other items include eel (prepared in a heavy garlic sauce) and sweet-and-sour river fish. "Beggars' chicken" (small chunks cooked slowly in caked mud) is said to have originated in this area.

Unlike Peking and Kwangchow, however, Shanghai has few large restaurants that cater to foreigners. Smaller restaurants throughout the city and outdoor food stalls gladly welcome foreign visitors, but the best meals are usually found at the hotels. For a pleasant experience, try the **Hung Fang** ("Red House") **Restaurant**, situated one block west of the Chin Chiang Hotel (corner of Changlo and Shensi Roads). Here one can dine on delicious oysters (the garlic sauce is delicately spiced), fish meuniere (Y3.50), tournedos (Y5.00), and Grand Marnier Soufflé! Perhaps the ultimate gastronomic experience in Shanghai is to rent the Yu Yuan (Garden of the Mandarin Yu) for an evening. Up to 25 guests can be accommodated but only as a private party and at a minimum of about Y40 per person. Chefs who prefer not to work in hotels are hired, and a special feast is prepared. It is not possible to arrange such an affair on the general tourist itinerary; businessmen and others must make arrangements well in advance through their local hosts. There is a Moslem restaurant (vegetarian) on Foochow Street and a Szechwan restaurant on An Tang Lu. The Red House, named for its brightly painted exterior, specializes in French cuisine and features a good baked Alaska; it is located off Huai-hai Rd. Shanghai residents have a sweet tooth and among the places they favor is the Shanghai Cakes and Pastries Store on 805 Nanking Road (one block from the Peace Hotel), which prepares Western-style baked goods.

SHOPPING

If there is one place where China's new "consumerism" is evident, it is Shanghai. With more than 17,000 shops, (including 140 offering 24-hour service), Shanghai is by far China's most consumer-oriented city. The main shopping street, Nanking Road, has become so crowded that it is now virtually impassable by cars. Billboards, once dominated by political slogans, now more commonly advertise new products or the latest movies—including (in October 1978) a film starring Gregory Peck.

The Friendship Store has been transformed from a rambling multi-building affair to an efficient three-storied building. Located on the north end of the "Bund," just before the bridge over Soochow Creek, the Friendship Store's hours are 9 AM to 9 PM. One can also buy soft drinks, change money, and order taxis there. Its selection of high-quality silks and clothing make it well worth a visit. A curios and antiques shop has recently been added to the Friendship Store; a two-story building adjacent to the regular store, it carries some 25,300 different curios (what some Americans might call "chachkas"), antiques, reproductions, and ancient art works. Objects for sale include pearls and gems, ivory and jade carvings, imitation bronzes, redwood screens, traditional Chinese stationery, writing brushes, ink tablets, plates, boxes, and vases. There are also woodblock prints of famous calligraphy and painting. Some good examples are reproductions of the remarkable horses by the famous painter Li Lung-mian of the Sung Dynasty; bamboos by Ni Yun-lin of the Yuan Dynasty, mynahs and ladies by Tang Yin of the Ming Dynasty, bamboos and orchids by Cheng Pan-chiao; flowers, birds, and figurines of Jen Po-nien of the Ch'ing Dynasty; and horses by Hsu Pei-hung and shrimps, flowers, and birds by Chi Pai-shih, both contemprary artists. Other articles on sale include embroidery and stone, wood, and bamboo carvings. Shoppers should take care to note the many non-antique items on display next to the 100-year-old items (all antiques are marked with a wax seal). Prices are relatively high.

In the alleyways immediately south of Nanking Road are vegetable and meat markets, as well as several tiny restaurants that serve items such as Shanghai duck (juicier than its northern neighbor) and dumplings.

Shanghai's major section for shoppers is Nanking Road. Among its variety of shops, the visitor will find a store devoted solely to paper cuts (across the street from the department store), one specializing in *wu shu* (martial arts) paraphernalia, and a large bookstore.

The Number One Department Store, at the corner of Nanking and Hsi Tang roads, near People's Park, is the largest in all of China, with merchandise arranged over four floors. It is open from 8 AM until 9 PM, and includes a special section that stays open all night. The top floor has radios, gift items, and stationery. The middle two floors specialize in clothing, and the street floor has items ranging from hand luggage (the canvas bags with a picture of Shanghai stenciled on the side are a popular souvenir) to tea (prized Hangchow chrysanthemum tea is available here in bulk). Since the removal of the "gang of four" there has been a noticeable increase in consumer-oriented production in China. Featured items for Chinese now include bicycles, sewing machines, wrist watches, cameras, TV sets, cosmetics, and colorful textiles.

About 150,000 customers a day pass through the store, which employs a staff of 1,200. The manager, who earns about $500 a year, must submit his annual plans to the Ministry of Commerce. Prices are centrally fixed and some products, such as TV sets, are subsidized. Annual sales amount to Y134 million (US$78.8 million), of which 2% is profit.

Walking on Nanking Road from the Peace Hotel west towards the People's Park, the following stores are also notable:

66 **The Shanghai Branch of China International Travel Service** (practically adjacent to the Peace Hotel)

98 **Domestic and imported toy shop**

118 **Music Store:** probably Shanghai's best, including Chinese and western instruments.

156 **Sporting goods shop**

180 **Photographic supplies** Japanese photopaper was available here as of late 1978.

202 **Luggage store** Perhaps to show how up-to-date it is, there is a display sign—"America"—in the window. Chinese luggage is quite serviceable and inexpensive.

259 **Martial arts supplies store** Complete range of costumes, dummy swords, and similar paraphernalia.

309 **Signs and banners store** Recently renovated, this shop lacks its earlier "rummaging" spirit, but will still appeal to those interested in banners, Chinese flags, and Chinese home decorative arts.

311 **Portrait photographers** Worth mentioning because while these stores are common in all Chinese cities, those in Shanghai have samples in the window which are more personal, where people smile more, and where some subjects appear in lavish wedding apparel.

351 Hsin Hua Bookstore Shanghai's largest bookstore and a bee-hive of activity. Readers buy books as well as rent them.

360 Electrical appliance store.

390 Tea store Fine teas from the region, including Hangchow's Lung Cha ("dragon tea").

422 Arts store This shop features a wide selection of prints and scrolls by famous artists. Greater variety than Shanghai's Friendship Store or the No. 1 Department Store.

490 Cutlery store The Chinese make excellent knives and scissors, although they are perhaps not as design conscious as the Germans or French.

522 Artificial flowers store.

541 Stationery Store.

550 Ceramics store Both everyday service and better quality porcelains.

592 Yardage store Nanking Road's most "fashionable" place for silks, cottons, and some ready-made garments.

635 Department store There are a number of department stores along Nanking Road, including another one at 690. This one had an eye-catching display of Chinese sewing machines, which enjoy an excellent reputation and are sold all over Asia.

660 Ticket office For booking theaters; tickets range from 20 to 40 *fen* depending upon the theater and the section chosen.

694 Antique store This new antique store opened in 1978 (hours: 9 AM to 7 PM). The store is situated in a shopping district west of the People's Park. Telephone: 530975 or 538092.

751 Papercuts store Papercuts now make up a smaller portion of this store's ware, but there are some extremely intricate ones (Y20). Also featured are some scrolls, wall mountings, and an opportunity to have your photograph transferred onto an enameled wall hanging (Y11).

800 Number One Department Store Lift is for foreigners only; it is best to start on the fourth floor (with arts and crafts) and work downwards.

SHAOSHAN

blossoming mountain

Pinyin Spelling:
Shaoshan
("shao-shahn")

Shaoshan is located 131 km. (78 mi.) southwest of Changsha. It is accessible by motor coach (three hours) and train (since April 1978). The village is in Hsiangtan County and is so small it does not appear on many large-scale maps of China. Its importance in the history of the Communist movement, however, far surpasses its physical dimensions, as it is the birthplace of Mao Tse-tung.

The road to Shaoshan is well-paved and passes through some of the most verdant countryside in China. The distinctive styles of Hunan dress (the unique peasant hats, for example), carts, and architecture quickly become apparent.

Shaoshan itself is in a narrow valley surrounded by hills, the highest of which is the site of a Taoist hermitage. The main attractions, of course, are the birthplace of Mao Tse-tung and the Mao Tse-tung Museum. For overnight visitors, a walk through the surrounding countryside and the small village is recommended.

Mao Tse-tung Birthplace The house where Mao Tse-tung was born in 1893 will surprise many by its relatively large size. It contains three bedrooms (the third for Mao's brother, killed during the civil war), a spare guest room, rice granary, separate kitchen, adjoining bathroom, stable area, and sheds for cows, tools, and wood. Just in front of the house is a small pond with lotus flowers where Mao used to swim as a small boy. Nearby are the rice fields where he worked. (Everything is duly noted by signs in Chinese and English.)

Mao Tse-tung Museum Opened in 1967, the museum focuses on Mao's early childhood and his revolutionary activities spanning the three decades between 1920 and 1950. The museum's circumspect planners built two wings that exactly duplicate each other, picture for picture, so as to better accommodate the large crowds of visitors (foreign and Chinese).

Schoolchildren visit Mao's birthplace.

 HOTEL ACCOMMODATIONS

Shaoshan Guest House Although Shaoshan can be seen during a day's outing from Changsha, some tours may be housed overnight at this spartan but comfortable hotel. The furniture is simple and the floors are unrelieved concrete and terrazzo. Its two main buildings overlook the town, only minutes away on foot. The main building has a dining room, lecture halls, retail shop, and a ping-pong table—the scene of many friendly matches (or, more commonly, mis-matches) between visitors and their adept Chinese guides. The main sleeping quarters for foreigners are in a separate building to the rear.

Efforts to make the northern steppe agriculturally self-reliant are intensifying.

Shenyang, the capital of Liaoning Province, is a large industrial city with 3 million people. Formerly called "Mukden" (its name in the Manchurian language), it is the communications hub and industrial center of northeast China.

China's Northeast Region (Tung-pei), comprising the three provinces of Liaoning, Kirin, and Heilungkiang, was for centuries little more than a barren steppe sparsely populated by herdsmen. The discovery by Westerners in the 19th century that this part of Manchuria was the repository of vast natural resources brought rapid changes. At the same time, the region became a focal point of foreign contention and rapacity. The Japanese set up a puppet government there in 1932, calling the region "Manchukuo," and launched into large-scale coal mining. At the end of World War II, the Soviets sought unsuccessfully to fill the political and military void left by the defeated Japanese.

Since 1949, the region has been methodically developed, with activities focusing around Shenyang (steel) and Harbin (oil). Liaoning Province is still relatively underpopulated. Nevertheless, Shenyang's growth is underscored by the fact that in 1910 it had only 100,000 people. Today its wide tree-lined streets, tall buildings, and spacious squares lend an appearance more suggestive of the West than many Chinese cities. The city is located 841 km. (522 mi.) northeast of Peking by rail (the express train takes 12 hours; jet flights, about one and a half hours). The best time of year to visit Shenyang is in the summer. Winters are bitterly cold.

Shenyang in History

Although the origins of Shenyang can be traced back some 2,000 years, it did not emerge as a city of note until the 11th century when, under the Yuan Dynasty, it thrived as a trading center for nomads. Among the powerful tribes in the region were the Manchus (the origin of the name is obscure) who began their rise to power by conquering and politically consolidating the northern border lands in the early 17th century. Nurhachi

SHENYANG

north of the river Shen

Pinyin Spelling:
Shenyang
("shen-yahng")

(1559-1626), founder of the Manchu state, began his open war against China's Ming rulers in 1618. By 1625, he controlled enough of the northern region to be able to establish a capital at Shenyang. In 1636, his 14th son and successor, Dorgon, proclaimed the founding of the Ch'ing ("pure") Dynasty from Shenyang. Peking was finally seized in 1644 after a Chinese commander had literally invited the Manchus inside the Great Wall. Mukden remained a secondary capital, however, in part because the rulers did not want to give up the lucrative ginseng trade—the Manchu equivalent of the salt monopolies established under the Ming.

Shenyang played a role in the Boxer Rebellion of 1900 and was the site of a 17-day battle during the Russo-Japanese War of 1902-05. In 1932, the Japanese established military control over Manchuria. They created the independent state of Manchukuo, installing the last Ch'ing Emperor, Henry Pu'yi, as regent (the "Mukden Incident"). The Japanese converted the area into an industrial base, with virtually all resources funneled off to the motherland.

The city was renamed Shenyang in 1949. The PRC government continues to eschew reference to the former names of Manchuria and Mukden.

Economy and Culture

Shenyang, as the largest city in northeastern China, supports a diversified array of heavy industry. Major enterprises include electrical equipment (e.g., high-voltage transformers), machine building, metallurgy, chemicals, textiles, and food processing.

Efforts to make Shenyang agriculturally self-reliant have been stepped-up, and the dry northern terrain now yields soybeans, cotton, tobacco, peanuts, apples, and pears. Afforestation is also a major undertaking; and there are two large nurseries in the area.

The city itself has a home for aged workers, a Workers Cultural Palace, and 12 parks featuring numerous small lakes. Education facilities include the provincial university, several technical institutes, and a large medical institute. Extensive day-care and health-care facilities have been set up adjacent to factories.

The most famous cultural institution in Shenyang is its acrobatic troupe. Such forms of entertainment have been popular in China for centuries (acrobats were depicted in tomb figures as early as the T'ang Dynasty) and are today actively supported by the government. Although most of the major cities have their own troupes, the Shenyang group—which maintains its own school, dormitories, and training facilities—is better known in the West because of its tours (including one to North America in 1973).

▓ HIGHLIGHTS FOR TRAVELERS

The principal incentive for a visit to Shenyang is the chance to see something of China's industrial development. In addition, the local branch of CITS will include a tour of the city's historical points of interest.

The Imperial Palace When the Manchus established their capital in Shenyang in 1625, the first order of business was to build a proper palace. The result was a complex of some 70 buildings, occupying a space of 50,000 sq. m. (59,800 sq. yd.), and replete with lacquered roof tiles. The project was completed in 1637.

After the Manchus moved their capital to Peking, the Shenyang palace was kept up, serving as the second seat of power in the empire. The library (Wen Shu Gallery) once held 35,533 volumes, including a massive history of China completed in 1782.

Today, visitors still file past the stone tablets written in Chinese, Manchurian, Mongolian, Uighur, and Tibetan, informing those who enter that they must dismount from their horses before being admitted. The exhibits include the personal effects of the Ch'ien Lung Emperor (1736-96) and an assortment of bows, arrows, musical instruments, dresses, pottery, porcelain, carvings, and a bell weighing over four tons.

North Tomb (Pei Ling) The tomb bears the remains of Abukai (1592-1643), the founder of the Manchu Dynasty, and his wife. Succeeding Ch'ing emperors came here to pay homage to their ancestors. By the 19th century, however, the tomb had fallen into disrepair. Since 1949, it has been restored and a large park built around it with lakes, pavilions, and a forest of trees. In the style of the Ming emperors, animal statues line the walkway to the tomb and a stele is inscribed with Abukai's calligraphy. There is a hall of ancestors and an inner court with the burial mound lying just beyond.

East Tomb (Tung Ling) Located about 8 km. (5 mi.) east of Shenyang on the banks of the Shen River, this site is the tomb of Nurhachi, the father of Abukai. Nurhachi (who was given the posthumous title of T'ai Tsu—"grand progenitor") was a gifted leader, military commander, and scholar. His tomb is similar to that of his son, but less grand and less often visited. It was completed in 1626, a year after his death.

Liaoning Exhibition Center The Liaoning Exhibition Center, located in the southern section of the city, was built in the late 1950s in Soviet architectural style. With 41,800 sq. m. of display space, it was officially opened to the public in 1960. The exhibit is continually updated with new industrial products turned out in the Shenyang area.

235

HOTEL ACCOMMODATIONS

Shenyang's main hotel, formerly known as the Mukden Railway Hotel, is the Liaoning Guest House. It has high ceilings, wide corridors, and a marble lobby, making it something of a landmark in its own right. During the 1940s, it served as a meeting place for representatives of contending political factions in China's civil war. Among the more tangible legacies of those days are some of the finest slate billiard tables found in China. The hotel, whose rates are Y22 per day, has the standard tourist amenities: bank, post office, and retail shop.

Visitors to Shenyang are also accommodated at Liaoning Mansions, near Peiling Park in the north of the city, and at a secluded but beautifully appointed smaller guest house on the northern outskirts.

LIAONING CUISINE

The cooking of northern China is not as elaborate as in other parts of China, but the region has a famous dish said to have originated with the Mongols: Huo Kuo ("fire pot"). A charcoal brazier is placed on the table and water boiled. While the water is heating, the service workers will prepare a sauce from rice wine, vinegar, chili sauce, sesame oil, shrimp paste, and soy sauce. Plates of raw meat (beef, mutton, chicken, and, perhaps, a surprise or two), sliced razor thin, are placed around the table. Guests then cook their own meat. The pieces are dipped in the sauce before eating. The meats are followed by vegetables and, lastly, noodles. By the end of this sequence, the water has been transformed into a rich, flavorful broth.

SHOPPING

Handicrafts from Shenyang are relatively undistinguished. Fur items are the favored local purchases. Many tours include a visit to a feather products factory. There is an antique store in Taiyan Street, with a rather limited selection. Overseas Chinese prefer to purchase ginseng and antler powders here, both indigenous to the area.

Sheltered by the Taihang Mountains to the west and bordered by the fertile Hopei plain which fans out on its three other sides, Shihchiachuang is a railway junction on the Peking-Kwangchow line, about 150 mi. south of Peking. It has a population of 450,000. The city owes its existence almost entirely to the railway; before its construction in 1905, there was only a village of 500-600 people. The other major industry in the town is cotton milling.

Shihchiachuang is of special interest to Canadian visitors because its hospital is dedicated to the memory of Dr. Norman Bethune, a Canadian surgeon who came to China in the 1930s to assist the Communist cause (the official name of the hospital is the Norman Bethune International Peace Hospital of the People's Liberation Army). Dr. Bethune is still revered in China as a model of selfless sacrifice. His tomb lies in the cemetery just west of the town. Coincidentally, the cemetery is also the site of one of the few historical objects of interest in Shihchiachuang, two bronze lions dating from 1185.

The Shihchiachuang Guest House is located in the southwest corner of the city. A few blocks north is the Tung Fang Hung ("East Is Red") Exhibition Hall, featuring displays of local products.

SHIH CHIA CHUANG

Stonecutters village

Pinyin Spelling: Shijiazhuang ("sher-jah-jooahng")

237

SIAN

western peace

Pinyin spelling: Xi'an
("shee-ahn")

Of all cities on the China itinerary, Sian's history most vividly exemplifies the extraordinary continuity of Chinese civilization. Once the largest city in the world and a paradigm of imperial splendor, Sian served as the capital of 11 dynasties. It was an active link in the major trade routes between China and the commercial enclaves of Central Asia and Europe during the 7th and 8th centuries. Today, Sian is a model example of the PRC government's concerted efforts to create new inland centers of industry to counterbalance the traditional dominance of the large east coast cities.

Sian, now the capital of Shensi Province, is about as far west in China as most travelers get. It is situated at the western end of a roughly equilateral triangle connecting Peking and Shanghai. It lies about 900 km. (559 mi.) southwest of Peking by air; by rail, the trip covers 1,165 km. (724 mi.), consuming 24 hours. The distance to Shanghai is 1,511 km. (938 mi.).

To the north of this city of 1,900,000 people lie the rugged Western Hills, dotted with ancient tombs. The Wei River forms a natural boundary on the north and the entire area lies in a fertile basin suitable for cotton and coarse grain. Architecturally, modern Sian is rather undistinguished, with low buildings and wide streets typical of the PRC's urban restorations. In summer, the heat shimmers off the pavement; in winter, the climate is dry and cold.

Sian in History

Remains of a neolithic village in nearby Pan P'o indicate that the area was inhabited at least 8,000 years ago. Sian was effectively the capital of China as long ago as the 11th century BC with the founding of the Western Chou Dynasty (ca. 1030 BC). It became China's first true capital in 212 BC, presiding over the unified domain of Emperor Ch'in Shih-huang. Then known as Ch'ang An, the city flourished politically, culturally, and commercially. In 129 BC, it was linked by water to other regions of China by means of a canal that fed into the Wei River.

Sian subsequently served as a capital during the Sui and T'ang eras, during which time its area was considerably enlarged. The population then numbered about 1 million people. Its strategic location along Asian trade routes brought frequent contacts with foreigners (evidence of these contacts is provided in tomb figurines that depict bearded horsemen, an anomalous combination in China up to that time). Scattered remains of its palaces, imperial compound, city walls, and tombs of the T'ang emperors are still evident.

Following the demise of the T'ang Dynasty at the start of the 10th century, Sian entered a decline and, despite periods of revival, never regained its prior eminence. With the establishment of the Ming Dynasty (1368), a new palace was added to house the Emperor's son. The Manchus occupied the town during the Ch'ing Dynasty, but its

diminished stature by that point is indicated by the fact that 19th-century Sian was only one-sixth the size of the T'ang Dynasty capital eight centuries before.

Before the advent of modern communication links, Sian remained rather isolated. This condition began to change after 1930 with the completion of a rail spur that linked Sian to Chengchow and cities to the west and north.

In 1936, Chiang Kai-shek visited the nearby hot springs to rest from his campaign against the Communists and warlords. In an event later known as the "Sian Incident," Chiang was kidnapped by a local warlord who sought to compel Chiang to negotiate peace with the Communists and join in a united front against the Japanese. Chou En-lai was dispatched to Sian to negotiate on behalf of the Communisits and, despite Chiang's attempt to escape, a temporary agreement was effected.

The most dramatic changes in Sian have come about since 1949. The city has developed into the textile center of the northwest. Many other new industries (fertilizers, chemicals) have been introduced. Its great wide streets are now paved. New buildings, department stores, sports grounds, and a modern transportation system have contributed to its transformation.

Economy and Culture

When briefing visitors, local officials will often point out that Sian is now a city that "walks on two legs." That is, the industrial and agricultural sectors function in ways that are mutually supportive. Moreover, both account for a roughly equal contribution to the local economy. Traditionally, agriculture had predominated. The area is ideal for growing wheat and cotton, crops which have particularly benefited from mass programs to extend irrigation systems in the area. Corn is also produced, as are various fruits and vegetables.

Industrialization did not come to Sian until the 1950s, but has since taken root dramatically. Local enterprises produce textiles, fertilizers, plastics, boilers, machine tools, and electrical motors, with many products applied to local agricultural use. Sian artisans produce shell and feather paintings and carved lacquerware items. An enamelware factory turns out everything from ash trays to wash basins.

Sian is the site of 11 of Shensi's 15 universities and research institutions, together employing a staff of about 20,000. This region of China has its own theatrical and operatic traditions which continue to thrive. Huhsien, a county west of Sian, has become world-famous for its peasant painters, a tradition begun in the late 1950s. Exhibitions of their work have toured the UK, France, Canada, Australia, and, in 1978, the US.

Figure from "Digging a Well"
by Fan Chih-hua of Huhsien County

▦ HIGHLIGHTS FOR TRAVELERS

The chief interest in Sian is its archeological legacy. There are myriad tombs, temples, ruins, and other sites of interest in the area, although visitors generally have enough time to see but a few.

Ch'in Shih-huang Ti Tomb One of China's significant archeological finds of the 1970s was the thousands of life-size terracotta warriors and horses guarding the main entrance of the tomb of Ch'in Shih-huang Ti (221-207 BC), the first emperor of a unified China and builder of the Great Wall. A huge hangar-like hall is now under construction 20 mi. (32 km.) east of Sian to permanently house and display these objects. The museum is expected to open October 1, 1979 and will extend over 15,000 sq. m. (3.7 acres). The horses and warriors themselves were first discovered by chance in the spring of 1974 by local peasants digging an irrigation well. Officials now estimate that 6,400 figures had been buried in a rectangular pit that covers 14,260 sq. m. (3.5 acres).

Shensi Provincial Museum Housed in a former Confucian temple in the southern district of the city, this museum boasts one of the richest collections of ancient artifacts in all of China. Three main buildings and three annexes have been remodeled twice in the last five years and can accommodate as many as 4,000 separate exhibits. Notable objects include sandstone and granite animal figures, T'ang Dynasty stone friezes, bronzes, neolithic pottery, and jewelry. Detailed captions (in English) provide helpful descriptions of the items.

The museum's centerpiece is its "forest of steles," a collection of 1,095 stone tablets (some carved by emperors) on which ancient texts —including the Confucian classics—were etched, resulting in a magnificent array of classical calligraphy. The museum also houses a replica of an old Buddhist temple.

Bell Tower As Sian has grown and changed contours over the centuries, its Bell Tower, built in the 15th century, has been moved repeatedly so as to always display the time at the center of town. The 69-foot-high structure has a square brick foundation and is surmounted by a two-story wooden tower adorned by gracefully arched roofs. The first floor is now used as a briefing room (it held prisoners during the civil war). In the interest of utility, the original 15th-century iron bell has been replaced by a garish lamp. The second-floor veranda provides an excellent view of the city, including the Drum Tower just one block to the west.

Small Wild Goose Pagoda This 140-foot-high pagoda was first built in 706 AD and soon afterwards destroyed by the ravages of war. It was again damaged during a major 16th-century earthquake. Still bearing its scars, the frail structure was repaired and reopened to

241

*The Big Wild Goose Pagoda,
first built 652-704*

visitors in 1977. A pleasant garden surrounds the pagoda, with a stunning selection of poppies. There are no wild geese in evidence, however, and the origins of the pagoda's name remain obscure.

Big Wild Goose Pagoda Originally built as a Buddhist retreat (7th century), it is said to have been first used to translate Sanskrit Buddhist texts (brought from India) into Chinese. Like many similar structures, it was destroyed and rebuilt several times during the ensuing centuries. The 240-foot, seven-story pagoda that survives dates from 1580.

The pagoda was restored in the early 1950s and today it is a popular place to get an overview of the city and the surrounding countryside. Some idea of the size and importance of the ancient city of Sian may be gained from noting that although the pagoda today stands south of the edge of the city, during T'ang times it was well within the city walls.

Pan P'o Village About 10 km. (6 mi.) east of Sian, on a site overlooking the Chan River, is a neolithic site of the Yang-Shao culture (ca. 6000 BC). It was discovered accidentally in 1953 when the foundations for a factory were being laid. Subsequent digging revealed a village of 45 houses, with remarkably preserved examples of stone-age pottery (bearing playful designs), tools, and animal bones. The objects are displayed in a large exhibition hall at the entrance to the grounds.

The site of the village itself has been protected through the construction of a freestanding building that covers the entire site. The visitor views the excavation from a wooden walkway that produces the uncanny sensation of footsteps echoing through 8,000 years of history. Original foundations are visible, along with reconstructed replicas of the houses.

Sian Hot Springs On a typical morning outing, visitors are driven some 24 km. (15 mi.) to the east of Sian for a quick tour and/or a quick bath, then on to the nearby tomb of Emperor Ch'in Shih-huang, and back to the hotel in time for lunch.

Records reveal that the springs were used by royal families as early as the 8th century BC, when a palace was built on the site. In the 10th century AD, it served as a monastery for the Taoist community, but was later reopened to the general public. The Hot Springs were the site of the Sian Incident. A steep trail leads up to a pavilion overlooking the valley where Chiang Kai-shek was recaptured while trying to escape.

The area has been rebuilt since 1949 as a resort for the general public. The central garden surrounds a large pond with water lillies. There are several tea houses and a series of low-slung buildings equipped with individual baths. Visitors are usually encouraged to "briefly" sample the 40° C (104° F) waters. The place attracts visitors from all over China.

Tumulus of Ch'in Shih-huang Ti The Emperor Ch'in Shih-huang was the founder of the Ch'in Dynasty. Despite evidence of extreme harshness, he is acknowledged in China today for his success in unifying the country, first militarily and then culturally and economically. A consummate pragmatist, he decreed that all carts be made the same width so that they could travel over standardized trails and produce uniform grooves on muddy roadways. Two large stone steles mark the path through the wheat fields to the tomb's summit. Today, the hill is covered with pomegranate trees.

Li Shih-min Tomb In mid-1978, the tomb of Li Shih-min, who became T'ai-tsung (618-907 AD), the second emperor of the T'ang Dynasty, was opened to the public. T'ai-tsung, who reigned from 626 to 649, launched China into one of its greatest eras of political and cultural achievement. Through his patronage, both Taoist and Confucian traditions flourished, while the growth of Buddhism in China was given its greatest impetus—T'ai-tsung himself came out to receive the scholar Hsüan-tsang upon his return from India with texts of the *Mahayana*.

The site, called Chao Ling, is the first imperial tomb to employ the technique of burial on a mountainside rather than in a tumulus raised on flat land. The site extends over a 20,000-hectare area located near Lichuan, some 60 km. northwest of Sian. The tomb itself has been restored as an underground museum, and contains a renowned set of stone tablets that provide a wealth of historical data on the peasant uprisings at the end of the Sui Dynasty (581-618 AD), and the unifying wars during the early T'ang. Also on display are an exquisite collection of painted and silt pottery figurines, murals, and utensils from subsidiary tombs at the site. Early T'ang craftsmen achieved detailed characterization through gesture, movement, facial expressions and costume, and used details such as tracing out eyebrows and moustaches stroke by stroke. Many minority peoples are represented in the pottery figurines. Pottery camels carrying silks give evidence of economic and cultural exchanges between China and other countries during this period.

Walking Tour

Walking around Sian, distances seem even longer than they are, probably because of the width of the streets and the absence of perspective afforded by high-rise buildings. For a short excursion, turn left outside the hotel gate, and left again at the first intersection. A walk along this street will convey a good flavor of urban living in this part of China—a remarkable contrast from Peking, Shanghai, or Kwangchow. After two long blocks, one reaches Tun Wu Road and the People's Park. Turning right, another long block ends at Chiehfang Road, Sian's major north-south boulevard. To the north is the railway station. Turning south, the walker passes through a shopping district. Upon reaching Tung Hsin Road, turn right again. On the right side, one block away, is the hotel.

HOTEL ACCOMMODATIONS

The People's Hotel, built in the late 1950s in leaden Soviet style, is Sian's only hotel for foreigners. It is located in the northeast section of town on Tung Hsin Street, a major east-west thoroughfare. Showing the effects of underuse, its atmosphere is rather forlorn and uninviting. Increased tourism can be expected to make the place more lively and, perhaps, the service more efficient.

The lobby has a service desk, bank, and post office combined, and a small retail shop for local handicrafts. The rooms are ample, with deep tubs in the bathrooms (as in all Chinese hotels there are only hand-held shower heads which must be used while seated in the tub, a skill quickly mastered).

SIAN CUISINE

The food in Sian is noticeably plainer than in other parts of China which, if nothing else, makes for a contrast in and of itself. Mutton (disdained by northerners) is a staple in this part of the country, as are river fish. Since Shensi is wheat country, noodles predominate as a source of starch, although a coarse-grained rice is also served at the hotel.

SHOPPING

Recommended purchases include weavings and cotton goods (note: these are rationed in China, and a guide is needed to arrange such purchases). Products from local handicrafts and enamelware factories are available, as are stone rubbings.

*A rubbing of a third-century AD
stone relief on a tomb*

苏
州

SOOCHOW

plentiful water

Pinyin Spelling: Suzhou
("soo-joe")

Soochow is an ancient city located on the old Imperial Canal in southern Kiangsu Province, just 86 km. (52 mi.) west of Shanghai. Noted for its scenic canals and gardens, the city has an area of 119 sq.km. (46 sq.mi.) and a population of 800,000. It is 12 miles from the banks of Lake Tai and sits astride the railway line connecting Shanghai, Wuhsi, and Nanking.

An old Chinese saying avows, "In Heaven there is Paradise, here below there are Soochow and Hangchow." Soochow today remains unique among Chinese cities in that it has preserved much of its traditional appearance and has largely retained its economic focus on handicrafts. Although factory chimneys now far outnumber Soochow's seven pagodas, the old city is remarkably undisturbed by new construction or motor traffic—the extensive network of canals still provides the city's major thoroughfares.

Soochow in History

Historical records indicate that Soochow was settled over 3,000 years ago. It rose to prominence as the capital of the Kingdom of Wu in 518 BC. At that time, the city was said to have "eight gates and eight water gates." The present name was granted in 589 AD, when work began on the Grand Canal that now runs immediately west of the city. Marco Polo visited Soochow in the 13th century and found it a "noble city and great." Its silk industry developed in the 14th century and its products are still among the most famous in China. During the Ming and Ch'ing dynasties, Soochow and its people earned repute for their subtle, graceful qualities. (The local Wu dialect was also highly regarded, as a popular aside had it: "Argument in Soochow is more pleasing than flattery in Kwangchow.")

Soochow was despoiled in the 19th century when the Taiping rebels briefly held the city. Treated as an adjunct to Shanghai by the Europeans, it was made a Japanese concession in the late 19th century. US and European economic interests were still prevalent throughout the first half of the 20th century.

Economy and Culture

Soochow's traditional silk industry dates back to the 14th century. Since 1949, its industry has greatly diversified, and Soochow's modern industrial output now includes mining, metallurgy, chemicals, machine tools, electronics, and precision instruments. According to local officials, the total value of industrial output in 1974 was 28 times that of the early 1950s.

Light industry includes jade carving, woodworking, tapestries, velvets, sandalwood fans, and lacquerware.

Agricultural productivity has benefited from the widespread introduction of mechanization. Because the land is flat, the former small plots have been converted into large holdings, with rice fields now mechanically drained and irrigated. Products of the region include winter wheat, cotton, and livestock.

The city has four institutions of higher learning, including the Soochow Embroidery Institute. There are 51 middle schools and 180 primary schools, with universal education provided through the primary level.

In addition to the natural beauty of the area, the local people uphold many aspects of their district cultural heritage, including Sukun Opera. Soochow's Pintan drama troupes perform works with a unique local flavor.

 HIGHLIGHTS FOR TRAVELERS

Gardens

It is difficult to dispute the local claim that Soochow has the most beautiful gardens in all of China. Natural ponds and waterways have been enhanced by exquisite gardens that combine traditional elements such as pavilions, temples, and rock sculptures (called rockeries) with distinctive arrangements of trees and flowers. The aim has been to create as many perspectives as possible within a confined space and to replicate in miniature scenes from nature not to be found locally.

Surging Wave Pavilion (Chang Lan) Laid out on the site of an estate founded in the 10th century, the garden itself was completed about 1044. Following a design symbolic of the "waves of life," it has itself been destroyed several times. Its last major reconstruction came in 1873, following the Taiping Rebellion. It was re-opened to the public in 1954. A stroll through the garden is supposed to evoke the feeling of rambling through thickly forested hills. Some of the names of specific viewing places are Fish-Watching Pavilion, Pavilion for Viewing Waters, and View of the Mountain Pavilion.

Lion Garden (Shih-tze Lin) Described in a local brochure as a "veritable labyrinth of hollow caves of spectacular shapes," the garden was first built in 1350, during the Yuan (Mongol) Dynasty. The grotesque stones come from Lake Tai. The garden has a large pond and stone boat.

Humble Administrator's Garden (Chou Cheng Yuan) Also known as "Plain Man's Politics Garden," a Ch'in Dynasty quotation purports to explain its name: "To cultivate one's garden to meet one's daily needs, that is what is known as the politics of a plain man."

Water is the main attraction of the site, covering three-fifths of the garden. Originally constructed during the Ming Dynasty, the East Garden was completely restored after 1949 (older portions are easily identified—the lines on old buildings are more subtle and greater attention was paid to detail in decorations). Bridges zig-zag at right angles across the ponds. Places of interest include the Hall of Distant Fragrance, Small Flying-Rainbow Bridge, Pavilion of Fragrant Snow and Azure Clouds, and Pavilion of Expecting Frost.

Tarrying Garden (Liu Yuan) Laid out under the Ming Dynasty, this garden is about a half-mile northwest of town. Originally a large country villa, it was rebuilt as a public garden and took its present name in 1876. The east section features halls and corridors decorated with calligraphy. Ponds and covered promenades mark the central section. The western section is known for its wooded landscapes.

Garden of Harmony (Yi Yuan) The most "natural" of the many gardens around Soochow, this site features pools with colored pebbles and innumerable flower beds. The garden is noted for four characteristics: stones from the lake, tablets above the entrances, pine trees, and animals.

Tiger Hill (Huchiu) This artificial hill is located two miles northwest of the main city, and is a "must" on the itinerary. It reaches a height of 36 m. and includes all of the traditional elements considered essential to the "perfect" hill: stones, rocks, plants, trees, pagodas, waterfalls, and a multitude of legends.

The hill was built over 2,500 years ago (during the Spring and Autumn period) by the King of Wu (490 BC) as the tomb for his father. Legend has it that a tiger guards his tomb (hence the name). The Yunyan Pagoda at the summit was built in 961 AD. Over the centuries it began to tilt, but it has lately been reinforced with concrete and steel bars.

Among the noted sights on the hill is Han Han Spring, which supposedly could be diverted to flood secret passages to keep out in-

*In Soochow garden—
upper left: Fantastic stones
in Lion Garden
upper right: Zig-zag bridges
in Chou Cheng Yuan
bottom: Bamboo groves
set off white walls in
Lion Garden*

truders. A huge flat stone known as the Stone of a Thousand Men was so named because the stains on the surface of the stone were believed to be the blood of the thousand workers who built the tomb. There is also a Sword Testing Stone (the Chinese, as many other cultures, have their own version of the King Arthur legend), where archeologists have found some clues about the original tomb.

249

An artisan working on elaborate embroidery piece at National Institute.

Soochow Silk

'East Is Red' Silk Weaving Mill Growing from a small backyard workshop to a major facility with 730 pieces of equipment, the mill's 2,000 workers turn out 250 varieties of fabric.

Soochow Silk Printing Mill The factory was founded in 1958 and is almost completely mechanized. It produces nearly a thousand patterns of pure silk, rayon, and other fibers. Many of its products are made specifically for export.

Tungshan Tungting Commune This commune has a diversified economy of grain, fruit, fish, and silk, and is especially known for its tangerines and shrimp (gathered from Lake Tai).

National Embroidery Institute. Embroidery is acknowledged as an art form in China and the Institute's display is unparalleled.

Grand Canal

The Grand Canal is located immediately west of the city and is the largest man-made waterway in the world. Originally constructed to bear tribute rice from the Yangtse Plain north to Peking, portions of it are still active. The segment adjacent to Soochow is heavily traversed by long lines of cargo barges carrying agricultural products and raw materials from commune fields to urban processing plants or warehouses. The canal's embankments are well-constructed masonry structures with towpaths still in use. The width of the canal averages 100 ft. but narrows to about 30 ft. at the numerous picturesque stone bridges that arch gracefully above it. Depths average 7-10 ft., adequate for small river craft.

HOTEL ACCOMMODATIONS

Visitors to Soochow will find themselves comfortably situated in the Soochow Grand Hotel, located on Friendship Road. Near to the Chang Lan Pavilion and Garden, the hotel is set among farmhouses in a charming old section of the city and has a walled garden. Rooms are old-fashioned with comfortable furnishings and old-style bathrooms. Although not air-conditioned, the heat of the summer is moderated by its thick concrete construction.

A new, nine-story hotel was due to be completed for the 1979 tourist season.

LOCAL CUISINE

Soochow has a well-earned reputation for dining. The city's restaurants—usually small and simply furnished—have traditionally attracted patrons from as far away as Nanking and Shanghai. The restaurants do an especially brisk business during the city's numerous food festivals, the most popular ones coinciding with changes in season. Fish and rice, the two items that dominate the region's food output, are featured.

One of the most esteemed festivals is the crab feast, which occurs in early autumn. Area fishermen congregate at a small shallow lake 5 mi. to the northeast of Soochow. There, armed with bamboo traps, they snare crabs as they emerge from the crevices where they have just laid eggs. The resulting dish is called "Ta-cha-hsieh." Other items known around Soochow are candies, pickled ducks, and tea.

SHOPPING

Handicraft fanciers will also enjoy Soochow, which is known for its embroidery, sandalwood fans, jade carvings, wrought gems, and, of course, Soochow silks. Selections are available at the Friendship Store, across from the "Wonderful Lookout" on Kuan-ch'ien Street, or at the department store, located on Ren Min Road just across the street from the Pleasure Garden. Both are within two and a half miles of the hotel.

TACHAI

great outpost

Pinyin Spelling: Dazhai
("dah-jai")

In recent years it's been difficult to walk anywhere in rural China without encountering the slogan "In agriculture, learn from Tachai!" Tachai is a small village in the Taihang Mountains in Shansi Province. It is situated near the city of Yangchuan. Tachai is on the China traveler's itinerary not by virtue of any great historical sights or even contemporary edifices, but because it exemplifies China's revolutionary principles put into practice. Tachai was once a poverty-stricken rural area marked by rock-strewn hills, poor soil, and flood-prone valleys. The area has now become highly productive farmland, well-irrigated and terraced, and supportive of forestry and animal husbandry, as well as agriculture. As a result, the Tachai Production Brigade has become the standard-bearer for agricultural production in China. Its enormous success prompted Mao to press for a nationwide "Learn-from-Tachai" campaign. Recently, the leadership has called for the massive transformation of China's rural counties into "Tachai-type" units. In 1975 and 1976, "Learn-from-Tachai" conferences set forth plans to convert one-third of China's counties into "Tachai-type" units by 1980.

Measured by any criteria, the achievement of Tachai is significant. Tachai's original agricultural cooperative was set up in 1953 when 50 men and women set out literally to transform nature without recourse to mechanization or advanced technology. Collective production succeeded in doubling the output of the land when it had been divided into individual plots. In 1958, a people's commune was established, with the Tachai community designated as one of its production brigades. Local peasants terraced the mountain slopes with picks and shovels and quarried rock with hammers and chisels in order to build embankments that would keep the mountain gullies from flooding over. They moved huge quantities of fertile soil from other localities to create viable farmlands within embankments.

The most arduous task was the construction of

Terracing of fields is necessary in China's loess highlands

the commune's longest irrigation gully (1.5 km.), called Langshai-chang (Wolf's Pad). During the winter of 1955, the people built 38 stone embankments along the gully and created terraced fields suitable for farming. However, summer flooding washed away these efforts. The embankments were rebuilt, only to be destroyed again by torrential floods during the summer of 1957. Unwilling to admit defeat, the brigade decided to try again, this time constructing embankments in curved rows with deeper foundations and larger boulders. Inspired by the determination of the local brigade, many other commune members pitched in to complete the embankments along the gully and collect the tens of thousands of cubic meters of fertile soil needed to create 44 terraced fields. Thus the project was completed (three days ahead of schedule). It has withstood storms and floods since 1957 and now boasts the highest agricultural yield in the area.

Today, Tachai has a varied crop output, electricity, aerial cableways, processing equipment, irrigation machinery, and new housing. It has ample grain reserves and is able to produce a surplus for sale to the state.

TACHING

great celebration

Pinyin Spelling: Daqing
("dah-ching")

Taching—the site of China's most famous oil-field—is situated between the cities of Harbin and Tsitsihar in southwestern Heilungkiang, China's northeasternmost province. In a pattern reminiscent of 19th century boomtowns of the American west, Taching has been transformed in a matter of a few decades from a virtually uninhabitable swampland into a bustling industrial and agricultural center with a population exceeding 600,000 (including 130,000 engaged in petroleum extraction and refining). The complex is located approximately 650 mi. (1,085 km.) northeast of Peking, with a direct rail connection consuming the better part of 12 hours.

Taching's land area forms part of the Sungliao Basin, the site some 140 million years ago of a large freshwater lake. The lake's rich plant and animal life provided the basis of the region's vast petroleum reserves. The story of contemporary Taching begins in the 1930s when Japanese geologists detected large oil reserves in the highland plains. After the founding of the PRC in 1949, exploratory drilling began with technical assistance from the Soviet Union. In 1959, before the work could produce results, Soviet technicians were withdrawn as a consequence of the Sino-Soviet split. Despite severe shortcomings in technology, the Chinese pressed on and, on September 26—a few days before the tenth anniversary of the founding of the PRC—the No. 3 Exploratory Well struck oil. By means of massive labor inputs and grass roots ingenuity and tenacity (as exemplified by "Iron Man" Wang [Wang Chin-hsi] and other workers now regarded as national heroes), work was completed on what was to become one of China's greatest natural resources and a major boost to the country's economic transformation. In 1964, Chairman Mao coined the slogan "In industry, learn from Taching," still used as a national rallying-cry for industrial development. For the Chinese, Taching's image conjures up the ultimate example of worker discipline, skillful planning, managerial efficiency, and the triumph of spirit over circumstance.

Building a new refinery

Since 1960, production is said to have increased by an annual average of 28% (despite slowdowns in the mid-1970s attributed to political disruptions by the "gang of four"), reaching an estimated level of 40 million metric tons (280 million barrels) in 1977. Local crude oil contains high quantities of paraffin and is too viscous to flow at cold temperatures. As a result, many of the pipes and storage tanks are buried underground. The Taching complex itself (actually made up of two fields) extends over 1,000 sq. km. (386 sq. mi.).

In a style now emulated throughout China, Taching has not limited itself to a single activity, but rather has developed into a multi-faceted agro-industrial complex. It now comprises a constellation of over 50 villages where wives and families of oil workers farm 2,300 hectares (5,543 acres) of land to supply food and auxiliary income to the region. Schools, nurseries, medical centers, and experimental stations form an integral part of the complex.

TALIEN

great link

Pinyin Spelling: Dalian

("dah-leean")

Talien (formerly known in the West as "Dairen") lies at the southern tip of the Liaotung Peninsula in northeast China. It is the country's third largest port engaging in foreign trade. Although the city is located only about 500 km. (310 mi.) due east of Peking, the train route must cover an additional 1,450 km. (900 mi.) in its journey around the Pohai Gulf.

Talien has broad streets and spacious squares, and is known both for its industry and its scenic setting. Rounded, green hills form the backdrop on three sides. The deep blue bay to the south is skirted by four excellent beaches. The main industrial zone has been built in the suburbs to alleviate crowding in the city.

Talien in History

Construction of Talien's port began in 1899 and was completed in 1930 by the Japanese. Under terms of the 1945 Yalta Conference, control of the city passed from Japan to the Soviet Union, which occupied the city until the early 1950s (ironically, it was the Soviets who helped complete Talien's vast network of underground defense shelters). The Soviet presence still lingers, as evidenced by the bilingual street signs and cenotaph with Rus-

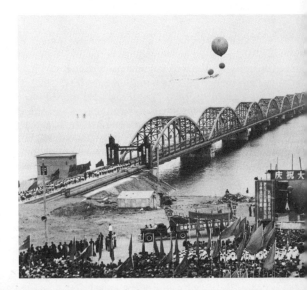

sian and Chinese inscriptions that dominates Stalin Square at the city's center.

HIGHLIGHTS FOR TRAVELERS

On the way to Talien, the train passes through fields of sorghum and soybeans. The outskirts of the city are dominated by factories that produce diesel engines, ships, metals, chemicals, textiles, refinery products, processed food, and blown glass. The city is the second most important cultural center in Liaoning Province (after Shenyang). In addition to its university there is a teachers' college, technical institute, and agricultural college.

Sightseeing in Talien usually includes the port, some factories, and the beach resorts. The port employs about 13% of the population and its ice-free harbor receives ships from over 100 countries. Modern dock facilities can handle containerized shipping and oil and coal from northeast China. In addition to touring the factories themselves, visitors are often taken to see new residential neighborhoods for workers, affording a view of daily life in the city. Recreational areas such as Tiger Park (Laohutan) are quite popular, especially in the summer.

Talien celebrates the opening of China's largest deep-water oil port.

257

TATUNG

great joining

Pinyin Spelling: Datong
("dah-tuhng")

Tatung, an industrial center of northern Shansi Province, is located some 150 mi. due west of Peking and 20 mi. south of the Great Wall boundary now demarcating the southern border of Inner Mongolia. Situated on a dry, relatively infertile plain, the town owes its economic importance to its development as a rail juncture for north-central China and as a major bituminous coal-mining area in a province that leads China in the production of that commodity.

Tatung's coal industry grew rapidly during the 1920s, when its coal was used to fuel the steam engines once built in the city. Today, both industry and agriculture in the city have become considerably diversified, with cement, light industry, and shoe manufacturing (which originally grew out of the hide trade with Inner Mongolia) also significant.

Tatung is perhaps better known to the world as the 15th-century capital of the Buddhist Northern Wei Dynasty. The major legacy of that period is the Yunkang Grotto, which ranks among the three or four greatest examples of traditional Buddhist art in all of China. The 21 caves of Yunkang, located some 10 mi. from central Tatung, comprise more than 100,000 painted sandstone sculptures dug out of a hillside one-half mile long. Carved over a period of 145 years (386-534 AD), the images range in height from over 50 feet to less than an inch, expressing an endless variety of moods and demeanors. Since the mid-1970s, extensive restorations have been carried out at the caves, which have lately been increasingly included on tourist itineraries.

Within Tatung's limits are two other sites of interest, the exquisite Nine Dragon Screen, built during the early Ming of multicolored glazed tiles and extending 147 ft. in length; and the Hua Yen Monastery complex, with wood and stone structures dating from the 11th and 12th centuries. Tatung's religious edifices are today effectively devoid of ceremonial uses.

Tientsin, China's third largest city, is located some 120 km. (74 mi.) southeast of Peking and 50 km. (30 mi.) from the Po Hai Gulf. It possesses China's largest artificial harbor and is a key transportation hub serving the populous North China Plain. The city is also a leading industrial center.

Tientsin has a population of 6.7 million spread over an area of 11,000 sq.km. (4,200 sq.mi.) and is the smallest of China's three centrally administered municipalities (with Peking and Shanghai). Tientsin proper extends for almost 10 miles along the banks of the Hai River, a factor which in the past made the city (with an average elevation of 16 ft.) constantly vulnerable to flooding. In recent years, water control projects have all but eliminated this threat.

TIENTSIN

entrance to the
heavenly capital

Pinyin Spelling: Tianjin
("teean-jin")

Tientsin in History

Recently unearthed records indicate that Tientsin's original site dates back to the Warring States period (403-221 BC). However, continuous settlement apparently did not begin until about 800 years ago, when the city was known as Chih-ku ("buying and selling"). Tientsin received its present name in 1404, at a time when it began to assume its characteristic role as a transshipment point between the southern coast and Peking. A military garrison was posted, city walls built (destroyed during the Boxer Rebellion), and storage facilities expanded. The next phase of Tientsin's development began in 1858 when the city was designated as a treaty port. The city was parceled out among British, French, and other Western concessions. Western-style buildings were constructed, port facilities improved, and light industry (mostly textiles) expanded.

Early in this century, the heavy silting of the Hai River forced the rebuilding of the port 50 km. downstream from the city of Taiku. During the Japanese occupation (1937-45), a major construction program was begun to develop an artificial harbor and deep-water berthing facilities. These were completed under the PRC in 1952. A second major expansion, including containerization, was carried out in 1976.

259

Tientsin carpet workers produce famous cut-pile designs.

The city suffered heavy damage during the Tangshan earthquake (1976) but by 1978 full production had been restored and tourists were once again allowed to visit the city.

Economy and Culture

Tientsin's economy is dominated by its port and heavy industry. Ships up to 10,000 tons can berth in the new artificial port, with ships up to 3,000 tons serving Tientsin itself. Heavy industry includes iron and steel, motor vehicles and parts, heavy machinery, chemicals, electronics, and watches. Tientsin-made elevators are used in hotels and office buildings throughout China.

Perhaps its most famous products are Tientsin carpets. Eight major factories produce an estimated 150,000 sq.yd. of carpet annually.

The area is also rich in natural resources. Some of China's largest coal mines are in nearby Tangshan. The major Shengli oil field is now being supplemented by extensive new offshore discoveries. In agriculture, Tientsin produces wheat, corn, and rice and has a thriving dairy industry. Fruit is also grown, and the local pears are notable.

⬛ HIGHLIGHTS FOR TRAVELERS

The Number One Carpet Factory employs 1,400 workers, two-thirds of whom are women. This industry dates back to 200 BC in China. For Tientsin carpets no weaving machinery is used. To impart an embossed effect, designs are etched with scissors.

The Hai River caused a major flood in 1963, and since then major water-control projects have been underway, including construction of new streams (to bypass the river), locks, and pumping stations.

Other sites of interest include a terra-cotta ceramics factory (the figures make excellent souvenirs), several large parks (Shuishang Park contains a museum with Ming and Ch'ing dynasty paintings), and the old city with its maze of narrow streets and bazaars.

Tientsin's steamed dumplings rival those made in Peking. The Kiesling Restaurant is noted for its European dishes.

Tsinan, the capital of Shantung Province, is known as the "City of Spings," having over 100 bubbling hot springs. Lying in a valley between the Yellow River and the T'ai Shan mountains, Tsinan is an industrial city on the Peking-Shanghai railway, some 350 km. (217 mi.) south of Peking. Tsinan's population is 1,200,000.

The major industries in Tsinan include metallurgy, machine-building, chemicals, and textiles. Agricultural products include wheat, corn, cotton, tobacco, and a good variety of fruits (peaches, pears, grapes, and dates). It also is known for its peanuts. There is a university serving the region, several medical schools, and a large industrial exhibition hall.

Tsinan has some historical sites of interest (a pagoda, "Buddha Cliff," and a T'ang Dynasty temple), but its chief attractions are the hot springs that appear all over the city. The four main springs have parks built around them and sport colorful names: Paotu (Gushing from the Ground); Heihu (Black Tiger); Wulungtan (Five Dragon Pool); and Shentzu (Pearls). These streams find their way into Taming Lake, which has an area of 460,000 sq. m. and occupies about one-fourth of the town's total area. It provides an idyllic setting, with water lilies and numerous gardens.

TSINAN

southern crossing

Pinyin Spelling: Jinan
("tsee-nahn")

TSINGTAO

green island

Pinyin Spelling: Qingdao
("ching-dow")

Tsingtao, a seaside resort and busy seaport, is situated on the southern coast of the Shantung Peninsula overlooking the Yellow Sea. The city, some 250 miles southeast of Peking, with a population of 1.5 million, is also the most important industrial town in Shantung Province. Surrounded on three sides by the sea, with Mt. Laoshan as the backdrop, Tsingtao's red-tiled roofs and verdant foliage complement its picturesque setting.

The city was a small fishing village until the Germans "selected" it as a port in 1898 and forced a treaty on China's imperial government. Within a decade, the Germans threw up a modern city with deep-water harbor, business district, and—characteristically for areas under foreign control—a separate area for Chinese residents. With 2,000 soldiers stationed in the city, the Germans mined the coal in the area to fuel their ships. During World War I, Japan took over rights to the city. It was not until 1922 that the Chinese regained control of Tsingtao.

Before 1949, the city's economy relied on trade, silk weaving, essential oils, and a brewery (perhaps the only positive reminder of the German occupation is the excellent beer, still served in its familiar green bottles). Laoshan Mountain produces the famous mineral water of the same name (also used as the base for Tsingtao beer).

Since the founding of the PRC, Tsingtao's industrial output has increased more than ten-fold and includes textiles, textile machinery, machine tools, and a diesel locomotive plant. Sites of interest to the visitor now include the port itself, fine bathing beaches (the cool current keeps the city comfortable during the hot summer months), an aquarium, and Lu Hsun Park.

URUMCHI

Pinyin Spelling: Ürümqi
("ur-room-chee")

U rumchi is the capital of Sinkiang Autonomous Region, China's most western province. The most "inland" city in the world (that is, the furthest from any major body of water), Urumchi is 3,270 km. (2,050 mi.) from Peking (a five-hour flight). The city lies as a green-blanketed oasis amidst Sinkiang's barren and uninhabited deserts, loess highlands, and the snow-capped peaks of the Tienshan Mountains.

Sinkiang covers 16% of the total land area of China and is populated by 13 of China's 54 nationalities. Of the total population of 11 million, 5.4 million are Uighurs, a colorful Central Asian people who favor dressing in gay costumes and have distinct cultural traditions. Other prominent minorities of this region are the Han (i.e., Chinese nationality), Kazakhs, Hui, and Mongolians.

Although forbidding in winter, Urumchi's summers are pleasant, with warm days and cool evenings. An extensive series of tree belts planted around the capital has helped to reduce the effect of wind, dust, and cold.

Economy and Culture

Long a poor region, Sinkiang has been making progress in both agriculture and industry. Because rainfall is scarce, many parts of Sinkiang are barren. The main source of water for irrigation is the snow and ice at the higher reaches of the Tienshan range. To harness this water supply, rivers have been rechanneled and irrigation canals dug. Sinkiang now has over 400 large and small reservoirs, 10,000 underground wells, and over 30,000 km. (18,800 mi.) of rechanneled waterways. About 65% of its available area of 3 million hectares (7.4 million acres) have been mechanized for ploughing.

In talking about the period before 1949, a local worker recently recounted that "at that time, one could get an ampoule of penicillin only by exchanging it for a horse, a battery flashlight for a lamb, a meter of cloth for 30 catties of wheat, and a small box of matches for a kilogram of wool." Now Sinkiang produces steel, oil, chemicals, sugar, tractors, and various other kinds of farm machinery. Trucks are the main method of transportation and thousands of miles of roads have now been paved.

There are eight universities in Sinkiang, including two medical schools. One medical college specializes in cancer research (Uighur people have a high incidence of laryngeal cancer, attributed to their habit of drinking hot liquids).

Islam is the dominant religion in Sinkiang. In cities such as Urumuchi and Kashgar, huge mosques are still in use. Religious festival days are still observed and it is even possible to encounter older women using veils.

HIGHLIGHTS FOR TRAVELERS

Apart from the very exotic nature of the region, visitors are likely to be taken by the large-scale efforts underway to turn this part of China into an agriculturally and industrially productive area.

Around Urumchi, tourist spots include Tien Chi (Heaven's Pool), a lake in the Tienshan Mountains, and the former Eighth Route Army (Communist forces) headquarters which is now a memorial hall to martyrs of those expeditions.

Local food specialties feature mutton. Assorted small cakes, called "nang," are sold at stands along the street and are a favorite of local people.

W uhan, the capital of Hupei Province, is the collective name given to the three closely linked municipalities—Wuchang, Hankow, and Hanyang. The three cities were physicially connected in 1957 upon completion of the Changchiang Bridge, the first and only span to cross the Yangtse between Chungking to the west and Nanking to the east (prior to 1957, all of China's north-south railway traffic had to be ferried across the river). Located in central China, in the middle of the Yangtse Plain, Wuhan is roughly 1,000 miles from each of China's four large cities: Peking and Kwangchow (on a north-south axis) and Shanghai and Chungking (on an east-west axis).

Wuhan is situated at the confluence of the Han and Yangtse rivers. Its three urban sections have a combined population of 1,900,000 people, with an additional 600,000 residing in the suburbs. It is the foremost city in a region noted for its population density and heavy industry. Wuhan is also a major transportation center. As an inland port, it can handle 8,000-ton vessels coming up river from Shanghai, some 1,000 miles away. It is also a key rail center.

Wuhan's three urban components have similar geographical features in that they are all situated on low, flat land and are interspersed with numerous ponds, canals, and other waterways. Formerly vulnerable to flooding, Wuhan is today well-protected by a newly reinforced series of dikes.

Wuhan's strategic location has also made it the third most important military center in China, a role that has considerable historical precedence. Battles fought here at the turn of the century accompanied the fall of the Ch'ing Dynasty. In 1949, Communist forces in this sector won key victories over the last pockets of Kuomintang resistance, paving the way to final victory.

Wuhan in History

Hankow Hankow occupies the northwest section of Wuhan, bordered by the Yangtse on the east and the Han River to the south. Hankow be-

WUHAN

"Wuhan" is a contraction of three city names—"Wu" from Wuchang and "han" from Hankow and Hanyang

Pinyin Spelling: Wuhan ("woo-hahn")

gan as a fishing village (with origins as early as the 3rd century BC) and it remained so until the mid-19th century. Under terms of the Treaty of Nanking (1861), it was designated a treaty port and its status gradually began to change as foreign firms started opening branches in the city. However, it was not until the building of the railway in the first decade of the 20th century that Hankow began truly to expand. In the course of its rapid industrial build-up, Hankow became the scene of the bloody "February 7th" strike of 1923, the first large-scale industrial strike in modern China history. Today, Hankow is the most modern section of Wuhan and the site of an important military installation.

Hanyang Located south of the Han River and west of the Yangtse, Hanyang is the smallest of Wuhan's three municipalities. It was founded as a municipality about 600 AD. The city gained prominence in the late 19th century as a focal point for political reform. Hanyang's political leaders were part of a movement that sought to revitalize China through "self-strengthening"—it was felt that by learning from the West rather than ignoring it, China could become strong enough to oust the foreign powers. Within the industrial sector, this policy led directly to the construction in Hanyang of China's first modern iron and steel complex in 1891. By the early 1900s, an arsenal and several other factories had been added along Hanyang's river front. The city's industrialization program collapsed during the depression of the 1930s. During the Sino-Japanese War (1937-45), much of the industry that remained was destroyed. Since 1949, however, the area has entered a new era as a center for light industry.

Wuchang Wuchang, located on the eastern side of the Yangtse, is the oldest of the three municipalities and has long functioned as an administrative center for the region. In the 14th century (during the Yuan Dynasty), Wuchang served as the capital of a large administrative region (encompassing what are now four central provinces). Today, it serves as the administrative seat for Hupei Province.

On October 10, 1911, the first victorious battle of the 1911 Revolution took place in Wuchang (Sun Yat-sen himself was absent—he was in Hawaii raising funds for the revolution). The site of the battle is commemorated by a bronze statue of Sun (on Shouyi Road). The Central Institute of the Peasant Movement, an important political training ground during the early years of the Chinese Communist movement, was set up in Wuchang. It was headed by Mao himself in 1927.

Economy and Culture

The name Wuhan is metaphorically synonymous with iron and steel as it is the site of some of China's most important foundries (surpassed only by the Anshan complex). With the assistance of West German and Japanese engineers, the Wuhan Iron and Steel Complex is being expanded to include a 3,000,000-metric-ton steel rolling mill. The area also produces a substantial array of chemicals, fertilizers, construction materials, and railway ties, as well as cotton fabrics and a number of light industrial products. An open-pit iron mine about 65 km. (40 mi.) southeast of Wuhan (Taiyeh Iron Ore Mines) provides almost all of Wuhan's iron ore (and limestone).

Although Wuhan is not primarily an agricultural region, rice and cotton output have increased greatly as the area strives to attain self-sufficiency. The growing season lasts 300 days and permits two yearly crops of both wheat and tea. Freshwater fisheries also contribute to the local economy.

Wuhan is above all else a working city and most aspects of its cultural life relate to this characteristic. Given its long history of intensive settlement and commercial activity, Wuhan retains visible links to the major cultural and political currents of China from at least the times of the T'ang emperors. In a country that today stresses political evolution and economic development above all other goals, Wuhan's pace and lifestyle are telling indicators of the direction China now seeks for its industrial centers.

 # HIGHLIGHTS FOR TRAVELERS

Hankow

The most modern of the Wuhan municipalities, Hankow serves as a model for Chinese urban planning. Its broad tree-lined boulevards are flanked by modern apartment houses, offices, and landscaped parks.

The city's legacy from the days of Western occupation is still visible along the Yenchiang Tatao, a street that runs parallel to the Yangtse in the northeast section. As with the Bund in Shanghai, government offices now occupy what were once banks, department stores, and palatial homes. Tourist sites include the Handicrafts Display Center, Sun Yat-sen (Chung Shan) Park (formerly a race track), the Institute of Medicine, and the Wuhan Zoo.

Hanyang

Hanyang, a densely populated district made up of a jumble of one-story, slate-roofed houses, is typical of old Chinese cities. The low-lying area just south of the Han River is now Hanyang's industrial district, connected to Hankow by the Changchiang Bridge. As Hanyang was formerly a popular residential retreat for the area's gentry, it includes numerous reminders of the pre-1949 era.

Lotus Lake (Lienhua Lu) This small, picturesque lake, now cast in the shadows of the Changchiang Bridge, was formerly the site of a European settlement.

Tortoise Hill (Kuei Shan) So named because of its resemblance to a tortoise, it is the only hill of any size in Wuhan. The area includes a well-maintained park and many points of interest, including pavilions, caverns, and a former monastery. One can now scale the "mountain" by means of stone steps.

Workers' Cultural Palace The Palace is the focal point of a park that also contains the Terrace of the Ancient Lute, overlooking gardens and the river.

Wuchang

The old part of Wuchang clings to a low ridge (She Shan—Serpent Hill), along which runs the railway spur that bisects the municipality. The old flavor of the city is well-preserved in its northern section, with modern offices and industrial areas relegated to the south.

Yangtse River Bridge (Changchiang Bridge) This bridge, along with its counterpart in Nanking, was built under "impossible" geological conditions, and is regarded as a symbol of China's modern industrial progress and self-reliance. The first modern bridge to span the Yangtse, it was completed on September 25, 1957 (two years ahead of schedule). Both levels of the structure are flanked by broad sidewalks for pedestrains and cyclists. The lower deck supports the railway; the upper, six lanes of vehicular traffic. The bridge is 1,156 m. (3,792 ft.) long, and reaches 80 m. (263 ft.) above the water. It has 8 piers and 9 spans.

Hsiang Pagoda The Hsiang Pagoda, also known as Yellow Crane Tower (Huang He Lou), was erected in the beginning of the 3rd century AD, and is the main attraction in the park that surrounds Serpent Hill (She Shan). Through the verse of the T'ang Dynasty poet Tsui Han, the Pagoda attained repute for the panoramic view it affords (now an ideal spot to survey the bridge). Since its construction, it has been restored three times, most recently by the present government which retained its Ming and Ch'ing dynasty elements.

Site of the Central Institute of the Peasant Movement Prior to the founding of the PRC, the Communist Party built an institute to train cadres and organize peasants. Its headmaster in 1927 was Mao

269

Tse-tung. This site now houses Middle School No. 22. However, Mao's former residence and some classrooms have been preserved and are open to the public.

East Lake (Tung Hu) Larger than Lake Tai and several times the size of Hangchow's West Lake, this picturesque lake is surrounded by a park covering 94 sq. km. (36.3 sq. mi.). Among the park's numerous tourist sites are the Ting Tao Temple—the Taoist master Lao Tzu's place of meditation; Lung Tsuen (Dragon Spring); the Hsing Ying Court— a pavilion in a wooded area commemorating the ancient poet Chu Yuan; and the Chiu Nu Tuen (Tomb of the Nine Heroines).

The Hupei Provincial Museum, noted for displays of recent archeological excavations, traces the province's history from its origins to the Opium War. Wuhan University, set in bucolic surroundings, is a popular tourist attraction.

HOTEL ACCOMMODATIONS

The Sheng Li Hotel (tel: 22-531) is a structure in the old style, located in the heart of Hankow. Its restaurant is among the best in any hotel in China.

WUHAN CUISINE

The Yangtse River serves not only as a geographical boundary but also as a gastronomic border. The staple north of the river is noodles whereas to the south rice predominates along with more elaborately flavored dishes. The Wuhan area is noted for its fresh fish and wild ducks from East Lake.

Wuhsi (also spelled Wusih), in Kiangsu Province, is an industrial and resort city on the north bank of Lake Tai (Tai Hu), one of China's five largest lakes. Important as a transportation junction, Wuhsi is situated astride the Grand Canal, and along the Nanking-Shanghai railway line, 145 km. (87 mi.) west of Shanghai. Wuhsi has an area of 204 sq.km. (78.7 sq.mi.) and a population of 650,000. The original name of the city, Yu Hsi ("with tin"), referred to local tin mines first worked in the Chou Dynasty. When the tin was depleted during the Han Dynasty, the name was changed to "Wuhsi" ("without tin").

WUHSI

without tin

Pinyin Spelling: Wuxi
("woo-shee")

Wuhsi in History

Wuhsi's long history dates back some 3,000 years to the Shang and Chou periods, when scattered settlements existed in the area. The city was formally founded during the Han Dynasty when it became the capital of a feudal state in the region. Yet, few details appear in later dynastic histories and Wuhsi remained for the most part a small country town. This image did not begin to change until the 1930s, when the town began rapidly to expand its industry, the keystone of which were 45 silk filature factories. Wuhsi also gained some importance as a transport center, transhipping manufactured goods and silks by water to Shanghai. Its greatest period of expansion, however, came after 1949.

Economy and Culture

Wuhsi has long been associated with silk production, an activity that had its origins in the area some 1,500 years ago. Silk-reeling and weaving workshops were set up in the mid-19th century, but the industry remained relatively stagnant during the first decades of this century. After the founding of the PRC in 1949, the silk filature factories (which separate silk fibers from the cocoons and wind them onto spools) were rebuilt, and related activities such as silk weaving, dyeing, and printing were started up.

Today, the city is also known for high-technology products such as diesel engines, air

271

compressors, electric cables, boilers, precision instruments, machine tools, and electronics parts. In total there are 470 factories in Wuhsi employing some 249,000 skilled workers. Light industry includes the production of bicycles, enamelware, glassware, and the famous Huishan Pottery Works. The city also produces concrete boats for use on the region's numerous small canals (these boats are actually lighter than wooden craft and have greater maneuverability and speed; moreover, they require less upkeep).

Wuhsi is surrounded by rich agricultural land capable of yielding three rice crops a year. Pig breeding and fishing are also important in the Lake Tai area.

The city has 150 primary and middle schools and one university; enrollment at all levels is approximately 140,000 students. In addition, some of the factories have their own part-time technical schools for training workers. Wuhsi also has 12 hospitals and a prominent historical library.

HIGHLIGHTS FOR TRAVELERS

Hsihui Park Located on the western outskirts of Wuhsi, this park encompasses the neighboring Hui hills, including "Tin Hill." Two famous sites are its temples and the Chi Chang Garden ("Garden for Ease of Mind"), all dating back to the Ming Dynasty. The garden at the foot of the hill was rebuilt recently as an exact replica of the 16th-century original. The temple on top of Hui Hill was built in 420 AD and affords a broad view of the surrounding region. Several pavilions and tea houses are scattered throughout the park. On hot summer days, the exquisitely decorated stone-slab chairs are always cool to the touch.

Huishan Clay Figure Workshop Local artisans of the Ming era were the first to discover the qualities of Hui Mountain clay. Excellent for molding, it also dries to a remarkable hardness and is thus excellent for firing. The local pottery factory underwent a modern revival in 1954 and now employs some 600 persons, about 60% female. Most of the figures now made reflect contemporary literary and political themes. More than one-third of the output is exported. The factory has a small retail outlet for visitors.

Wuhsi Number One Silk Filature Factory Another common spot on the visitor's itinerary is the Number One Silk Filature Factory. The vast majority of its workers are women. The mill dates from 1933 and prior to 1949 had an average annual production of 40 tons of raw silk. The present output is well over eight times that amount, and the newly installed semi-automatic machines enable a worker to tend 60 threads of silk at a time.

Grand Canal Wuhsi sits astride the Grand Canal and is among the last major stops on the way to Hangchow from Peking. The Canal is excluded from most itineraries, possibly because it still reflects aspects of "old" China—much canal traffic is still manually propelled. The main canal dates from 605 AD, when it connected the Yellow River in the north (at Loyang) with the Yangtse in the south. By 610, the entire canal route from Peking to Hangchow was opened. Later, in

273

the Yuan (Mongol) Dynasty, the northern segment of the canal was redredged and, over the centuries, it has remained a basic means of supplying the capital city and its border armies with food from the south. The main bridge over the canal is a short distance from the central square of the city.

LAKE TAI

Lake Tai (Tai Hu) has an area of some 2,240 sq.km. (864 sq.mi.) and includes about 100 islands. Many of its sights may be visited by boat in the course of a morning or afternoon excursion.

Worker's Sanitorium Although several of these are located around the lake, most visitors tour the facility on Chungtu Island. The sanitorium provides treatment for non-infectious chronic diseases. It comprises three compounds with over 300 beds and commands a superb view of the lake and surrounding area. Both traditional Chinese medicine (acupuncture, moxibustion) and Western medicine are used to help patients, as well as physiotherapy and physical training programs.

Bridge on Turtle Head Peninsula, Lake Tai

Turtle Head Island (Yuantou Tsu) This small, pleasant island is situated on the south shore of the lake. The island forms the head of a turtle, hence its name. There are several arched bridges, pavilions, and walkways, but the emphasis is on the natural scenery, especially the lake itself with its barges and fleets of sailing vessels. On the "head" of the turtle stands a small lighthouse, near which is a stone inscribed with the island's name.

Three Hills in Lake Tai The main peak has a restaurant that overlooks the lake and Turtle Head Island. Pears and apples, the source of considerable local pride, are featured.

Li Garden (Liyuan) One of three famous gardens in Wuhsi, Li Garden lies south of the city on Lake Li, a smaller body that feeds into Lake Tai. The public garden reflects classic Chinese design, with grotesque rockeries, bow bridges, pavilions, walkways built on dikes that cross the lake, and varieties of flora. There is a miniature five-story pagoda at the mid-lake pavilion. It is reached via a covered promenade with wooden walls perforated by 89 flower-shaped windows. Ancient legend has it that the garden was founded by a local king who courted a princess there.

 HOTEL ACCOMMODATIONS

Taihu Hotel This is a modern structure with a magnificent view of the lake. It is a two-story building with spacious, high-ceilinged rooms and small, screened windows that overlook the lake. Hotel services include a good restaurant, retail shop, and post and telephone facilities. Room rates are Y9 (US$5.10) per day. In front of the hotel is a garden with a duck pond. Recreational equipment is available to guests. The hotel's shop is excellent, offering examples of local crafts (semi-precious stones and hand-carved pipes). It serves as the local Friendship Store and money can be exchanged here.

Less than a mile from the hotel is a cluster of mulberry farms with a small village at its core. A walk to this area affords an excellent view of rural China. The local people are open and receptive, and school children are likely to greet visitors with a warm "Hello!"

REGIONAL CUISINE
It is probably more difficult in Wuhsi than in most cities in China to "drop in" on a local restaurant. The hotel dining room generally serves the standard fare (although excellently prepared). Fish dishes, of course, are quite popular, with shrimp, crab, and crisp-fried eel heading the list. Spare-ribs are another good local dish, prepared with a bean-curd sauce.

275

Pig breeding is important in the countryside around Wuhsi.

▦ SHOPPING

Shoppers will be attracted by the fine regional handicrafts, including pottery figurines, briar pipes, and linen embroideries. Silk products, the local specialty, range from finely woven "paintings" to fabrics suitable for dresses. Wuhsi also has a rarely frequented antiques store that has been known to feature items long since "bought up" in the larger cities.

Yenan, a market town of 30,000 people, is located some 270 km. (168 mi.) north of Sian in Shensi Province. Having served as the headquarters of the Communist Party in 1936-47, it is symbolically and historically one of the most revered sites in the People's Republic.

The Yen River cuts a deep path between the dry loess hills, repositories of the innumerable cave dwellings characteristic of the area. The hills have been extensively terraced to provide an agricultural base for the local economy.

Other than sites connected with the revolution, the city has few standard tourist attractions. There are several factories, a university, and an assortment of historical sites (Buddhist caves, a Taoist hermitage, and a Sung Dynasty pagoda—the town's symbol). The main points of interest are the Museum of the Revolution and the caves where Mao Tse-tung and other Chinese leaders directed the revolution during its "Yenan Period."

YENAN

Yen River tranquility

Pinyin Spelling: Yan'an ("yeh-nan")

Yenan in History

In 1936, the Communist Eighth Route Army reached this remote area at the end of one of the great epics in military history—the 8,000-mile Long March, a two-and-a-half-year trek through central and western China that survived the incessant ravages of climate, terrain, and numerous encounters with the Nationalist forces of Chiang Kai-shek. It was during the Long March that Mao Tse-tung consolidated his control of the Party, and it was in Yenan that Mao, Chou En-lai, Chu Teh, and others re-assessed the failures of the formerly urban-based revolution and forged the political and military strategies that led to victory in the civil war and the establishment of the People's Republic of China.

The ordeals of the Long March had compelled its leaders to place survival ahead of orthodox doctrine. Once in Yenan, ideology was again tempered by circumstances. The concerns of class struggle paled before the need to mount a national war of resistance against Japan. Appealing to the latent nationalism of the rural population, the Party be-

The symbol of Yenan, a Sung Dynasty pagoda, overlooks the Yen River.

gan to rebuild itself on a peasant base. The Red Army gained considerable support for its guerrilla campaigns. Its ranks swelled by peasant volunteers, the Army became a strong, cohesive force, both politically and militarily.

The Yenan Legacy The specific policies developed at Yenan succeeded in winning broad, enthusiastic support from the peasantry. Indeed, their contribution to the eventual success of the revolution prompted the continued application of many of these policies (for example, land reform and mass mobilizations) throughout Mao's 28 years at the helm of the People's Republic. (Indeed, the Great Proletarian Cultural Revolution of 1966-76 may be seen in part as an

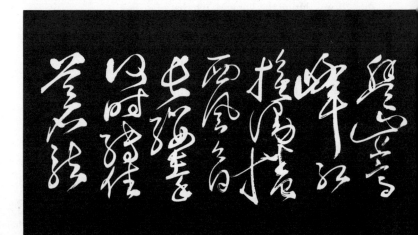

attempt to re-infuse the Yenan spirit into the workings of government.) The main theoretical legacies from Yenan may be characterized as:

1. Heavy reliance on the creativity of the "masses," particularly the peasantry, in their ability to overcome the ravages of nature, poverty, and political exploitation;

2. Rejection of administrative control through a closed, unresponsive, and elitist bureaucracy;

3. Periodic rotation of intellectuals and other elites to the countryside to engage in manual labor so as to break down barriers between them and the masses (i.e., workers and peasants);

4. Reliance on cooperative movements to reorganize local economies (forerunners of the commune system);

5. Development of a mass culture and education movement whose primary aim was the integration of literature, art, and formal schooling with politics. "Criticism and self-criticism" and "seeking the truth from facts" are traditions that also have their roots in Yenan.

Since 1977, the leadership's emphasis on modernization has led, in many instances, to a more circumspect approach to these policies, although their themes continue to be interwoven in political pronouncements. Yenan had been a frequent stop on the itinerary of foreign groups in the 1960s and early 1970s (particularly politically oriented delegations), but has since been less often visited.

[Readers are referred to Mark Selden's *The Yenan Way in Revolutionary China* (Harvard University Press, 1971) and to Fairbank, Reischauer, and Craig's *East Asia: The Modern Transformation* (Houghton Mifflin Company, 1956) for a more detailed account of the Yenan legacy.]

A 1935 poem by Mao Tse-tung in calligraphy by Shan Mui San

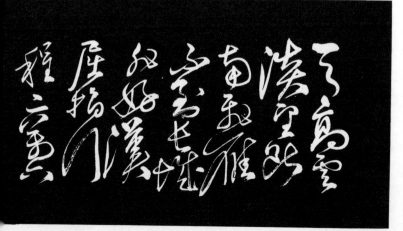

IV
BIBLIOGRAPHY

A READING LIST FOR CHINA TRAVEL

The list that follows seeks to provide a sampling of general works on the People's Republic of China. A more comprehensive bibliography can be found in Arlene Posner and Arne J. de Keijzer (eds.), *China: A Resource and Curriculum Guide*. Second edition, revised. Chicago: University of Chicago Press, 1976. A variety of bibliographies and background materials on China are available free or at very low cost from China-friendship organizations (see list, p. 24). A number of bookstores also specialize in China materials (e.g., Books New China in New York; China Books and Periodicals in New York, Chicago, and San Francisco; and China Arts and Crafts in Vancouver).

Background

China Council of the Asia Society (comp.). *People's Republic of China: Press Briefing Materials*. Revised edition. New York: Learning Resources in International Studies, 1976. Originally prepared for President Ford's visit in 1975. Concise data, particularly on political background.

China Phone Book and Address Directory: Hong Kong: China Phone Book Company (G.P.O. Box 11581), 1978. Despite its price ($25), an indispensable reference for business travelers and journalists.

Cohen, Jerome and Joan. *China Today and Her Ancient Treasures*. New York: Harry N. Abrams, 1974. An excellent visual introduction to China's past and present.

Committee of Concerned Asian Scholars. *China! Inside the People's Republic*. New York: Bantam, 1972.

Coye, Molly Joe and Jon Livingston. *China Yesterday and Today*. New York: Bantam, 1975. An inexpensive (US$1.95) compendium of readings, documents, and observations.

Fairbank, John King. *The United States and China*. Third revised edition. Cambridge: Harvard University Press, 1972.

Fan, K.H., and K.T. (eds.). *From the Other Side of the River: A Self-Portrait of China Today*. New York: Anchor, 1975.

Gamberg, Ruth. *Red and Expert: Education in the People's Republic of China*. New York: Schocken, 1978.

Hinton, William. *Fanshan: A Documentary of a Revolution in a Chinese Village*. New York: Vintage, 1966. An absorbing, intimate

CHINA
CONIC PROJECTION

SCALE OF MILES
0 100 200 300 400 500

SCALE OF KILOMETRES
0 100 200 300 400 500

Capitals of Countries.... ☆   International Boundaries _._._
Provincial Capitals........ ◉   Provincial Boundaries _.._.._
Canals ━━━   Walls ∿∿∿

*Wuhan municipality consists of Hankow, Hanyang and Wuchang

© Copyright HAMMOND INCORPORATED, Maplewood, N.J.

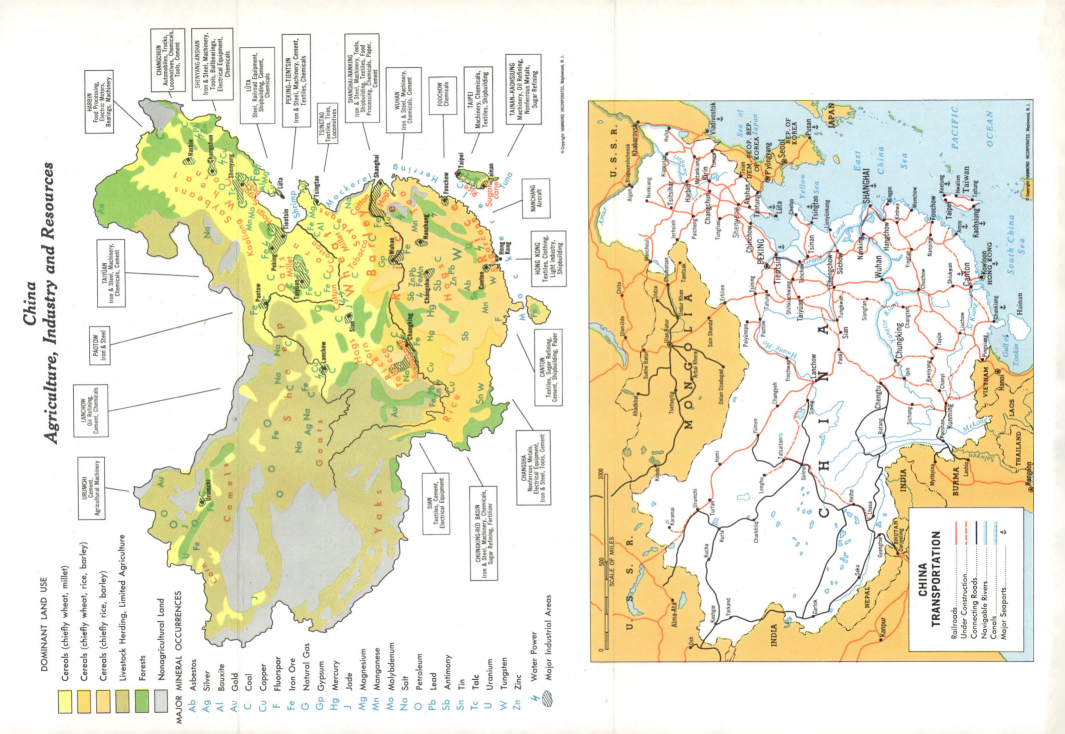

China
Agriculture, Industry and Resources

DOMINANT LAND USE

- Cereals (chiefly wheat, millet)
- Cereals (chiefly wheat, rice, barley)
- Cereals (chiefly rice, barley)
- Livestock Herding, Limited Agriculture
- Forests
- Nonagricultural Land

MAJOR MINERAL OCCURRENCES

Ab	Asbestos	Mo	Molybdenum
Ag	Silver	Na	Salt
Al	Bauxite	O	Petroleum
Au	Gold	Pb	Lead
C	Coal	Sb	Antimony
Cu	Copper	Sn	Tin
F	Fluorspar	Tc	Talc
Fe	Iron Ore	U	Uranium
G	Natural Gas	W	Tungsten
Gp	Gypsum	Zn	Zinc
Hg	Mercury		
J	Jade	⚡	Water Power
Mg	Magnesium	▨	Major Industrial Areas
Mn	Manganese		

HARBIN
Food Processing, Electric Motors, Bearings, Machinery

CHANGCHUN
Automobiles, Trucks, Locomotives, Chemicals, Tools, Cement

SHENYANG-ANSHAN
Iron & Steel, Machinery, Tools, Ballbearings, Electrical Equipment, Chemicals

LÜTA
Steel, Railroad Equipment, Shipbuilding, Cement, Chemicals

PEKING-TIENTSIN
Iron & Steel, Machinery, Cement, Textiles, Chemicals

TSINGTAO
Textiles, Tires, Locomotives

SHANGHAI-NANKING
Iron & Steel, Machinery, Tools, Shipbuilding, Textiles, Food Processing, Chemicals, Paper, Cement

WUHAN
Iron & Steel, Machinery, Chemicals, Cement

FOOCHOW
Chemicals

TAIPEI
Machinery, Chemicals, Textiles, Shipbuilding

TAINAN-KAOHSIUNG
Machinery, Oil Refining, Nonferrous Metals, Sugar Refining

TAIYÜAN
Iron & Steel, Machinery, Chemicals, Cement

PAOTOW
Iron & Steel

LANCHOW
Oil Refining, Cement, Chemicals

URUMCHI
Cement, Agricultural Machinery

SIAN
Textiles, Cement, Electrical Equipment

CHUNGKING-RED BASIN
Iron & Steel, Machinery, Chemicals, Sugar Refining, Fertilizer

CHANGSHA
Nonferrous Metals, Electrical Equipment, Iron & Steel, Tools, Cement

CANTON
Textiles, Sugar Refining, Cement, Shipbuilding, Paper

HONG KONG
Textiles, Clothing, Light Industry, Shipbuilding

NANCHANG
Aircraft

© Copyright HAMMOND INCORPORATED, Maplewood, N.J.

CHINA TRANSPORTATION

Legend:
- Railroads
- Under Construction
- Connecting Roads
- Navigable Rivers
- Canals
- ⚓ Major Seaports

SCALE OF MILES

0   500   1000

© Copyright HAMMOND INCORPORATED, Maplewood, N.J.

account of the revolutionary transformation of a farming village in Shansi Province.

Hsu, Kai-yu. *The Chinese Literary Scene: A Writer's Visit to the People's Republic.* New York: Vintage, 1975. Literary observations from a six-month visit to China in 1973.

Kaplan, Fredric M., Julian M. Sobin, and Stephen Andors. *Encyclopedia of China Today.* New York: Eurasia Press and Harper & Row, 1979. A single-volume reference work focusing on the post-1949 period.

Kessen, William, ed. *Childhood in China.* New Haven: Yale University Press, 1974. First-hand encounters between US educators and teachers, pupils, and parents in China.

Milton, David, and Nancy Dall Milton. *The Wind Will Not Subside: Years in Revolutionary China, 1964-1969.* New York: Pantheon, 1976. A first-hand account of the Cultural Revolution during 1964-69 by two resident teachers from the US.

Nagel's Encyclopedia Guide to China. Anne L. Destenay (trans.). Geneva, Switzerland: Nagel Publishers, 1974. Exhaustive descriptive information, especially on cultural aspects.

Newnham, Richard. *About Chinese.* Baltimore, Md. and Hammondsworth, England: Penguin, 1973. A readable introduction to the workings of the Chinese language.

Oksenberg, Michel, and Robert B. Oxnam. *China and America—Past and Future.* New York: Foreign Policy Association, 1977.

Schell, Orville. *In the People's Republic: An American's First-Hand View of Living and Working in China.* New York: Vintage, 1977. The personal account of a China scholar's two-month experiences working in a PRC community and factory.

Schram, Stuart. *Mao Tse-tung.* New York: Pelican, 1967. A standard Western biography.

Sidel, Victor W. and Ruth. *Serve the People: Observations on Medicine in the People's Republic of China.* Boston: Beacon Press, 1973.

Snow, Edgar. *Red Star Over China.* New York: Vintage Books, 1971. Based on Snow's personal interviews with Mao and others in 1938, this is probably the most evocative first-hand account of the Chinese Communist movement in the period following the Long March.

Sullivan, Michael. *The Arts of China.* Revised edition. Berkeley: University of California Press, 1977. Perhaps the best concise survey available on traditional arts.

Terrill, Ross. *800,000,000: The Real China.* New York: Laurel Press, 1972. Measured observations of Chinese life and politics, based on a visit by an Australian journalist now teaching at Harvard.

————*Flowers on an Iron Tree: Five Cities of China*. Boston: Little, Brown, 1975. Vivid descriptions of Shanghai, Talien, Hangchow, Wuhan, and Peking.

Tregear, Thomas R. *The Chinese: How They Live and Work*. London: Christopher Hurst, 1973. Daily life in the PRC.

Books from China

Most foreign-language titles from China are published by the Foreign Languages Press in Peking. They are available from bookstores specializing in PRC materials, or may be ordered from China Publications Center, P.O. Box 399, Peking. Most of the titles listed below are available in Spanish and French, as well as other languages.

Alley, Rewi. *Travels in China, 1966-1971*. 1973. Informal, wide-ranging narrative by a New Zealander long resident in China.

China—A Geographical Sketch. 1974. A basic introduction to China's principal geographical features.

China Travel Guide. 1975. Contains street maps for 27 cities on the traveler's itinerary.

A Glance at China's Culture. 1975. Includes medicine, science, education, and sports, as well as literature and art.

A Glance at China's Economy. 1974. A brief narrative survey.

Lu Hsun. *Selected Stories of Lu Hsun*. 1972. A collection of 18 short stories by China's most prominent revolutionary writer.

Mao Tse-tung. *Four Essays on Philosophy*. 1968.

————*Mao Tse-tung Poems*. 1976. 39 poems that span the revolutionary period.

————*On the Ten Major Relationships*. 1977. Essays on China's economic and social development.

————*Quotations from Chairman Mao Tse-tung*. 1972. Mao's "little red book," first published in 1966 as the handbook of the Red Guards.

————*Selected Works of Mao Tse-tung*. Vols. I-V. 1961-77. Official translation of Mao's writings, spanning the 1926-57 period.

————*Talks at the Yenan Forum on Literature and Art*. 1967. An important commentary on the relationship between art and politics in China.

Tachai—The Red Banner. 1977. A detailed history of the brigade's development since 1949.

Wu Ching-tzu. *The Scholars*. An 18th-century satirical novel still avidly read in China.

Periodicals

Peking Review, a weekly publication from China, offers a good means of keeping abreast of official PRC views on domestic and international developments. The illustrated PRC publications intended for general audiences are *China Reconstructs* (monthly) and *China Pictorial* (quarterly). Periodicals published outside of China include *New China*, a colorful, general-interest magazine produced by the US-China Peoples Friendship Association; *The China Quarterly*, an authoritative scholarly journal published in the UK; *Far Eastern Economic Review*, a Hong Kong weekly covering current political and economic developments; and *China Business Review*, an in-depth bimonthly publication of the National Council for US-China Trade.

V
CHINESE PHRASES
FOR TRAVELERS

GENERAL

ENGLISH	CHINESE CHARACTERS	CHINESE PRONUNCIATION
I, me; mine	我；我的	*waw; waw-duh*
You; your	你；你的	*nee; nee-duh*
He, it/she	他／她	*tah/tah*
His, its/hers	他的／她的	*tah-duh/tah-duh*
We, us	我们	*waw-muhn*
You (pl.)	你们	*nee-muhn*
They, them (m./f.)	他们／她们	*tah-muhn/tah-muhn*
Their (m./f.)	他们的／她们的	*tah-muhn-duh/tah-muhn-duh*
Hello, how are you?	你好；你好吗	*nee how; nee how mah*
Good morning!	早；早安	*dzow; dzow ahn*
Good evening!	晚安	*wahn ahn*
Good-bye!	再见	*dzai jee-an*
I don't understand.	我不懂	*waw boo dung*
Yes, I agree; correct	是；对	*shir; doo-ay*
. . . don't agree	不同意	*boo tung-ee*
Please . . .	请	*ching*
Thank you; many thanks	谢谢；多谢	*shee-eh shee-eh; daw shee-eh*
It's nothing/don't mention it	不客气	*boo kuh-chee*
I'm sorry.	对不起	*dway boo chee*

Thank you, but I . . .	谢谢，我……	*shee-eh shee-eh, waw . . .*
am unable to . . .	不能	*boo nung*
don't want to . . .	不要	*boo yow*
don't like . . .	不喜欢	*boo shee-hwahn*
Good; very good	好；很好	*how; huhn how*
No (not) good	不好	*boo how*
Pleased; happy	欢喜；快乐，高兴	*hwahn-shee; kwy-luh, gao-shing*
Very; extremely	很；非常	*huhn; fay-chong*
Slow	慢	*mahn*
Fast	快	*kwy*
Hot	热	*ruh*
Cold	冷	*lung*
Who?	谁	*shay*
When is . . .?	什么时候……	*summah shir hoe*
Where . . .; . . . is where?	什么地方····；···· 在哪里	*sumonah dee fahng; . . . dzai nah-lee*
Friend	朋友	*pung-yo*
Friendship	友谊	*yo-ee*
Friendly	和气	*huh-chee*
May I please ask your name?	请问贵姓	*ching-one gway shing*
My name is . . .	我的名字是……	*waw-duh ming-tzuh shir*
I am	我是	*wah shir . . .*
American (i.e., US citizen)	美国人	*may-guo run*
Australian	澳大利亚人	*ow-dah-lee-ah run*
British	英国人	*ying-guo run*
Canadian	加拿大人	*gah-nah-dah run*
French	法国人	*fah-guo run*
German	德国人	*duh-guo run*

285

Italian	意大利人	*ee-dah-lee run*
Japanese	日本人	*ur-bun run*

TRAVEL

Right	右	*yo*
Left	左	*dzaw*
Front	前	*chee-an*
Back	后	*hoe*
Luggage	行李	*shing lee*
Customs	海关	*high wahn*
Car	汽车	*chee chuh*
Bus	公共汽车	*gung-gung chee-chuh*
Taxi	出租汽车	*choo-dzoo chee-chuh*
Airport	飞机场	*fay-jee-chahng*
Railroad station	火车站	*whaw-tsuh dee-an*

AT THE HOTEL

Hotel	旅馆	*lew kwahn*
Room	房间	*fahng-jee-an*
Key	钥匙	*yow shir*
Floor (story)	楼；层	*low; tsung*
Elevator	电梯	*dee-an dee*
Telephone	电话	*dee-an wah*
Light (electric)	电灯	*dee-an dung*
Laundry	洗衣店	*shee ee dee-an*
Toilet	厕所	*tse-swo*
Bath	洗澡	*shee-dzau*
Water	水	*shoo-ay*
Please come in!	请进来	*ching chin-lye*
(Please) wait a moment.	等一等	*dung-ee-dung*

| Sleep | 睡觉 | *shway-jao* |

SIGHTSEEING

Welcome		*hwahn-ying*
We would like to visit a . . .	我们要去⋯⋯	*waw-muhn yao choo . . .*
commune	公社	*goong shuh*
factory	工厂	*goong tsahng*
museum	博物馆	*bwo woo gwahn*
park	公园	*goong yoo-ahn*
school	学校	*shoo-eh shao*
store	商店	*song dee-an*
university	大学	*da shoo-eh*
Take a picture	照象	*jow see-ahng*

SHOPPING

Antique	古董	*goo-dung*
Artworks	工艺品	*goong-ee pin*
Book	书	*shoo*
Bookstore	书店	*shoo dee-an*
Department store	百货商店	*bye-hua shahng dee-an*
Handicrafts; art	手工艺；艺术	*show goong-ee; ee-shoo*
Stamps	邮票	*yo pee-ow*
How much (money)?	多少钱	*daw shao chee-an*
Expensive	贵	*gway*
Cheap (inexpensive)	便宜	*pee-an ee*
Dollar	块，元	*kwy, wahn*
Ten cents; cent	毛；分	*mao; fun*
Where can I buy . . .?	在哪里可以买⋯	*dzy nah-lee kuh-ee my*
I would like [that] . . .	我 要那个⋯⋯	*waw yow nay-guh*
black one	黑的	*hay-duh*
blue one	兰的	*lahn-duh*

287

green one	绿的	*lee-oo-duh*
red one	红的	*hoong-duh*
white one	白的	*bye-duh*
yellow one	黄的	*hoo-ahng-duh*

FOOD

I'm hungry.	我饿了	*waw uh-luh*
I'm thirsty.	我渴了	*waw kuh-luh*
Eat	吃	*chir*
Drink	喝	*huh*
Restaurant	饭馆	*fahn gwahn*
Breakfast	早餐；早饭	*dzau-tsahn; dzau-fahn*
Lunch	午餐；午饭	*woo-tsahn; woo-fahn*
Dinner	晚餐；晚饭	*jeng-tsahn; jeng-fahn*
Snack	点心	*dee-an shin*
Chopsticks	筷子	*kwy-dzuh*
Knife	刀	*dew*
Fork	叉	*tsah*
Spoon	汤匙	*tahng-shir*
Spicy	辣	*lah*
What is your specialty?	有什么特别的好吃？	*yo summah-tuh bee-ed-dah how-chir*
I've had enough to eat!	吃饱了	*chir-bow-luh*
The food was delicious!	这好极了	*tsy how jee-lah*
Bottoms Up!	干杯	*gahm-bay*
Water (cold)	冷水	*lung shway*
Coffee	咖啡	*kah-fay*
Tea	茶	*tsah*
Beer	啤酒	*bay-joe*
Beef	牛肉	*nee-oh row*
Chicken	鸡	*jee*

Duck	鸭子	*yah-dzuh*
Pork	猪肉	*joo-row*
Fish	鱼	*yu*
Shrimp	虾	*see-ah*
Eggs	鸡蛋	*jee-dahn*
Rice	饭	*fahn*
Vegetables	青菜	*ching-tsy*
Soup	汤	*tahng*
Fruit	水菓	*shway-gwaw*
Apple	苹果	*ping-gwaw*
Banana	香蕉	*see-yahng jow*
Orange	桔子	*chung-dzuh*
Peach	桃子	*tau-dzuh*
Pear	李子	*lee-dzuh*
Watermelon	西瓜	*shee-gwah*
Ice cream	冰淇淋	*bing-chee-lin*
Western food	西餐	*shee-tsahn*

HEALTH CARE/MEDICINE

Medicine	药	*yow*
Pharmacy	药店	*yow dee-an*
Where can I find medicine?	哪里有药	*nah-lee yo yow?*
Aspirin	阿斯匹林	*ah-shee-pee-lin*
I have a cold.	我伤风了	*waw shahng fung-leh*
I don't feel good.	我不舒服	*waw boo soo-foo*
I am ill.	我有病	*waw yo bing*
Please call a doctor.	请医生来	*ching ee-shung lai*
Dentist	牙医	*yah-ee*
Hospital	医院	*ee you-ahn*
Headache	头痛	*toe toong*

Toothache	牙痛	*yah toong*
Dizziness	头晕	*toe yoon*
Diarrhea	泻肚	*syeh-doo*
Stomach sickness	胃病	*way bing*
Stomach pain	胃痛	*way toong*
It hurts me here.	我这里痛	*waw juh-lee toong*

MISCELLANEOUS/TIME, NUMBERS

What time is it?	几点钟	*jee dee-an joong*
[number] o'clock	……点钟	*. . . dee-an joong*
Morning; mid-day; evening	早上；中午；晚上	*dzau-shahng; joong-wo; wan-shahng*
Yesterday; today; tomorrow	昨天；今天；明天	*dzaw tee-an; jin tee-an; ming tee-an*
Day; month; year	天，日；月；年	*tee-an, rir; yoo-eh; nee-an*
One	一	*ee*
Two	二	*are*
Three	三	*sahn*
Four	四	*suh*
Five	五	*woo*
Six	六	*lee-oh*
Seven	七	*chee*
Eight	八	*bah*
Nine	九	*gau*
Ten	十	*shir*
Eleven	十一	*shir-ee*
Twelve	十二	*shir-are*
Thirteen	十三	*shir-sahn*
Fourteen	十四	*shir-suh*
Twenty	二十	*are-shir*
Thirty	三十	*sahn-shir*
One hundred	一百	*ee-bye*
One thousand	一千	*ee-chee-an*

VI
TRANSLITERATION
GLOSSARY
OF PLACENAMES

COMMON ENGLISH SPELLING	PINYIN SPELLING	CHINESE
Geographical Features		
East China Sea	Dong Hai	东海
South China Sea	Nan Hai	南海
Yangtse River	Chang Jiang	长江
Yellow River	Huang He	黄河
Provinces and Autonomous Regions		
Anhwei	Anhui	安徽省
Chekiang	Zhejiang	浙江
Fukien	Fujian	福建
Heilungkiang	Heilongjiang	黑龙江
Honan	Henan	河南
Hopei ·	Hebei	河北
Hunan	Hunan	湖南
Hupei (Hupeh)	Hubei	湖北
Inner Mongolia Aut. Reg.	Nei Mongol Zizhiqu	内蒙古自治区
Kansu	Gansu	甘肃
Kiangsi	Jiangxi	江西
Kirin	Jilin	吉林
Kwangsi Aut. Reg.	Guangxi Zhuangzu Zizhiqu	广西壮族自治区
Kwangtung	Guangdong	广东
Kweichow	Guizhou	贵州

Liaoning	Liaoning	辽宁
Ningsia Hui Aut. Reg.	Ningxia Huizu Zizhiqu	宁夏回族自治区
Shansi	Shanxi	山西
Shantung	Shandong	山东
Shensi	Shaanxi	陕西
Sinkiang Uighur Aut. Reg.	Xinjiang Uygur Zizhiqu	新疆维吾尔自治区
Szechwan	Sichuan	四川
Taiwan	Taiwan	台湾
Tibet Aut. Reg.	Xizang Zizhiqu	西藏自治区
Tsinghai	Qinghai	青海
Yunnan	Yunnan	云南

Cities and Other Localities

Anshan	Anshan	鞍山
Changchun	Changchun	长春
Changsha	Changsha	长沙
Chengchow	Zhengzhou	郑州
Chengtu	Chengdu	成都
Chungking	Chongqing	重庆
Hangchow	Hangzhou	杭州
Harbin	Harbin	哈尔滨
Huhehot	Huhhat	呼和浩特
Kunming	Kunming	昆明
Kwangchow (Canton)	Guangzhou	广州
Kweilin	Guilin	桂林
Loyang	Luoyang	洛阳
Nanking	Nanjing	南京
Nanning	Nanning	南宁
Peking	Beijing	北京
Shanghai	Shanghai	上海
Shaoshan	Shaoshan	韶山
Shenyang	Shenyang	沈阳

Shih Chia Chuang	Shijiazhuang	石家庄
Sian	Xi'an	西安
Soochow	Suzhou	苏州
Tachai	Dazhai	大寨
Taching	Daqing	大庆
Talien	Dalian	大连
Tatung	Datong	大同
Tientsin	Tianjin	天津
Tsinan	Jinan	济南
Tsingtao	Qingdao	青岛
Urumchi	Ürümqi	乌鲁木齐
Wuhan	Wuhan	武汉
Wuhsi	Wuxi	无锡
Yenan	Yan'an	延安

Pinyin Alphabet Pronunciation Guide

(Letters in parentheses are equivalents used in traditional Wade-Giles spellings.)

a (a) Vowel as in *far*

b (p) Consonant as in *be*

c (ts) Consonant as in *its*

ch (ch) Consonant as in *chip*; strongly aspirated

d (t) Consonant as in *do*

e (e) Vowel as in *her*

f (f) Consonant as in *foot*

g (k) Consonant as in *go*

h (h) Consonant as in *her*; strongly aspirated

i (i) Vowel as in *eat* or as in *sir* (when in syllables beginning with c, ch, r, s, sh, z, and zh)

j (ch) Consonant as in *jeep*

k (k) Consonant as in *kind*; strongly aspirated

l (l) Consonant as in *land*

m (m) Consonant as in *me*

n (n) Consonant as in *no*

o (o) Vowel as in *law*

p (p) Consonant as in *par*; strongly aspirated

q (ch) Consonant as in *cheek*

r (j) Consonant as in *right* (not rolled) or pronounced as *z* in *azure*

s (s, ss, sz) Consonant as in *sister*

sh (sh) Consonant as in *shore*

t (t) Consonant as in *top*; strongly aspirated

u (u) Vowel as in *too*, also as in the French *tu* or the German *Munchen*

v (v) Consonant used only to produce foreign words, national minority words, and local dialects

w (w) Semi-vowel in syllables beginning with u when not preceded by consonants, as in *want*

x (hs) Consonant as in *she*

y Semi-vowel in syllables beginning with i or u when not preceded by consonants, as in *yet*

z (ts, tz) Consonant as in *zero*

zh (ch) Consonant as in *jump*

VII
INDEX

I

J

K

Arne J. deKeijzer is founder of A.J. deKeijzer & Associates, Inc., a consulting firm specializing in the development of trade between the United States and the People's Republic of China. He was previously the New York representative for the National Council for US-China Trade. Mr. deKeijzer has been involved in the opening of relations between the US and China since the days of "ping-pong diplomacy," having served for seven years on the staff of the National Committee on US-China Relations. Since 1973, he has visited China 12 times. He is co-editor of *China: A Resource and Curriculum Guide* (University of Chicago Press, 1976); co-author of the *JAL Guide to the People's Republic of China* (Eurasia Press, 1978); and is the author of a number of articles on US-China trade.

Fredric M. Kaplan is founder and publisher of Eurasia Press and former Executive Editor of *Worldmark Encyclopedia of Nations*. A specialist on contemporary China, he is co-author of *Encyclopedia of China Today* (Harper & Row and Eurasia Press, 1979) and the *JAL Guide to the People's Republic of China*, and is Co-Chairperson of the US-China Peoples Friendship Association (New York).

CONTRIBUTORS   **John Israel** is Associate Professor of Chinese History, University of Virginia, and is author of *Student Nationalism in China, 1927-1937*. He was interpreter-escort for the Local Education Leaders Delegation to the People's Republic of China (June 22-July 8, 1978). **Victor W. Sidel, M.D.** and **Ruth Sidel, Ph.D.** were among the first American health professionals to visit the People's Republic, with their initial invitation coming in 1971. Victor Sidel is a physician specializing in community medical care and comparative studies of medicine; Ruth Sidel is a psychiatric social worker. They are co-authors of *Serve the People: Observations on Medicine in the People's Republic of China* (Beacon Press, 1974). **Annette Juliano** is Associate Professor in the Art Department, Brooklyn College, with a specialty in Chinese art and archeology. She is author of *Teng-hsien: An Important Six Dynasties Tomb* (Artibus Asiae, 1979), and is US correspondent for *Oriental Art* magazine.